# A Pinch of Incense

*"The worship involved merely throwing a pinch of incense on a civic altar, but to refuse indicated contempt of the emperor and merited capital punishment."*

Joseph Wilson Trigg, historian
*Origen: The Bible and Philosophy in the Third Century*

# A Pinch of Incense

**Martyr's Farewell**

The Alexandrian mob is outraged when Origen gives the kiss of peace to one of his students who is on his way to martyrdom.

Details of illustration by Greg Harlin, page 214

A.D. 70 to 250

From the Fall of Jerusalem to the Decian Persecution

The Christians

THEIR FIRST TWO THOUSAND YEARS

Second Volume

CHRISTIAN HISTORY PROJECT

THE EDITOR:

Ted Byfield has been a journalist for fifty-five years and a western Canadian magazine publisher since 1973, the founder of *Alberta Report* and *British Columbia Report* weekly newsmagazines, and founding editor of *Alberta in the Twentieth Century*, a twelve-volume history of his province. A columnist for Canada's *Sun* newspapers and sometime contributor to the *National Post* and *Globe and Mail* national newspapers, he is active in evangelical journalistic outreach. He was one of the founders of St. John's School of Alberta, an Anglican school for boys where he developed a new method of teaching history.

THE ASSOCIATE EDITOR:

Calvin Demmon of Marina, California, has worked as an editor of *Alberta Report* newsmagazine; as city editor of the *Huntington Park Daily Signal* and of the *Daily Southeast News* in Los Angeles County; and as a columnist and editor for the *Monterey County Herald*. He has contributed articles and short stories to a number of magazines and to several books.

COVER:

The painting by Glenn Harrington of Pipersville, Pennsylvania, depicts a Christian who had been forced to choose either to burn incense in obeisance to the pagan religion or risk incurring a death sentence.

**CHRISTIAN HISTORY PROJECT LIMITED PARTNERSHIP**

| | |
|---|---|
| President and CEO | Robert W. Doull |
| Controller | Beverly Arlow, CGA |
| Marketing Manager | Leanne Nash |
| Contact Center Manager | Terry Petherbridge |
| Contact Center Administrators | Kathy Obrigewitch, Keith Bennett |
| Trainer | Brian Lehr |
| Distribution Manager | Lori Arndt |

*For the volume:* **A PINCH OF INCENSE, A.D. 70 to 250, From the Fall of Jerusalem to the Decian Persecution**

| | |
|---|---|
| Writers | Charlotte Allen, Mark Galli, Steve Hopkins, Ian Hunter, Frederica Mathewes-Green, John David Powell, David Shiflett, Gary L. Thomas, Steve Weatherbe, Joe Woodard |
| Art Director / Illustrations Editor | Jack Keaschuk |
| Page Production & Graphics | Dean Pickup |
| Illustrators | Carlo Cosentino, Michael Dudash, Matthew Frey, Greg Harlin, Glenn Harrington, Jamie Holloway, John Mantha, Tom McNeely, Richard Sparks, Rob Wood |
| Director of Research | Moira Calder |
| Researchers: | Gail Bajaj, Marilyn Bertsch, Erika Brown, Regina di Castro, Rev. David Edwards, Ken Gee, Michelle Gee, Louise Henein, Gregory Kopchuk, Diane Machel, Nathan Manning, Leanne Nash, Ryan Roth |
| Production Editor | Rev. David Edwards |
| Proofreaders | P.A. Colwell, Faith Farthing |
| General Academic Consultants | Dr. Kimberley Georgedes, Dr. Douglas Sweeney Special consultants: Dr. William McDonald, Dr. Samuel H. Moffett, Professor Eugene TeSelle |

*For the series:* **THE CHRISTIANS: Their First Two Thousand Years**

| | |
|---|---|
| Series Planner | Barrett Pashak |
| Assistant Planner | Louise Henein |

© 2002 Christian Millennial History Project Inc.
© 2002 Christian Millennial History Project Limited Partnership.

| | |
|---|---|
| Chairman | Gerald J. Maier |

NATIONAL LIBRARY OF CANADA CATALOGUING IN PUBLICATION DATA

Main entry under title: A pinch of incense

(The Christians : their first two thousand years ; 2)

Includes bibliographical references and index.

ISBN 0-9689873-1-1

1. Church history—Primitive and early church, ca. 30-600. 2. Persecution—History—Early church, ca. 30-600. I. Christian Millennial History Project. II. Series: Christians : their first two thousand years ; 2.

BR162.3.P56 2002    270.1    C2002-910577-3

PRINTED IN CANADA BY FRIESENS CORPORATION

# CONTENTS

# ILLUSTRATIONS

(Artists)

Margin character sketches     (Jamie Holloway)


## MAPS

For additional copies of this book or information on others in the series,
please contact us at:

The Christian History Project
10333 178 Street
Edmonton AB, Canada, T5S 1R5
www.christianhistoryproject.com

1-800-853-5402

# FOREWORD

Most readers of this book will find themselves on foreign ground. In the first volume of this series, they had been at home. They knew the players and they knew the roles they played because the first book mostly furnished a historical background for the New Testament. With this volume, however, they venture forth into unknown lands, where both the people and many of the places are unfamiliar. The reader may even become suspicious of the individuals encountered here, inwardly asking: Were Ignatius and Irenaeus really Christians? Did Origen believe the same things I believe? Did Justin have the same ideas of right and wrong? Were Blandina and Perpetua born again?

What they were, the reader must decide. But one thing is clear. Never before or since has the Word of God been preached with such startling, positive, and sweeping effect. By the volume's end, the early believers are well on the way to converting the world as they knew it, though at a fearful price, most of it paid by "little people," undistinguished by anything beyond their astonishing courage and heroism.

It was an age when faith and commitment were measured, not only in words, but in terms of blood, suffering, sorrow, humiliation, and pain. And had they not paid this price, the very word Christian would probably be unknown today. As one of them said, "The blood of the martyrs is seed." It was indeed, and Christians today are the distant fruit, born of that seed.

We have been careful in this volume to place the growth of the faith in its political, social and cultural context, so careful that some readers may wonder whether they're reading a history of Christianity or a history of imperial Rome. But we believe you cannot understand the one without the other, any more than you could understand the role of twentieth-century Christianity in modern America without describing the vast cultural and moral change that went on around it. For neither then nor now can Christians divorce themselves from the world—a world for which, they say, Christ died.

"It is finished!" he cried, in his all-but-last word from the cross, meaning that it was completed, accomplished, that his human job was done. But for his followers, it was not finished. It was barely started, and with this volume they begin to discover the staggering magnitude of the work he has assigned them to do.

Ted Byfield

DUDASH

The deeply paternal attitude of the apostle John, evident particularly in his letters,
is demonstrated in the hills outside Smyrna. Learning that one of his followers
had enthusiastically embraced the life of a brigand, the "Son of Thunder" rides
off to confront the prodigal. John's headstrong response sees him taken prisoner
by the band, but also brings the errant young man to his knees in repentance.

# CHAPTER 1

# *The man with the inside story*

## Jesus posed bewildering questions. Was he God? Was he man? The memories of the disciple who knew him best provided some answers

In the last thirty years of the first century, the faith already known as Christianity existed in a world that gave every evidence it was coming to an end. Jerusalem, home of all that the Christians had inherited from the Jewish past, lay in ruins. Its great Temple, once supposed to be the indestructible abode on Earth of the unchanging God, had been reduced to a pile of rubble. True, Jesus had foretold all this, but what would happen now? Surely, Christians assumed, the end must be at hand.

Meanwhile, in their communities scattered around much of the Mediterranean world, they lived with fear. Imperial Rome, which they had at first seen as their protector, had suddenly turned savagely against them, the emperor Nero himself burning the Christians in his capital city as living torches. The indefatigable Paul, who had founded so many of their communities, had perished beneath an executioner's sword in the same imperial rampage.

And what of the original Twelve? There were strange and dramatic reports—Thomas, for instance, was said to have been executed in far-off India; Andrew, missionary to distant Scythia, north of the Black Sea, home of a fierce nomadic people, was later crucified in Greece. Then there were the three whom Jesus so often singled out—Peter and the brothers James and John Zebedee. James had been executed at Jerusalem, Peter crucified at Rome. That left John, aged but still living, it was said, at Ephesus, the big port on the east coast of the Aegean.

What a story John could tell, if he ever told it. For he, even more than Peter, seemed closest to the mind and heart of Jesus. He was sometimes called the disciple "whom Jesus loved." Jesus loved them all, of course, but John was special. Some thought he would live until Jesus returned. Night after night, day after day, for three years Jesus had talked to them, often with words and ideas they could not begin to understand. But John pondered these things, discussed them, struggled to comprehend them. So if anyone now knew the answers, John did. Was Jesus God? Was the world ending? What would John say about these things?

Already accounts of Jesus' life and ministry were circulating widely, diligently copied by hand and bound in a book-like codex, so much more manageable than the old scrolls.[1] Nearly every Christian community had one or two of them. One recorded Peter's memory of the events, taken down by John Mark, or so everyone seemed to agree. There was a beautifully written account ascribed to Luke, the doctor who traveled with Paul and who, it was said, drew upon Mary's memories of Jesus' childhood. Some communities had a third, mostly a record of Jesus' sermons, with which Matthew's name was always associated. Then there were other accounts of what Jesus had said and done, either excerpted from one of the three or incorporated into them.

Hearing these read reinforced a Christian's confidence and helped direct his or her life, but it was not the basis of a person's commitment. Faith was more commonly based on the very strong sense a Christian had of Jesus' immediate presence in his life. That was the important thing. At some points, he felt it more strongly than at others, almost as though Jesus were testing him to see if he could walk on his own without help. But if a Christian stumbled, no matter how terribly, Jesus was always there to pick him up. This is what Paul had meant. Nothing can separate us from the love of God, he had said—death, life, angels, principalities, powers, height, depth, things present, nothing whatever (Rom. 8:38–39). This powerful sense of Jesus' presence was what held whole Christian communities together.

Even so, Jesus had never left the impression he didn't want his people to think for themselves. And he had left them with a monumental puzzle to think about: Who was he? The fact is, he continually spoke as though he were God. He "forgave" people's sins, and only God can do that. He referred to everyone as sinful, though he never applied this to himself. And at the crucial point in his trial, he identified himself with the Almighty, making inevitable his conviction for blasphemy—which, of course, his claim certainly was. Unless it was true.

But how, after all, could God be here on Earth but also up in Heaven? Jesus

---

1. The pre-Christian Jewish scriptures were recorded on papyrus made from reed pulp and preserved in large rolls or scrolls, one continuous page, usually ten inches wide and up to thirty-five feet long, with the text on one side only. In the first century, however, the Christians were among the first to cut the papyrus into sheets, six to eight inches wide and ten to twelve high, with text on both sides and bound together in the form of a primitive book called a "codex."

*A tale of two eagles: The first, this ninth-century ivory carving (above), which is on display at the Victoria and Albert Museum, London, is the emblem of the evangelist and apostle John. It stood for his gospel that "soared to the heavens" in witnessing to the divinity of Jesus. Later the eagle appeared on lecterns in Christian churches as the symbol of the rebirth brought by the gospel. It stood in conflict, both figuratively and practically, with the second, the eagle that was the totem of the Roman empire, of which the bronze standard below is one of the oldest representations. It is now ensconced in a side wall of the Dodici Apostoli (the Church of the Holy Apostles) in Rome.*

prayed to God, to his "Father," as he called him. Could God pray to God? Were there two Gods? Surely, the whole message of the Jewish tradition was that there was only one. Perhaps John knew the solution to the puzzle—if he were ever to tell his story.

If indeed he were even alive. Luke's history of the church, the Acts of the Apostles, which runs from the Ascension in about A.D. 30 to the mid-60s, makes its last mention of John in the late 30s, when he joined Peter in the Samaritan mission. Later Christian historians record John as leaving Palestine, probably in the 50s, after the death of Jesus' mother whom he had been assigned by Jesus to care for. He moved, they say, to Ephesus, capital of the Roman province of Asia (later western Turkey), where the first Christian mission had been established by Priscilla and Aquila under the direction of Paul. As an apostle, John supervised the bishops that led the congregations throughout the province.

Toward the century's end, John had reached a great age, somewhere in his eighties, naturally reinforcing the belief that he would not die, a theory he himself pointedly denied. Stories about him were everywhere repeated. For instance, Clement of Alexandria, writing more than a century later, tells how John had left an intelligent and promising boy, probably an orphan, in the care of the bishop at Smyrna, another Aegean port about thirty miles north of Ephesus, with instructions that he raise the youngster in the faith. The bishop tried, but when the boy became a young man he fell in with a crowd of criminals and soon had a gang of his own, brigands and killers who lived in the hills preying on passing travelers.

When John asked how the boy was doing, the bishop burst into tears and reported, "He's dead." Not dead as a man but "dead to God," and he explained the boy's fall. "Some guardian!" snapped John, still the "Son of Thunder" that Jesus had once called him (Mark 3:17). Groaning, John tore his garment, demanded a horse, and galloped immediately for the hills. He was soon made prisoner by the gang and demanded to be taken to its leader. When the latter saw him he turned and fled.

"Why are you running away from me, son?" called John. "From your own father, unarmed and very old? You should feel sorry for me, not fear me. You haven't

## Although the Christians lived under a cloud, suspect to officialdom and increasingly repugnant to their neighbors, their numbers kept growing and they kept spreading.

lost your life. I will make account to Christ for you. I would suffer death for you, just as he suffered death for us. Stop what you're doing! Believe! Christ sent me to you!"

The young man stopped, dropped his weapons to the ground, and wept bitterly. John threw his arms around him and baptized him with his tears, says Clement. They returned to Smyrna. John pleaded his case and restored him to the community.

The fact there was a Christian community at all in Smyrna—or anywhere else for that matter—evidenced the curious irony peculiar to these people known as Christians. While on the one hand they lived under a cloud, always suspect to officialdom and increasingly repugnant to their neighbors, on the other, their numbers kept growing and their cult kept spreading.

From Jerusalem, it had swiftly moved to the Mediterranean coast, to the Roman provincial seat at Caesarea, then south to Alexandria, where there was a flourishing Christian presence. At Cyrene (whence came the man Simon who had carried Christ's cross) there was another Christian congregation, and at the burgeoning Roman port of Carthage, the Christian numbers rivaled those at Alexandria.

North of the Mediterranean, the same thing was occurring. From the original seed missions established by the apostle Paul, the movement spread east to Byzantium, at the western terminus of the Black Sea, then along the sea's northwest coast as far as Odessus, which would become Varna in Bulgaria. Christian congregations dotted the Adriatic coast and the cities and towns of Italy. Even at Rome, where the horror of Nero's executions had all but wiped out the new faith, it soon revived, and Christian groups were quietly reappearing throughout the city. There were Christian communities along the south coast of Gaul, which would become France, and a few in the provinces of Tarraconensis, Lusitania, and Baetica, which one day would be Spain.

Strangest of all and most worrisome to those in authority, the army itself was being penetrated by Christianity. Christ had shunned violence, yet Christianity had a particular appeal to soldiers and men under discipline. The Twelfth Legion, now back at its base in Armenia after long service in Judea, was said to be especially tainted. And it had to be admitted that the Christians often made good soldiers, fought valiantly, and died honorably. Nevertheless, how could any sane commander trust them?

To the imperial bureaucracy, the whole Christian phenomenon was akin to a plague. It spread insidiously from one man to another, then to his whole family, then to his neighbors. Moreover, it was difficult to make a rational case against these people. They paid their taxes, even cheerfully. Their support for community projects with both their time and money was distinctly generous. They were law-abiding, sober, diligent, eminently good workers; even as slaves, they characteristically served their masters tirelessly, particularly if their masters were also Christian.

So why, one might reasonably ask, was the empire so ill disposed toward them? Because they were, and even saw themselves as, *outsiders*. Their ultimate loyalty lay beyond Caesar, beyond the empire, to this mysterious person they called Christ. It was disgusting. The man had been crucified like a common criminal. Could anything be less suggestive of deity?

The empire from the start had proclaimed itself tolerant of all authorized religions, and it had certainly authorized some strange ones. But these religions must be considered by the Roman subject as "a personal thing." The only common "public" religion must be the state paganism of the empire—often embodied, by law, in the person of the emperor. To reject this, to refuse to enshrine the imperial ideal as uppermost in the very soul of the subject, was viewed therefore as a blatant defiance, tantamount to rebellion. And it was precisely this commitment that the Christians refused to make.

Nero had shrewdly discerned in the Christian mind this implicit insurrectionism, and on this ground had pronounced Christianity illegal. In Roman law, this was unprecedented. You could be prosecuted for *doing* something but not for *believing* something. Thereafter, by proving a person Christian, the state could establish him as a criminal. But how could it *prove* a person Christian?

An ingenious formula was devised. The suspected Christian need merely be

*Incense shovels, such as this one discovered near Bethsaida's Roman temple, were used not only in pagan worship but later in Byzantine-era synagogues.*

asked to take a pinch of incense and ceremonially burn it to the "genius" of Caesar.[2] Surely a modest demand. But, astonishingly, Christians refused to do it. Their God, they said, was *not* Caesar. The sentence could then be passed immediately: seizure of property, imprisonment, often death—by the sword, by fire, by the cross, by being fed to starving animals in the arena as a public spectacle, whatever local sentiment called for.

What it called for could be nasty, chiefly because of the other enemy the Christians had to contend with, notably the mob. The mass of the people utterly loathed them, for reasons both good and bad. As everyone but the Christians understood, the fate of any city depended on the gods. Whether there was sufficient food depended on the harvest, which depended on the weather, which depended on the gods. Whether plagues came, whether enemies broke through the cordon of legions protecting the empire, depended largely on chance or fortune, which depended largely on the gods. Pleasing the gods, therefore, was the first duty of the wise and conscientious.

Now these Christians not only failed to do this, they actually denounced the whole state religion. The gods, insofar as they existed at all, were plainly evil, they said. Their images and idols should not just be ignored; they should be destroyed. The Christians were, in other words, atheists—to the mob a downright danger. Every plague, famine, fire, or flood could properly be ascribed to their contempt for the gods.

Such was the reasonable case against them. The unreasonable basis of the other was, ironically, their undoubted generosity. They were such very, very good people. Their women were virginal until married, their men loyal to their wives, respecting their female slaves and shunning the whorehouses. Prissily good. Boringly good. Prudes, in fact. Let's have them to the arena. Let's see how virginally good they are there. Such, often, was the local sentiment.

These persecutions, however, came sporadically, depending chiefly on the emperor's view of Christianity, secondarily on that of the local governor. Since Christianity was technically illegal, either authority could arrange a roundup of the Christians at any time. But the governor usually looked to Rome for direction. In the 70s and 80s, this meant to Emperor Vespasian, or later to his eldest son Titus, both best known for suppressing the rebellion of the Jews and destroying their city and temple in A.D. 70. Their policy toward the Christians was simplicity itself: They didn't have one.

In such a hiatus, the faith spread more rapidly than ever, penetrating not only all cities but also all classes. To the imperial administrators this last was particularly disturbing. That a slave should embrace this new creed was understandable enough. The poor wretch often had nothing whatever to look forward to in this life—death slumped over the oar to which he had been chained for years, then to be pitched into the sea; or death in the hot sun of the field in which he had

2. Emperors required their subjects to worship and swear by their divine "genius," a term that implied something between a soul and a guardian angel. This worship involved only throwing a pinch of incense on a civic altar, nothing more. To refuse, however, was an insubordination indicating contempt of the emperor.

worked every painful day of a hopeless and painful life. Common laborers were only a little better off. To such woebegone creatures, the figure of a crucified god might understandably appeal.

But how could you account for a man like Flavius Clemens, consul of Rome, father of the declared successors to the imperial throne? Why in the name of all sanity would *he* become one of these Christians, along with (or perhaps because of) his wife? Why would a respected senator, aristocrat, and former consul of Rome like Marcus Acilius Glabrio become Christian? These and others from the top ranks of Roman society were charged with "atheism," and it was altogether likely their actual crime was Christianity. What could they have possibly gained from this crucified Jew?

Vespasian ruled the empire with a refreshing sanity from his accession in A.D. 70 until he died nine years later after a brief illness. Sensing his moment of death, he leapt to his feet. "An emperor should die standing!" he cried, and he collapsed into the arms of a servant. It was the stamp of the man. Titus, a mirror of his father, promised a similarly benign reign but fell ill and died of fever two years and twelve weeks later. This brought to the throne Titus's brother Domitian, ten years his junior, and conditions for both the Christians and the empire began to decline.

How rapidly and how steeply they declined is difficult to know, since both of the foremost historians of the era, Tacitus and Suetonius, appear to compete with one another in so blackguarding Domitian that it's difficult to distinguish the facts from the invective. He is vain, arrogant, an emulator of Nero, they say, and a practiced seducer of other men's wives. Not of his own wife, it seems, for the year 90, his ninth in office, found him still without an heir. He named as his successors the two sons of his cousin Flavius Clemens. Even skeptical historians allow that their mother, Clemens' wife Domitilla, was assuredly Christian. So, probably, was Clemens himself.

The avenues by which Christianity had so infiltrated the imperial household remain a secret of history. Some speculate that Sabinus, Vespasian's brother, in his day a gentle and humane prefect of Rome, evidenced distinctly

*This marble frieze, which might be titled "Flavian Family Portrait," now resides in the Gregorian Profane Museum in Rome. Carved about A.D. 90, it shows (left to right) the emperors of the Flavian Dynasty: Domitian, Titus and their father Vespasian. Domitian seems to be the less-favored of the two sons in this marble representation, as Vespasian reaches to rest an approving hand on Titus. In fact, this is a telling representation of the family's relationships as Domitian appears to have alternately idolized and envied his elder brother Titus. The colossal head of the "bad boy" of the family, Domitian (measuring nearly four feet high) comes from a temple dedicated to him in Smyrna, Asia Minor (modern Izmir, Turkey). Worship of Domitian, however, did not necessarily imply respect on the part of the empire's citizenry.*

DUDASH

Christian tendencies and might very well have influenced Domitilla. In any event, it was a secret unknown to Domitian until five years after he had named Clemens' sons as heirs of the empire.

Then he discovered it and unleashed a sudden purge of the atheists in the imperial circle. Clemens was arrested, tried for neglecting his state religious duties, and executed; his wife Domitilla was banished to the island of Pandataria, off the coast at Naples, on the same charge. Glabrio was sentenced to death,[3] his family persisting in the faith through the bloody century that would follow, making their cemetery on the Salarian Way one of the most ancient of all the Christian burial grounds.

How far beyond the court the Domitian crackdown extended, however, is debated by historians. In one instance, it took a strange path. Determined to discover

3. Senator Glabrio proved a difficult man to execute, according to the historian Cassius Dio. Domitian first ordered him to fight with a lion. Glabrio overcame the animal and presumably killed it. Domitian then ordered him exiled and later to be put to death.

what lay behind this insidious influence that was infesting his own household, Domitian ordered the arrest and examination of the surviving members of Jesus' family, the grandchildren of the apostle Jude.

Quoting the early Christian historian Hegesippus (whose works have since been lost), the fourth-century church historian Eusebius describes how these simple Palestinian farmers were arrested and led terrified under escort before Domitian himself at Rome. There the emperor asked them whether they were descendants of David. Yes, they said, they were. It was a dangerous admission, writes Eusebius, because Domitian, by now persuaded that Christianity was a Jewish conspiracy, had ordered the roundup and execution of all Jews descended from King David.

How wealthy were they? Domitian demanded. Together they had land worth about nine thousand denarii, they replied. How much actual property did they

## The emperor asked these simple Palestinian farmers if they were descendants of David. Yes, they said, they were. It was a dangerous admission, one that could lead to execution.

own? Thirty-nine acres, they said, out of which all of them had to make a living. They then showed him their callused hands by way of proof.

What was this about Christ's "kingdom?" came the next question. It was not of this world nor of anything on earth, they said, but had to do with the angels and Heaven, and would be established when this world came to an end.

Domitian sneered, dismissed them as beneath his notice, and ordered as pointless the arrests of other "sons of David" to stop. The brothers returned to Palestine, where they were honored by the Christians for having borne Christian witness to the emperor.

Meanwhile, writes Eusebius, Domitian had exiled John, the preeminent Christian in Asia, to the island of Patmos in the Aegean. But Domitian then faced consequences of his own back at Rome, where the aristocracy decided they had had enough of him. If men of the status of Clemens and Glabrio weren't safe from him, who was?

The three Flavians, as the dynasty of Vespasian and his two sons is known to Roman history, had never been wholly accepted by Rome's old and established aristocratic families. The Flavians were what a later empire would know as "commoners," their bloodline uncertain since they had risen by their own effort from the business class. Vespasian himself had even worked at one point as a mule trader. Although he and Titus, having distinguished themselves in the battlefield and ruled intelligently, won a grudging acceptance, Domitian, despite efforts to gain for himself similar battle honors, had never succeeded. He ruled with increasing brutality, needless cruelty, and, in the opinion of Pliny the Younger, eventual insanity.

The conspirators who eventually murdered Domitian were neither politicians nor even noblemen, writes Domitian's biographer, Pat Southern (1997). They

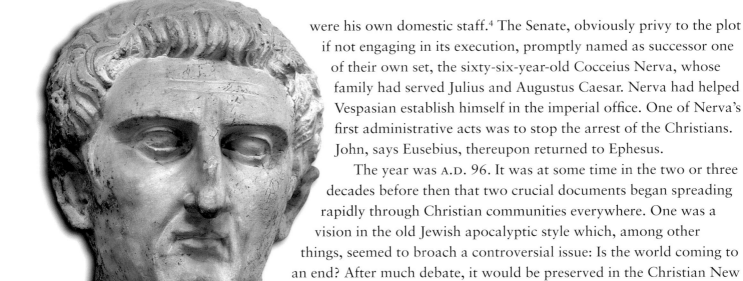

*Descended from a family linked to the Senate and the first emperors, the emperor Nerva stood in marked contrast to the rough and ready military roots of the Flavians. Though Nerva ruled the empire for only two years (A.D. 96–98) they were years that brought some respite for Christians from the brutal reign of Domitian.*

were his own domestic staff.[4] The Senate, obviously privy to the plot if not engaging in its execution, promptly named as successor one of their own set, the sixty-six-year-old Cocceius Nerva, whose family had served Julius and Augustus Caesar. Nerva had helped Vespasian establish himself in the imperial office. One of Nerva's first administrative acts was to stop the arrest of the Christians. John, says Eusebius, thereupon returned to Ephesus.

The year was A.D. 96. It was at some time in the two or three decades before then that two crucial documents began spreading rapidly through Christian communities everywhere. One was a vision in the old Jewish apocalyptic style which, among other things, seemed to broach a controversial issue: Is the world coming to an end? After much debate, it would be preserved in the Christian New Testament as the Book of Revelation. The author repeatedly identifies himself in the text as "John," though not specifically as John the Apostle.

The other document undertook an even thornier question: Was Jesus God? This one, all agreed, was indeed produced by John the Apostle. It was just what Christians had been hoping for, giving John's memories and subsequent reflections on Jesus' ministry. It was to become the Gospel According to St. John, fourth book of the New Testament.

One early Christian, Irenaeus, a pupil of one member of John's circle at Ephesus and destined to play a major evangelical and teaching role in the coming century, ascribes both books to the apostle, not just the Gospel. So do most early Christian writers. Eusebius, however, ascribes the Gospel to John the Apostle but mentions no author for Revelation. Dionysius of Alexandria, another early Christian scholar, says the language of Revelation was so different from that of John's Gospel that both could not possibly have been written by the same man.

Certainly, the Greek of the Revelation was remarkable for its incompetence. "The crudities, grammatical errors, and quite extraordinary juxtaposition of words," writes twentieth-century translator J. B. Phillips, "make many scholars find themselves unable to believe that both it [and the Gospel] could be written by the same person." Revelation "piles word upon word remorselessly, mixes cases and tenses without scruple, and shows at times a complete disregard for normal syntax and grammar." The Fourth Gospel, on the other hand, "is written, within limited vocabulary, smoothly and correctly and would have caused no literary qualms in a contemporary Greek reader."

Even so, Phillips is persuaded of the validity of the vision. "The intense

---

4. Fearing themselves under impending sentence of execution, Domitian's personal servants assassinated him. His chamberlain Parthenius overtook the emperor as he made his way to the baths. An important man must see him immediately, he said. Returning, Domitian found Stephanus, steward of Domitilla who was Clemens' widow, waiting for him, his arm bandaged as from a wound. Domitian had put Clemens to death. He had information of a conspiracy, said Stephanus, and handed Domitian written evidence. As the emperor read it, Stephanus drew a dagger from beneath the bandage and stabbed him in the groin. Desperate to live, Domitian grappled with Stephanus, trying to gouge out his eyes. A gladiator then appeared to finish the job. Historian Archibald Robertson (1954) observed: If Stephanus acted on instructions from his exiled mistress, there was at least one Christian who didn't turn the other cheek.

emotion of being, as it were, 'in the heavenlies,' the excitement of seeing what is normally invisible to human eyes, and the frustration of having to use human words to describe what is beyond human expression would, it seems to me, fully account for the incoherence." Once he had absorbed the initial shock of the Greek, Phillips said, "the effect of the language of this book is most powerful."

The style of the Revelation is called "apocalyptic," a form of religious writing widely used by the Jews for the previous two centuries, in which lurid visions of God, Heaven, Hell, angels, devils, and monsters, often engaged in superhuman conflict, serving to reveal realities beyond normal human understanding.

And yet, writes Leon Morris in the *Tyndale New Testament Commentaries*, Revelation has numerous qualities which separate it from other Jewish apocalyptical literature. Revelation's author calls his book a prophecy; the others do not. Far more than the others, he relates man's salvation or his condemnation chiefly to man's moral conduct. And while he certainly condemns the Roman empire as an instrument of wickedness, he does not see the world as hopelessly dominated by evil, as the others do. Most notably, Revelation does not look forward to a coming Messiah. To its author, the Messiah has already arrived, and the fearsome "Lion of Judah" has turned out to be "the Lamb."

In his striking vision that follows, the author perceives a great scroll, foretelling the future of humanity but locked shut by seven seals that no one in Heaven or on Earth can open. Then the Lamb appears and proves worthy to break the seals, "for thou hast been slain and by thy blood hast purchased for God men from every tribe, and tongue, and people, and nation!" One by one, the Lamb breaks the seals. When he breaks the fifth seal, he "could see, beneath

*The writer of the Revelation plainly felt the emotion of being 'in the heavenlies,' the excitement of seeing the invisible, the frustration of trying to express the inexpressible.*

the altar, the souls of those who have been killed for the sake of the Word of God and because of the faithfulness of their witness."

How long shall it be, they ask, before the Lord shall judge and avenge their blood upon the inhabitants of the earth? "Then each of them," the passage concludes, "was given a white robe, and they were told to be patient a little longer, until the number of their fellow-servants and of their brethren, who were to die as they had died, should be complete" (Rev. 6:9–11 JBP).

The conflicts that the Revelation depicts are not confined to the supernatural. The spiritual condition of seven specific churches in Ephesus and vicinity is described intimately, two depicted as in excellent shape, three as wavering between Heaven and Hell, and two as in grave spiritual danger (Rev. 1:20–3:22).

From the start, the book puzzled and divided Christians, says Morris. It can be regarded in four ways. By the "preterist" view, it can be taken to have relevance only to those seven churches to whom it is addressed and to no one else. The "historicists,"

The fifth seal of the scroll is broken. The voices of the witnesses slaughtered for their faith in Jesus (in Greek, the martyrs) cry out for their blood to be avenged. They're told they must wait until the number has been reached of those who must suffer as they had suffered. Thus does the author of Revelation foresee the lot of some Christians, whether in the second and third centuries or in the twenty-first.

by contrast, see it as a forecast of events through the whole of human history. The "futurist" perspective sees it as a pre-depiction of events at the end of the world. Finally, the "idealist" version regards it as setting forth the principles under which God determines the outcome of human history in all ages. Some combination of at least two of these views, observes Morris, "is essential."

The imperial authorities, once they had acquired copies of it, were for their part not at all divided on what it meant. In it, Rome is shown as "Babylon," as the "harlot of the Seven Hills" who is "drunk on the blood of the saints" (Rev. 17:6ff) who deceives the nations with her "sorcery" (18:23). As the Roman bureaucracy saw it, therefore, the book clearly demonstrated the Christians as anticipating and plotting the empire's overthrow, and it would be cited against them for the next two centuries and more as evidence of their subversive intent.

However, it was the other document, John's story of Jesus' ministry, that Christians everywhere would have sought most avidly to read or hear. More than any of the other three gospels, it gave evidence throughout of the firsthand eyewitness, the man who was there and had seen for himself exactly what happened.

It abounded in detail—the behavior of crowds, the position of the boats along the Galilee shore following the feeding of the five thousand (John 6:22–24), the confrontation between the healed blind man and the irritated Pharisees (9:1–7), the exchange between Jesus and Martha over the meaning of the Resurrection (11:20–27), the specific name of the soldier whose ear was cut off in the Garden of Gethsemane (18:10), and the dialogue between Jesus and the Samaritan woman at the well (4:5–26). She left the water pot behind, we are told (4:28–30). But so what? Why is such a detail included in the story? No doctrine or moral lesson is implied by it. It's there simply because the author remembers seeing it.

Far more than in the other three, it named names. Where they referred only to "the disciples," the fourth would specify *which* disciples. "Philip answered him . . ." (6:7); "Andrew, Simon Peter's brother, said to him . . ." (6:8); "Simon Peter answered him . . ." (6:68); "Then said Thomas which is called Didymus . . ." (11:16); "Philip came and told Andrew . . ." (12:22). Peter, Thomas, Philip and Judas are individually mentioned in the long discourses between chapters 13 and 16. All this requires an eyewitness.

So too does the topographic detail: "Bethany beyond Jordan" (1:28); "Aenon near to Salem" (3:23); "Jacob's well at Sychar, near to the parcel of land that Jacob gave to his son Joseph" (4:5); "the pool of Bethesda" (5:2)[5]; "the boats from Tiberias" (6:23); "Solomon's porch" (10:23); "the place beyond Jordan where John baptized" (10:40); "Bethany about fifteen furlongs from Jerusalem" (11:18); "the city called Ephraim in the country near to the wilderness" (11:54); "the

brook Cedron" (18:1); "the place called the Pavement" (19:13). Only someone who had been there could have furnished such detail.

Again and again, the author insists on his own reliability. "He that has seen it has borne witness and he knows that his witness is true" (19:35); "This is the disciple who bears witness of these things, and we know that his witness is true" (21:24). Yet, the reader scarcely needs all this. The text breathes credibility. Not for

*Seen from the ramparts (left) of the fortress-like Monastery of St. John and over the rooftops of the village of Chora (foreground), this hill on the island of Patmos looks out over the islands of the Aegean. In addition to the main monastery which dominates the island, a smaller one (right) was built around the cave in which the exiled John the Evangelist is said to have received his astonishing vision, known as the Revelation.*

---

5. John's description of the porticoed place of healing at Bethesda seemed implausible to many biblical scholars because the pools known to exist in the area were wide, deep reservoirs inappropriate for the purpose. However, the excavation in the 1960s of an area east of the major pools revealed one containing a number of small grottoes with paved steps leading down to them, a rectangular stone washing basin, and relics of votive offerings of a healing sanctuary. As for the "troubling of the water," mentioned in the text, this too finds ratification in the Jewish historian Josephus, who refers to intermittent springs in the area that he calls by the Aramaic name *Bethzatha*. A copper scroll found with the Dead Sea Scrolls at Qumran confirms the Hebrew name to be Bethesda. Once again, the Fourth Gospel's accuracy had been affirmed.

*Until excavations were undertaken adjacent to the crusader-era Church of St. Ann in Jerusalem, scholars doubted John's description of the pool of Bethesda, its location and even its existence. Archaeological digs in 1888 and 1956 proved the evangelist accurate in this and numerous other details he mentions in his gospel.*

another eighteen centuries, with the appearance of the modern novel, would writers learn to invent otherwise irrelevant details to make imagined scenes seem real. This man wrote these things because he heard and saw them. How else could they be accounted for?

It's plain also that the writer had the other three accounts before him. He omits a great deal that they include because he considers their description adequate. The genealogical tables and the infancy and childhood stories that begin Matthew and Luke are not there. But he also solves problems the others left unresolved. They record only one visit of the adult Jesus to Jerusalem, an improbability since devout Jews customarily made the pilgrimage annually. John records a visit in each year of Jesus' three-year ministry.

Like Mark's, the Fourth Gospel begins its narrative with the ministry of John the Baptist. But from there on to the arrest and trial, Mark's is a compendium of one miracle after another. In John there are only seven miracles, each cited to convey a theological point. A blind man's sight is restored to show Jesus as "the light of the world." Jesus walks on the water to show himself as a guide. Water is turned into wine to relieve a hostess's embarrassment at a wedding banquet and to demonstrate that God has kept back the best wine until now, meaning presumably Jesus.

There is no mention in the Fourth Gospel of the directive about the bread and wine at the Last Supper. Since the churches were everywhere following it, there would be no need to cover it again. What the fourth does give, however, is a description of an appalling incident on the Galilee shore after the feeding of the five thousand, when the crowd sought to proclaim Jesus as a king. "Unless you eat the flesh of the Son of Man and drink his blood," Jesus declares, "you have no life in you" (6:53). Understandably revolted, people deserted him in droves. Even the Twelve were shaken.[6]

John's account of the Last Supper does provide the striking example Jesus left for every succeeding generation. Taking a towel and washing the feet of his fol-

## Was Jesus God? First-century Christians saw that the answer was not simple. Nature is not simple, so why then should we expect the Creator of nature be simple?

lowers, he drives home the point that the Christian leader must see himself as the servant of those he leads. (He thereby furnished the title assumed by the bishops of Rome—*Servus Servorum Dei*, "the Slave of the Slaves of God," a description a considerable number of them would actually live up to, though certainly not all, as events over the centuries would disclose.)

Finally, the Fourth Gospel's record of the Last Supper includes four full chapters of discourses the author recalls Jesus making, whether then or on other occasions, infused no doubt with John's own reflections over the years. These and other discourses in the Gospel would provide maxims and sayings of Jesus that would inspire Christians throughout the ages: "I am the vine and you are the branches" (15:5); "I am the door of the sheep" (10:7); "I am the Light of the world" (8:12); "I am the Resurrection and the Life" (11:25); "I am the Way, the Truth and the Life" (14:6); and finally the beloved, "I am the good shepherd . . . and I lay down my life for the sheep" (10:14, 15).

Little in the Fourth Gospel directly contradicted the other three accounts. Rather, it complemented or completed and explained them. The narratives of Matthew, Mark and Luke, wrote Anglican Archbishop William Temple in his *Readings in St. John's Gospel*, "are unintelligible unless something like John's story is accepted." The others, he says, give a photograph of Jesus where John

---

6. Some Christians question the assumption that Jesus was referring to the bread used in the Last Supper in this instance. They see the words "eat" and "drink" as metaphors for "believe," so that Jesus was in effect saying something like: "If you cannot swallow that the Word has become the kind of creature you are (human flesh and blood), you can have no share in God's kind of life."

paints a portrait. The photograph is literally accurate, but the portrait brings out what a photograph cannot.

Jesus' confrontation with Nicodemus, for instance, with its strange assertion that a man must be "born again," is a story not told in the other three gospels. It leads directly to the staggering assertion: "God so loved the world that he gave his only begotten Son, that whoever believes in him should not perish but have everlasting life" (3:16). Temple calls this the "central declaration" of the Christian faith.

More instructive still to first-century Christians, however, was the fourteen-verse prologue with which the Fourth Gospel begins, since it directly addressed the question: Was Jesus God?

"In the beginning," it declares, "was the Word." In the Gospel's original Greek, the term used was *logos*. It was an expression they knew well, since it appeared recurrently in the Septuagint, the Greek translation of the Hebrew scriptures, to render the Hebrew word *dabar*, as in, "By the *word* of the Lord were the heavens made" (Ps. 33:6). Or, "At his *word* the waters stood in a heap, and the reservoirs of the waters at the *word* of his mouth" (from 39:17–18 of the apocryphal Book of Sirach).

But the same term, logos, had ancient usage in Greek philosophy as well. It appeared frequently in Plato, who used the term to describe the rational

*The first chapter of John's Gospel, here seen in a lectionary of the Greek Orthodox Church, majestically introduces Jesus Christ as the Eternal Word, "O Logos." The stirring passage, a statement of faith, is solemnly read in Western churches during Christmas celebrations, while Eastern Christians assign it to be read at the central Easter service.*

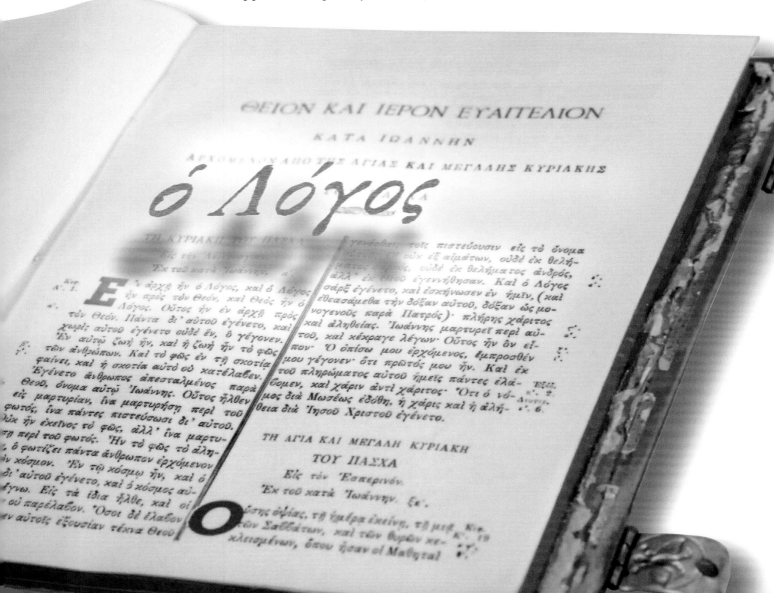

principle that must lie behind all nature. The Hellenistic Jewish philosopher Philo, a contemporary of Jesus who sought to reconcile the Greek Hellenistic tradition with that of his own people, combined the Greek and Hebrew usage of the word. He saw the logos as the image or reflection of God, through which the universe was originally ordered and continued to function.

The term "in the beginning" was also instantly recognizable. It echoed the opening verse of the Book of Genesis. So the Fourth Gospel isn't talking about the beginning of Jesus, nor even the beginning of the world, but the beginning of everything that ever existed. It then makes two seemingly contradictory statements. "The Word," it says, "was *with* God, and the Word *was* God."

A succession of such declarations follow, each as sweeping as the last. Through the Word all things came to exist that do exist. Nothing exists apart from the Word. What came to be in the Word was "life," and "the life was the light of men."

The light "shines in the darkness," it declares, and its next assertion would tax the vocabularies of English translators. "The darkness comprehendeth it not," say the Authorized Version of the English King James I and the traditional Catholic Douay-Rheims translation. "The darkness did not absorb it," says Temple. "The darkness did not overcome it," says the New International Version. "The darkness did not overpower it," says the Revised King James. But the translator Phillips, with a blunt simplicity that strained the Greek but better made the point, averred: "The light still shines in the darkness and the darkness has never put it out."

The text next introduces John the Baptist, who was, it says, not himself "the light" but came to bear witness to it, this being the light "that enlightens every man who comes into the world." The light was in the world and the world didn't know "him." It came to its own people and they didn't receive him. However, those who did receive him gained a new life, became in fact the children of God, born not through nature, nor through the power of man, but through the action of God himself.

Then with a grand finality, the prologue closes. The Word became a living human being and "dwelt among us." So there is the answer. Jesus is the Word. He is "with God" and also "was God." The prologue concludes: "We beheld his glory, the glory as of the only begotten of the Father, full of grace and truth."

Startling though it was, the gospel's first hearers would have realized that much the same description had been used by St. Paul. In his epistle to the Christians at Colossae, he had portrayed Jesus as the "image" of God. (Col. 1:15); all things were created through him (1:16); all wisdom and knowledge are concentrated in him (2:3); in him the fullness of God dwells (1:19); he reconciles all things to himself, and through the cross he vanquished all the principalities and powers of Heaven and Earth (1:20).

Along with John's Gospel and the Revelation, three other documents appeared, all letters or epistles ascribed to the name "John" and sharing the language of the gospel. The first repeats the terminology of the Fourth Gospel's prologue. "The Word of life," it begins, "that which was from the beginning, which we have heard, which we have seen with our eyes, which we have looked upon, and our hands have handled . . . this is what we declare unto you" (1 John 1:1–3). These three letters would likewise be incorporated into the New Testament.

So the question was answered. Was Jesus God? Yes, and yet not quite yes, since he was also "with God." The nature of God, so it appeared, was not simple.

*The traditional tomb of John the Evangelist is a regular stop in Ephesus for Christian tours and pilgrims. The four columns mark the apparent location of the tomb amidst the ruins of the Byzantine basilica. In the background is a restoration of the fifth-century Christian fortress that dominated the newer areas of ancient Ephesus.*

Yet, why should it be simple? they could ask. Nature is certainly not simple, and the more men discover about it, the less simple it becomes. So why, then, should we expect the Creator of nature to be simple?

Something else became abundantly clear to them. If the Word of God, which had existed from the beginning of time, had become in fact and in deed a living human being on this Earth, then that event must be paramount over all other events, at least as important as the first appearance of life itself.

Beside this, everything else must be inconsequential. Rome, the emperor, the pagans, the mob, all the forces ranged against them would be as nothing. For the light would shine in the darkness, and the darkness would not put it out.

# The skeptics sought to destroy John's Gospel, but textual discoveries badly let them down

**Modern finds made the New Testament the most reliable of the ancient classics**

In the year 1826, when Ferdinand Christian Baur became a professor of theology at his old alma mater, Germany's 350-year-old Tübingen University, the thirty-four-year-old academic launched a war on the historical credibility of the New Testament in general, and on the Gospel of John in particular. It was a concerted assault that rapidly gained the support of nearly all of Germany's nineteenth-century "modern scholars."

Seventy years later, the most respected biblical historian of the age, who had once been an ardent disciple of Baur, formally announced that the war was over, and that the "school of Baur," as it had come to be called, had lost. The attack on the New Testament had failed, he said, and in the four decades that followed, one archaeological and textual discovery after another confirmed the defeat.

But the war was not over. In the twentieth century's last half, scholars yet more modern resumed the assault, strongly supported, if not by the evidence, at least by the news and television media.

Baur's mode of attack was to apply the philosophical method of another Tübingen graduate, George Wilhelm Friedrich Hegel, to Christian origins. According to Hegel, truth is not something that exists in a single time and place, but rather something that emerges from an evolving pattern of human conflict. Controversies began with some *thesis* that is challenged by an *antithesis*, finally resolving in the emergence of a *synthesis*. The entire New Testament, said Baur, cannot be understood as a simple record of things that actually occurred, but rather as a conflict between the forces that supported Peter (thesis) and those that supported Paul (antithesis), resolved finally by the rise of Catholicism (synthesis).

The New Testament books had been written many years after the events they purported to describe, Baur said, and always to espouse either Peter's version of Christianity or Paul's. On this ground, he assigned new dates to their composition. The synoptic Gospels—Matthew, Mark, and Luke—had been written between A.D. 100 and 150, and therefore could not possibly represent a reliable record of things that happened perhaps a hundred or more years before. Of the Pauline epistles, only Romans, the two to Corinth, and Galatians could be accepted as written by Paul, because they showed evidence of conflict with Peter. The First Epistle of Peter was too much like Paul's to be genuine. Acts must go, because it represents Paul as being on friendly terms with Peter. Finally, least reliable of all was John. It was written, asserted Baur, sometime between A.D. 150 and 200.

The attack struck the Christians at a vulnerable point. Was this really true? Had the Bible been *proved wrong*? To peoples for whom the Bible, generation after generation, had provided the whole moral, spiritual, and philosophical rationale for everything that mattered in life, this was a devastating blow.

The "Bible," to English-speaking Protestants, whether American or British, meant the Authorized or "King James" Version, produced at the directive of James I, the first Stuart king of England, early in the seventeenth century. But the Greek texts from which it was translated went back only to the twelfth century. The Martin Luther Version, similarly cherished by German-speaking Protestants, suffered the same vulnerability. The Douay-Rheims Version, used by English speaking Catholics, had better credentials, having been translated from St. Jerome's fourth-century Latin. Of them all, however, Baur's disciples could ask: Accounts written a century or more after the event? Translated often from texts dated a thousand or more years after that? How could such things claim historical veracity?

The Christians did have a rejoinder. After all, they said, classical historians like Tacitus, Suetonius, and Herodotus were likewise translated from copies made eight hundred or more years after the originals. Why did this not challenge their credibility? Why just the Bible? But this response, as was so often to prove the case, received nothing like the public attention given the original criticism.

Most Christians simply refused to believe Baur's contentions and ignored them. But some embraced them, particularly the intellectually enterprising of the rising generation, and these began the twentieth century with the seeds of biblical skepticism firmly sown. Those seeds would take root, strongly reinforced by Darwin's theory of natural selection. Arising alongside Baur's

*Ferdinand Christian Baur was just the first of the scholars at Tübingen university in Germany to take critical aim at the credibility of the Gospel of St. John.*

claims, Darwin's theory further weakened the tradition, by demonstrating, or so it was claimed, that nature's species came about, not through specific design, but through sheer happenstance.

Long before the nineteenth century closed, however, the school of Baur found itself faced with a formidable foe. A circle of British scholars, led by Joseph Barber Lightfoot, bishop of Durham,[1] established that evidence for a century-long conflict between the disciples of Peter and Paul simply did not exist, and the content of the books themselves provided more than adequate rational grounds to accept the dates Christians had traditionally assigned to them, if not even earlier ones.

---

1. Besides J. B. Lightfoot, nineteenth-century British scholars who successfully defended the credibility of the New Testament against the attack by the school of Baur included William Sanday, George Salmon, Brooke Foss Westcott, and Fenton John Anthony Hort.

It remained then for Adolf von Harnack, once a Baur sympathizer, and described by *The Oxford Dictionary of the Christian Church* as "probably the outstanding patristic scholar of his generation," to pronounce the claims of the school of Baur as unfounded. In an unexpected public statement that shocked the school's friends and foes, he declared in 1897: "In all main points, and in most details, the earliest literature of the church is, from a literary point of view, trustworthy and dependable. . . . The assumptions of Baur's school, one can almost say, are now wholly abandoned."

However, he conceded that great damage had been done: "There remains an indefinite lack of confidence in the validity of the early Christian literature, a method that clings to all sorts of small details, which it seeks to use as arguments against the clear and decisive evidence."

Archaeology, meanwhile, was vindicating the Old Testament. At the turn of the twentieth century, skeptics could assure the public that writing did not exist in Moses' day (some time between 1500 and 1200 B.C.); therefore, the first five books of the Pentateuch must represent mere mythology, handed down orally, including, of course, the Ten Commandments.

*It fell to another Tübingen theologian, Adolf von Harnack, to pen the epitaph for the Baur school. Baur's assumptions, he suggested, were "wholly abandoned."*

But with the 1900s, one find after another reduced the skeptical case itself to mythology. Excavations by the Americans at Nippur (1900), by the Germans at Ashur (1903–1914), and by the Americans and British at Ur (1918–1939) and at Kish (1922–1926) produced thousands of inscribed tablets ranging back to 2000 B.C. and beyond. Papyrus scrolls just as old were found in Egypt. All these clearly evidenced writing that predated Moses by as much as eight hundred years. Scores of other discoveries turned up examples of writing contemporary with Moses.

Much stronger validation was forthcoming for the New Testament. In 1844, a complete text of it had been found at St. Catherine's Monastery on Mount Sinai. Written on vellum and known as the Codex Sinaiticus, it was dated back to the fourth century A.D. when vellum, made from animal hide, began replacing papyrus, made from reed pulp, as the standard writing material. Nothing earlier than this was expected, because papyrus either dries out and flakes, or becomes damp and rots. Yet as the twentieth century unfolded, legible papyrus fragments were found in Egypt, where the dry climate prevented decomposition. Except for fragments, however, few of these were from New Testament writings.

Then, in 1931, came a bonanza.

Codices were discovered in Egypt with eleven Christian manuscripts, seven from the Old Testament; one a sermon by Melito, bishop of Sardis, written in the late 100s, and three from the New Testament, including parts or the whole of all the books. These were dated in the early 200s and included, of course, the Gospel of John. They were acquired by a New York-born mining engineer named Alfred Chester Beatty and are known as the Chester Beatty Papyri.[2]

*Bishop J. B. Lightfoot of Durham in England not only defended the New Testament against Baur's attacks but argued convincingly for even earlier dating of its books.*

A far more astonishing discovery had been made eleven years before the Chester Beatty find, but had not been recognized until the mid-1930s. At the turn of the twentieth century, two British papyrologists, Bernard P. Grenfell and Arthur S. Hunt, discovered that a number of trash mounds in the Faiyum Oasis region southwest of Cairo, which the local farmers were using as a source of fertilizer, were largely composed of hundreds of papyrus rolls of great antiquity. In the ensuing years they brought them out and turned them over to the John Rylands Library in Manchester, England, where scholars began to segregate and catalog them.

In 1935, one of those scholars, C. H. Roberts, produced a single fragment of papyrus which he definitively dated between the years A.D. 100 and 150. It was about the size of the palm of a man's hand. On one side of it, he said, were the thirty-first, thirty-second, and thirty-third verses of the eighteenth chapter of John's Gospel, on the other the thirty-seventh and thirty-eighth verses of the same chapter.

The implications were momentous. It meant that the oldest extant fragment of the New Testament is from the Fourth Gospel. More important, it meant that early in the second century, that Gospel was circulating in the interior of Egypt, seven hundred miles away from Ephesus, where it had been written. From the standpoint of textual validity, the Fourth Gospel became the most authenticated book in the New Testament, and it was instantly evident that the book must have been written before the turn of the second century, possibly long before it. The school of Baur was very dead indeed.

But not the skepticism it had helped give rise to. Following the Second World War, another attack on the New Testament began, led off this time by Anglican

2. Alfred Chester Beatty (1875–1968) assembled the biggest oriental manuscript collection ever held privately. He donated it to the Irish Republic, which made him the Emerald Isle's first honorary citizen.

Bishop Ernest William Barnes of Birmingham, whose book, *The Rise of Christianity*, confessed his rejection of most Christian doctrines and, of course, the historical reliability of all the Gospels, but especially John's.

This drew a reply from one of the ablest scholars of the day, Sir Frederic Kenyon, former director and principal librarian of the British Museum, who in about fifty pages of his book *The Bible and Modern Scholarship* took the bishop's book to pieces point by point, all demonstrating that in essence it was a restatement of Baur, 120 years later.

Since the 1960s put virtually all traditional institutions under attack, it was almost obligatory that the Fourth Gospel be assailed again by biblical critics. No longer able, however, to portray it as an accretion of legend because of the disconcerting Rylands Fragment, its foes were driven to new innovations.

Attention was focused on its authorship. It was certainly not John the Apostle, most critics agreed, because he was a simple fisherman and probably couldn't speak Greek, let alone write one of the most spiritually moving religious masterpieces in human history.

So there must have been another author. For years, Christians had speculated that a certain John the Elder, a disciple of John Zebedee, had in fact produced

## Modern scholars always seemed to start out with the assumption that the biblical accounts of Jesus could not be historic, and to end up with bizarre speculation.

the gospel and the three epistles that accompanied it. Their third-person reference to the "beloved disciple" as the eyewitness authority for them, they said, was obviously a reference to John the Apostle, whose memories they record.

No, said the new critics, John Zebedee had no doubt been killed years before at the same time as his brother James, just as was recorded by the historian Papias, writing early in the second century. But Luke, replied the Christians, records the death of James (Acts 12:2). Why would he have not mentioned John if they had both been killed together? Perhaps he didn't know about it, or perhaps it was an oversight, came the reply.

Moreover, said the critics, John Zebedee could not possibly have been the gospel's "beloved disciple." But then where, Christians asked, did John Zebedee go? If he isn't the "beloved disciple," then what happened to him? He appears repeatedly in the other three Gospels, but isn't mentioned at all by name in the fourth.

The answer to this question never seemed to get made, because another, even tougher one kept coming up: If the "beloved disciple" wasn't John, then who was he? Why do the other gospel writers take no notice of him?

"He may not have been an apostle," replies author Greville Cooke in his book *Who Wrote the Fourth Gospel?: A Short Summary of the Evidence*, "but a young man with whom Jesus became deeply intimate, who resided in Jerusalem,

# Preserving the New Testament in the desert

**At the foot of Mount Sinai, Greek Orthodox monks have for seventeen centuries guarded Christian texts**

A Greek Orthodox archbishop once likened St. Catherine's Monastery, nestled in the desert sand at the foot of Gebel Musa (Mount Sinai), to Noah's Ark—because for seventeen centuries its monastic community has zealously protected a treasure trove of Christian art and manuscripts from the tossing storms of natural weather and human strife.

Founded by the Byzantine Emperor Justinian (A.D. 527–565) on the site of a chapel built in 363, the isolated, granite-walled monastery includes a church said to occupy the very site where the voice of God spoke to Moses from the Burning Bush. Also within the stronghold stands a remarkable library with more than three thousand ancient manuscripts and five thousand early printed books.

Until 1865, the library's collection included the Codex Sinaiticus, a fourth-century vellum manuscript containing the complete text of the New Testament. Though the monks of St. Catherine's had cherished the codex for centuries, it was unknown to the rest of the world until a German-Russian researcher, Constantine Tischendorf, found it there in 1844.

News of its existence rocked skeptics who had long discounted biblical texts because they could be verified no earlier than the twelfth century. After announcing his "discovery," Tischendorf borrowed the codex in 1865—and, like many other patrons of libraries, he never got around to returning it. In 1933 it passed into the hands of the British Museum.

More recent research has pushed the dates of New Testament fragments back to the late first century or early second, and investigations of the texts indicate the actual writing might have begun even before the fall of Jerusalem in A.D. 70.

Hundreds of tourists visit St. Catherine's Monastery daily in peak season. Though their presence distracts the praying monks, visitors are charged no admission fee—the Greek Orthodox remind themselves that any guest could be Christ in disguise. ■

The ancient alleys and buildings of St. Catherine's give no exterior hint of the modern library (3) that houses the world's second-largest collection of illuminated manuscripts (the Vatican's being the largest) and an impressive group of ancient icons. It was here in the mid-1800s that a German-Russian researcher "discovered" (and later "borrowed") the Codex Sinaiticus (4), which now rests in the British Library. The codex (or book) is, along with the Codex Vaticanus at the Vatican Library, one of the earliest nearly complete versions of the entire Bible.

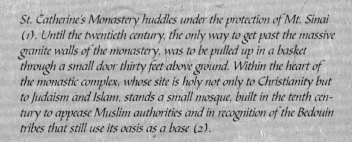

St. Catherine's Monastery huddles under the protection of Mt. Sinai (1). Until the twentieth century, the only way to get past the massive granite walls of the monastery, was to be pulled up in a basket through a small door thirty feet above ground. Within the heart of the monastic complex, whose site is holy not only to Christianity but to Judaism and Islam, stands a small mosque, built in the tenth century to appease Muslim authorities and in recognition of the Bedouin tribes that still use its oasis as a base (2).

occasionally joining Jesus and the Twelve in Galilee." He was proposing, that is, the existence of an unobtrusive spiritual genius that the other gospel writers had neglected to mention, or failed to notice—though he was Jesus' closest confidant, sat beside him at the Last Supper, was entrusted with the care of Jesus' mother, and was, by reputation, destined to live forever. Many people found this difficult. Was it not easier, they asked, simply to believe the book was written by John Zebedee? No it was not, not in the increasingly skeptical 1960s anyway, when it was becoming difficult to believe anything.

Meanwhile, the attack of other modern scholars took a variety of directions. The gospel is heavily influenced by Hellenism, some said. No, said others, it's decidedly Jewish, clearly aimed at a purely Jewish audience. No, still others replied, it's actually anti-Semitic, continually complaining about "the Jews." These felt the text should be rewritten to eliminate this taint.

Someone else must have written the prologue, said many critics. Someone else must have written the twenty-first chapter, which is an epilogue, said others. Someone else must have written the whole thing, said Rudolf Bultmann, another Tübingen man, born twenty-four years after Baur died, who revived the inclinations of his school minus its Hegelian methodology, and led the movement against the historical credibility of the Fourth Gospel in the twentieth century.

To Bultmann, the gospel was undoubtedly influenced by Gnosticism. Great credibility was by his time being conferred on the so-called Gnostic gospels; late second-century versions of Christ's life rejected by the early Christians as too far removed from the events they described to be included in the New Testament.

Whatever their date of origin, these scholars replied, they had at least been produced late enough to escape the doctrinal biases of the earlier gospel writers. They could therefore be counted on to give a far more accurate description of what Jesus had actually taught, they argued, than the Gospels, particularly the Fourth. The Christians noted an irony here. Where in the nineteenth century the Fourth Gospel had lost credibility because it had been written so late, it now lost credibility because it had been written so early. Biblical criticism, in other words, had come the full circle.

But by then, something else was evident. "Modern scholars," as the media reverently referred to them, inevitably seemed to begin with the assumption that the biblical accounts of Jesus could not possibly be historic. Their task, as they saw it, was always to answer the question: What did he *actually* do and say? Increasingly bizarre speculations followed. Their initial assumption, however, they rarely if ever questioned. ■

# CHAPTER 2

# *This revolting new sect: Who, exactly, are they?*

**After torturing two slave girls, an icy bureaucrat deems the cult harmless, but as Ignatius is led in chains to Rome, the Christian sky darkens**

Around the year 110, Gaius Plinius Caecilius Secundus, the Roman governor of Bithynia in the northern part of what is today's Turkey, discovered something truly disturbing: His province was crawling with members of a vile and dangerous religious cult called Christians. To Plinius—or Pliny, as he is known today to English-speakers—that was like opening a kitchen cupboard in your rich aunt's mansion and finding it full of cockroaches.

Pliny was someone your rich aunt might have known had she lived during the early second century. He hailed from one of Rome's wealthiest and most aristocratic families. His uncle, also named Pliny and known as Pliny the Elder, had been a famous amateur scientist whose intellectual curiosity had gotten the better of him; he had died of smoke inhalation in A.D. 70, after sailing into the harbor near Pompeii to take a closer look at the eruption of Mount Vesuvius. Pliny the Younger (his official name) had a talent for administration, and had chosen a life of government service in the bureaucracy of the Roman emperor Trajan, a military hero whom Pliny admired greatly.

Christians! Pliny had heard a little about them, and everything he had heard

COSENTINO

was bad. "Degenerate"—that was one word for the sect that stuck in Pliny's mind. Pliny's friend, the snobbish Roman historian Tacitus, maintained that the Christians were "notoriously depraved" and called their faith a "deadly superstition." They were rumored to indulge in lewd nighttime ceremonies that included group sex, even with the participants' own mothers and children, and the ritual slaughter of infants, whose blood they drank. To the Romans, who revered the family despite the debaucheries of some of their less lustrous emperors, such stories were shocking.

The worst feature of the Christian religion, however, was that dead Galilean carpenter, or criminal, or traitor, or whatever he was, who had been crucified—with good reason, no doubt—in Judea nearly a century before. A Jew! One of them! One of those stiff-necked, keep-to-themselves atheists who refused to worship the traditional gods (they claimed to have their own god, who was invisible and thus hardly counted as a god), and they were constantly whining about the rule of Rome and yearning for the arrival of a king of their own, whom they called the Messiah, or Anointed One. All educated Romans of the late first and early second centuries—Tacitus, his fellow historian Suetonius, and the writers Martial, Quintillian, and Juvenal among them—detested the Jews as haters of the human race, and they lumped Christians and Jews together.

The crucified carpenter had a Jewish name, *Yeshua* or, in Greek, *Iesous*, a version of Joshua, the name of the Jewish biblical hero, but Pliny and his Roman contemporaries probably didn't know that. They called the dead Galilean simply *Christus*, a ridiculous name, since it came from the Greek for "Messiah," and the carpenter had failed abysmally in that kingly role. Or perhaps his name was *Chrestus*, a common man's name in the ancient world that meant "lucky," was pronounced something like *Christus*, and was the name by which the Roman historian Suetonius, another of Pliny's friends, seems to have known Jesus. In their bizarre rites, the Christians worshiped this *Christus* or *Chrestus*, this Christ, this Jewish criminal. Worshiped him like a god, it was said. "A god." Pliny pondered that alien concept in his mind. This Christ was supposed to be alive somewhere or somehow—but hadn't he been dead for some eighty years?

It was illegal to be a Christian in 110, and it had been so for some time. Historians are not certain why the Roman imperial government regarded the sect, whose numbers at the time did not exceed eight thousand in an empire of perhaps sixty million people, as arch-enemies of the state. Clearly, however, the Christians refused to worship the Roman emperors as gods—and every emperor since Augustus, who reigned when Jesus was born, had been deified either in his lifetime or shortly after his death. Refusing to recognize the emperor's divinity was *maiestas*: treason, setting oneself up against the state, a crime punishable by death.

The Jews, of course, took exactly the same position as the Christians, but for nearly two centuries there had been a tacit arrangement that allowed the Jews to pray to their own god in their synagogues for the emperor's well-being, rather than have to sacrifice directly to either the emperor or the pagan gods. Certainly, the Jews could be hard for a Roman official to handle. While Pliny was governing Bithynia, Jewish groups, outraged at the special taxes that Rome required them to pay, were plotting riots against Rome in their large communities in Egypt, northern Africa, and the Middle East. And there had been that ugly business in Judea in the year 70, when the Jewish homeland was ablaze with nationalist uprisings and the Roman army had to raze the entire city of Jerusalem, including the Jewish Temple, in order to get rid of the insurgents.

But even the Jews seemed preferable to the Christians who wherever they lived inevitably provoked antipathy, even among their own kinfolk, because their primary loyalties were to their movement and to each other, not to their pagan families and friends. Many Christians were converted Jews themselves, because the first Christian missionaries, such as Paul of Tarsus and his first companions, had also been Jews who preached Christ in the synagogues of every city they visited. Jews who accepted Jesus as the Messiah provoked the antagonism of their fellow Jews who did not.

In A.D. 49, Suetonius reported, there had been an uproar in Rome's Jewish quarter "at the instigation of Chrestus" that had led the emperor Claudius to close down the synagogues and expel the Jews from the city. Nearly a generation later, the emperor Nero seized upon the general public aversion toward Christians to blame them for the Great Fire that raged through Rome in A.D. 64, a fire he was accused of having set himself in order to clear the land for some grandiose building projects. Nero ordered a series of sadistic punishments for them: crucifixions; dressing them in animal skins and having them torn to pieces by dogs; setting them afire as human torches.

*One of the oldest manuscripts of the letters of Pliny the Younger is held at the Pierpont Morgan Library in New York. Dating from the early sixth century, it is nearly two centuries more recent than the earliest complete versions of the Bible. No earlier fragments of the Roman governor's reports to Rome exist.*

*Even the most remote of Rome's provincial cities in Asia Minor boasted some feature reflecting the wealth and culture of the empire. The magnificent theater of Aspendos overlooks the Mediterranean coastal plain about two hundred and thirty air miles southeast of Ephesus, near the modern Turkish center of Antalya.*

# The Christians lived amidst the grandeur that Rome conferred on the world

## Asia Minor's luxury inspired the conquerors to expand upon the opulence they found there

Imperial Rome was nothing if not an occupier, but it was neither barbaric nor impoverished, and when it enveloped a country or a city it stamped everything it found there with its unmistakable imprint, often making significant improvements. In Asia Minor, in particular, Roman architects and craftsmen added opulent embellishments to the luxurious appointments that existed there long before they arrived. As a result, although distant from the center of the empire, those who lived in the Roman-occupied cities of Asia Minor were much more than remote agricultural workers, scraping by uncultured in rude tents and huts. Instead, their well-established cities drew the admiration and appreciation of their conquerors, who remodeled and expanded buildings, gardens and other facilities in much more than just a utilitarian manner. Thus the subject territories continued to provide artistic, cultural and educational opportunities unrivaled in most of the non-Roman world. Remains of what Rome created in the region show the breadth and ambition of its influence. ■

In addition to its ubiquitous amphitheaters, Rome built grand gymnasiums, such as the one at Sardis (1), its ruins still standing. Cities frequently developed opulent spas (2)—this one, near Laodicea, still echoes to the splashing of bathers. In some centers, Rome simply enhanced the glories it found, as it did with the breathtaking altar of Pergamum (3), which now resides in its own museum in Berlin. But large-scale grandeur was not the only hallmark of the affluent urban life of Asia Minor. Smaller details in the decoration of these cities, like this touching statue of a baby from the gymnasium at Ephesus (4), confirm the aesthetic reach of Rome.

Around A.D. 90, the emperor Domitian, notorious for his cruelty and his determination to crush all political and religious opposition, brutally persecuted "atheists"—suspected Jews and Christians—among Rome's aristocratic families, including his own. By the time Pliny became governor of Bithynia sometime after 106, Roman policy was clear: You could charge someone with being a Christian (it was as simple as writing up a bill of complaint and presenting it to the local magistrate), and that person was in possibly serious trouble.

It was the parade of accused Christians into his courtroom that first alerted Pliny to the fact that the "notoriously depraved" sect had spread all the way north to Bithynia, a rich agricultural and trading colony positioned on the southern shore of the Black Sea, and was growing rapidly there. That was perhaps inevitable. Just to the west of Bithynia lay the prosperous port cities of Asia Minor, Macedonia, and Greece—Ephesus, Philippi, Thessalonica, Corinth— where the Christian missionary Paul had preached his message of Christ crucified and sent his letters to Christian communities. Galatia, whose towns of Iconium, Lystra, and Derbe were among Paul's stops, directly abutted Bithynia, and Paul had even stopped briefly in Bithynia itself. The apostle Peter had addressed one of his letters to Christians in Bithynia and other nearby regions.

So, since nearly everyone in Bithynia hated the Christians (their refusal to eat meat from animals slaughtered in sacrifice to the gods was said to be depressing prices at butcher shops), Pliny was soon trying large numbers of them in the tribunal that he headed as a provincial governor. Despite the presence in the sect of well-born ladies and gentlemen like Flavius Clemens and Domitilla, Christianity had a reputation as a slum religion, a faith for shoemakers, laundry workers, slaves, and other lowlife, who had few, if any, legal rights to begin with.

Ragged, malnourished, their very bones deformed in many cases by years of hard labor, these despised men and women seemed drawn to their strange Christ, who had taken the "form of a slave," as Paul had written, even though he was supposed to be divine. The Christians repeated among themselves other words of Paul's: that in Christ, "there is no longer slave or free." Paul had written those words, which sounded to people of Pliny's class like a call for mass mutiny, in a letter to the Christian community in Galatia—right next door to Bithynia! Trajan had recently issued an edict from Rome banning secret societies and refusing to allow their members to eat together, an edict that seemed specifically directed toward Christians and their treasonous designs.

Still, Pliny, dutiful official that he was, did not quite know what to do with all these wretched folk, men and women, adolescents and oldsters, city dwellers and peasants, who were dragged cringing before him. Some of them were denying that they were now or ever had been Christians. Others admitted that, yes, they had once worshiped Christ, but that was then, and they were now perfectly willing to revile his name, offer incense to the divine emperor, or do anything else that Pliny demanded of them in order to show that they were as good Roman subjects as anyone else. So Pliny sat down and wrote to his superior in Rome, the emperor Trajan, asking for advice.

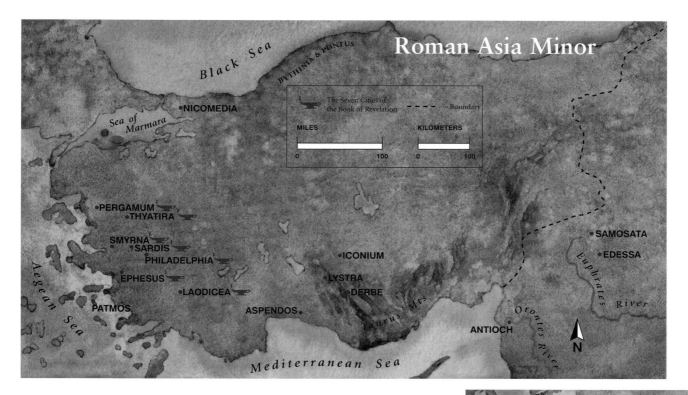

Roman Asia Minor

*Black Sea*

BYTHINIA & PONTUS

The Seven Cities of
the Book of Revelation ---- Boundary

MILES                    KILOMETERS

0              100        0              100

•NICOMEDIA

Sea of
Marmara

•PERGAMUM
•THYATIRA

SMYRNA
•SARDIS
PHILADELPHIA

•ICONIUM                    •SAMOSATA

•EDESSA

*Euphrates River*

EPHESUS                    •LYSTRA
•LAODICEA                   •DERBE

*Aegean Sea*

PATMOS            ASPENDOS•

*Taurus Mts.*

ANTIOCH

*Orontes River*

N

*Mediterranean Sea*

Pliny was famous for his elegantly written letters, batches of which
were periodically published—copied out by professional scribes and circulated—for the delectation of Roman literati who relished a good
Latin turn of phrase. He was also slavishly attached to his hero, Trajan,
who was widely liked by his subjects because of his humane and pro-
gressive administration and his blameless moral life—a relief to the
Romans after the depravities of Nero and Domitian.[1] Pliny pestered
Trajan with letter after letter on the most minute administrative details.
Neither he nor his emperor, however, regarded Christians as anything
more than passing nuisances, on the order of a malfunctioning sewage
system or a fire hazard in a public building that required official attention.

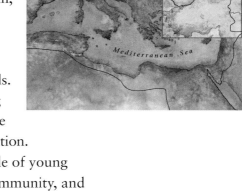

At the same time, Pliny took the precaution of arresting a couple of young
slave-women, who happened to be deaconesses in the Christian community, and
conducting an inquiry. That meant having the two girls tortured until he was sat-
isfied that they were telling the truth. It was standard Roman procedure: First
you stretched your victims out on a rack and cranked at both ends until you
yanked some of their bones out of the joints. Then you moved on to the "claw,"
a hook-like contraption that worked its way along the victims' exposed flesh,
tearing it to ribbons. And then . . . by then, nearly everyone talked.

The terrified deaconesses told Pliny everything they knew. Pliny duly passed

---

1. Domitian, who succeeded his brother Titus as emperor in A.D. 81, died in 96 and was followed on the
throne by Nerva, who spent just two years as emperor before dying of a "feverish chill." Nerva, with no
son of his own, had discovered Trajan on the battlefield, recognized him as a brilliant soldier, adopted
him, and set him up as his heir and successor. So it was that in A.D. 98 the emperor Trajan began a reign
that lasted to 117, during which time the empire grew to be as large and prosperous as it was ever to be
in its history, stretching east as far as Mesopotamia, north to Britain, and south along the entire
Mediterranean coast, including Egypt.

along the information to Trajan: the weekly worship services at which Christians chanted hymns "in honor of Christ as if to a god," as Pliny phrased it; the oaths that Christians swore to refrain from theft, robbery, adultery, and breaches of the peace; the gatherings they used to have before Trajan's ban on secret societies, at which they shared food "of an ordinary, harmless kind," not the blood of babies, Pliny wrote. Yes, the cult was "degenerate," he informed Trajan, but it also seemed innocuous. Christians struck Pliny as a bit strange, but also as ordinary, law-abiding people who happened to hold beliefs and engage in rituals that were incomprehensible to him and other Romans. Pliny also informed the emperor about how he planned to handle the trials: All the accused would be asked three times to abjure Christianity; those who refused after the third opportunity would be executed immediately, except for Roman citizens, who would be sent to Rome for trial—just as Paul, a Roman citizen, had been taken to Rome from Jerusalem for trial some fifty years before.

Trajan's response to Pliny came in the form of a "rescript," an official reply, carrying the force of law, to a local administrator's inquiry. The emperor agreed that Pliny was following exactly the correct procedure, one that should be followed henceforth. Here were the new rules: All Christians who appeared in court were to be given a chance to recant. If they repented of their faith and burnt a little incense to one of the gods or to Caesar, they were to be pardoned on the spot. Furthermore, Roman officials were not to initiate arrests of suspected Christians on their own, and no Christian could be condemned on an anonymous denunciation. Those bringing charges against them would have to prove their case in open court.

This "don't ask, don't tell" policy, which Trajan's successor, Hadrian, reaffirmed in another rescript in 124, became the official position of the Roman Empire toward Christians for nearly a century and a half. In some ways, Christians were worse off than they had been before, because it

was now spelled out in writing that professing their faith could cause them to be hauled in front of a court to face a possible sentence of capital punishment. The form of execution was usually horrible: crucifixion, burning alive, scorching with red-hot irons, being gored by wild bulls or eaten alive by lions or leopards in the violent circus shows that the bloodthirsty Roman masses enjoyed. Alternatively, Christians might be sentenced to slavery in the imperial mines, where they would be worked to death on starvation rations. Rome was clearly afraid of these people whose first loyalty was to Christ, not Caesar, and who had the courage to die for their faith.

In other ways, however, the Christians were vastly better off under Trajan and his successors than they had been before. The persecution of Christians was a sporadic and local matter that depended on the whim of provincial governors—or of the emperor himself, who was free to suspend the sanctions if he wished. Under those conditions, Christianity flourished. By 150, less than forty years after Trajan's rescript, the number of Christians in the Roman Empire had quintupled, to more than thirty thousand. By the middle of the third century, Christians numbered nearly 1.2 million—just under two percent of the empire's total population but an astounding figure for a religion that had begun with a few frightened people huddled in a room in Jerusalem.

Nonetheless, even under Trajan's relatively lenient policies, Christians were suffering for their faith. One of the most notable was Ignatius, bishop of the Christian community at Antioch in northern Syria. Ignatius was a remarkable figure, because he had personally, during his own lifetime, witnessed the entire growth of Christianity from the days of Paul onwards. Widely circulated stories held that Ignatius had even met Jesus himself as a little boy, perhaps while his parents were traveling on pilgrimage to the Holy Land. The Gospel of Mark (9:36, 37) recounts an incident in which Jesus took a small child in his arms in Capernaum and said to his disciples: "Whoever welcomes one such child in my name welcomes me, and whoever welcomes me welcomes not me but the one

*Like Roman emperors before and after them, Trajan (opposite page left) and Hadrian (opposite page right) put their personal stamps on the distant provinces of the empire by engaging in vigorous building programs. In particular, they constructed temples to themselves to ensure the proper attitude of allegiance and civil piety among the populace. In Asia Minor those of Trajan in Pergamum (center) and Hadrian in Ephesus (below) were visited by citizens wanting to show their loyalty by burning incense before the emperor's statue.*

who sent me." Some early Christians said the small child had been Ignatius.

The story is not implausible. Antioch, one of the earliest centers of Christianity outside the Holy Land, lay about three hundred miles north of Jerusalem. It was a sprawling, sophisticated city, the fourth-largest in the Roman world after Rome itself, Alexandria in Egypt, and Carthage in North Africa. Antiochenes worshiped every god and goddess in the Greek, Roman, and Syrian pantheons, but their favorites were Bacchus, the god of wine, and Tyche, the goddess of luck and patroness of Antioch, whose statues could be seen everywhere in the city. There was also a flourishing Jewish community at Antioch, into which Ignatius might have been born.

Within a decade after Jesus' death, there was a good-sized Christian community in Antioch as well. Both Paul and Peter preached at Antioch, converting both Jews and Gentiles. The Gospel of Matthew was believed to have been written there, and the evangelist Luke was said to have been born in that city.

It was in Antioch, some time around A.D. 40, that the followers of Jesus first acquired the name "Christians," the Acts of the Apostles (11:26) tells us—a name that Ignatius himself adopted with enthusiasm in his letters. Antioch's Christian community, thriving from its earliest days (although occasionally marked by quarrels between Jewish and Gentile converts) and headed for a time by Peter himself, was a gateway to the East for missionary activities.

It was into this Antiochene world, bustling with commerce, glittering with wealth—and in its Christian quarter, alive with excitement over the new faith in a son of God who had become human and taken on human suffering—that Ignatius came of age. Perhaps he remembered the Galilean from that childhood journey south so long ago: the strong arms that had lifted him high, the kindly eyes that told him not to be afraid of all those rough fishermen with their strange way of talking, the voice, gentle yet insistent with authority that seemed to come directly from God. Ignatius likely knew Peter and Paul, and perhaps Luke and Barnabas, Paul's companions, and also became close to the aged apostle and evangelist John, who was said to have died in Ephesus around the year 100. Certainly, Ignatius's writings show the influence of John, making it quite plausible that he was John's disciple.

We don't know very much else about Ignatius, however, except that he eventually became bishop of Antioch's Christian community, probably the third in line after Peter and another bishop named Evodius. According to one tradition, Peter laid his hands on Ignatius and gave him the mantle of leadership. Eventually, after he had served as bishop for thirty years, Ignatius ran afoul of the authorities on account of his Christian faith and was sentenced to die in Rome.

According to some, it was Trajan himself, sojourning at the imperial palace in Antioch, who personally passed judgment against the elderly bishop, after Ignatius defied an imperial command that Christians join with the pagans in worshiping the Roman gods. It is unlikely, however, that the enlightened Trajan would have bothered to attack the sect he regarded as only a minor nuisance. It is more likely that Ignatius somehow offended the local authorities in Antioch.

In any event, Ignatius was condemned to be eaten by wild animals in the arena, and he was transported to Rome in chains to meet his death there in front of the screaming crowds.

Why the execution was scheduled to take place in Rome is a matter for conjecture; perhaps Ignatius was a Roman citizen, or perhaps, as Christian leader in the empire's fourth-largest city, he was regarded as a prize prisoner to show off in the stadium. Under a guard of ten Roman soldiers, he made the long, slow, mostly overland trek westward, across Asia Minor, and along the Roman road

*A mosaic from Zliten in Libya (twenty miles east of Leptis Magna) demonstrates the technique used in Roman amphitheaters to provoke wild animals to savage victims. Tied to a stake set on a cart, the prey was moved back and forth, perhaps in sudden jerks, teasing the big cat into attack.*

that wound through the Balkan regions and Greece, where he was to be put on a ship headed for Italy. As he wrote in a letter:

> I am already battling with beasts on my journey from Syria to Rome. On land and at sea, by night and by day, I am in chains with ten leopards around me—or at least with a band of guards who grow more brutal the better they are treated. However, the wrongs they do make me a better disciple.

News of his fate preceded him, and everywhere he stayed, delegations of Christians came to greet him as a celebrity of their faith. He wrote letters to those Christian communities (seven of the letters are still intact) after he moved on to the next town. In fact, Ignatius spent many months on that last journey in some of the cities in Asia Minor—Ephesus, Smyrna, Sardis, and Philadelphia— that were among the "seven churches in Asia" listed in the Book of Revelation (1:11).

Ignatius was a living, second-generation connection between these wide-spread Christians and the apostles—Paul, Peter, and John—who had actually witnessed Jesus' ministry on earth. The pastoral letters that Ignatius wrote to the churches in Ephesus, Rome, Philadelphia, and Smyrna, were modeled on those of Paul, Peter, and John, quoting freely from Paul's own letters, the Jewish

scriptures (he knew their Greek translation very well), and the four Gospels, which were widely circulated in the Christian communities by then. "My spirit is devoted to the cross, which is a stumbling block to unbelievers but salvation and eternal life to us," Ignatius wrote in his letter to the Ephesians, echoing what Paul had written to the Christians in Corinth (1 Cor. 1:18–20) fifty years earlier. "Become wise as a serpent in everything and guileless forever as the dove," Ignatius wrote elsewhere in a paraphrase of lines from Matthew's Gospel (10:16). Jesus is the "door to the Father," he wrote in a language that echoed John's Gospel (10:7–9; 14:6).

*Held in chains by ten "leopards" (as he called his Roman captors), Ignatius is led on to the next city on the land route to Rome—and to his death. As everywhere on his journey, bands of Christians come out to honor their bishop and hero.*

COSENTINO

In his letters, Ignatius begged the Christians in the little communities he visited to remain steadfast in their faith, reminding them that their churches should unite behind the leaders they called bishops, and cautioning them to remember that the Jesus Christ at the center of their faith was truly God's son, but had also become a real human being who had suffered in the flesh—for there were already some who argued that Jesus was no more than a good man, and others who said he was a divine spirit in human disguise who had merely pretended to die on the cross. Ignatius worried that the Church would split up into quarreling factions and forget its roots in Judaism and the God of Israel.

> Avoid, therefore, the evil sprouts that bring forth deadly fruit. Merely to taste this fruit is to meet a sudden death. Such are not the plants of the Father. If they were, they would appear as branches of the Cross and their fruit would be immortal.

As for himself, Ignatius actually looked forward to his martyrdom. He refused the entreaties of the Christians in Rome to let them do something about having his sentence commuted. (There was probably little they could do anyway.) In a letter to the Romans, Ignatius proclaimed that under the grinding of the beasts' teeth into his flesh he would become the "wheat of God," ready to be made into "the pure bread of Christ." His dream of martyrdom came true. Sometime between A.D. 98 and the last year of Trajan's reign in 117, the brave old bishop reportedly died on the sands of the Flavian Amphitheater in Rome—the structure, still standing, known today as the Coliseum—and his remains were brought back to Antioch to be buried.

When he died, however, Ignatius left behind a disciple who would carry on the word-of-mouth Christian tradition that he himself had received from Jesus' apostles.

## 'On land and sea, by night and by day, I am in chains with ten leopards around me—or at least with a band of guards growing more brutal the better they are treated.'

That disciple was a man called Polycarp, a resident of Smyrna.[2] Believed to have been born in A.D. 69, he was at least thirty when he first heard Ignatius preach. But according to tradition, he was already a Christian by then, having been born into a Christian family. Like Ignatius, Polycarp was said to have been a disciple—one of the last disciples—of the aged apostle John at Ephesus, so he was another second-generation link to the time of Jesus' ministry. When John mentioned "an angel in the church of Smyrna" to whom Christ had promised "the crown of life" in the Book of Revelation (2:8–10), he may have had Polycarp in mind.

---

2. Smyrna was the beautiful port city on the Aegean Sea (known as Izmir in today's Turkey) where Ignatius had stayed for several months on his journey to Rome. Like Antioch, Smyrna probably had a large Jewish community, and it is likely that Paul preached in one of its synagogues on his travels. It was in a letter to the Christians of Smyrna that Ignatius begged the churches to stand in unity behind their bishops.

# Three very early Christian books that almost made it into the Bible

**Clement's letter, Hermas's angelic vision, and a manual called the Didache were probably used by Christians who didn't yet have the Gospels**

Some were just silly—recounting fabulous stories, for example, about the Baby Jesus playfully molding live sparrows out of mud. Some were considered dangerously erroneous and were therefore rejected by a majority of Christian communities. Some were known only in copies of copies, fragmentary and variable, their originals long lost. For whatever reasons, any number of ancient Judeo-Christian documents never made it into the anthology now known as the Holy Bible. Most were easily dismissed. For a few of the books that would be excluded, however, the call was very close.

Three such works in particular stand out: the *Epistle of Clement to the Corinthians*, the *Shepherd of Hermas*, and the *Didache* (meaning "Teaching" and pronounced *DID-a-kay*). All were written late in the first century or very early in the second. Clement's letter and the *Didache*, in fact, are among the oldest surviving works of Christian literature not included in the Bible.

Opened now only by historians and theology students if at all, the three contain little that is not included in the books that did become the New Testament. Yet each of them sheds its own light on Christian life in the late first and early second centuries. What's more, by the very fact that they could be omitted they demonstrate that there was a wealth of material available from which the biblical compilers could pick and choose. In short, assembling the New Testament was hardly a matter of having to scrounge up any little scrap that could be found.

The exact date of Clement's letter is controversial, ranging from as early as about A.D. 68 to not much later than about A.D. 97. Its author apparently spent time with Paul at Philippi in A.D. 57 (Paul mentions a Clement in Phil. 4:3), and perhaps traveled to Corinth as well. After Paul and Peter and most of the other apostles were martyred, Clement was a logical choice to govern the church at Rome, and he was selected to do just that. He had read Paul's letters of instruction to the early churches, and when that troublesome church at Corinth erupted in yet another scandal, he wrote to it, just as Paul had done. Though Clement's letter does not contain his name, historians are just

*Like the pastoral letters and books circulating in the early centuries of Christianity, the first art produced by Christians depicted the comforting aspects of Jesus' ministry—not surprising in an age of persecution. The miracle stories and portrayals of Christ as a youthful Good Shepherd were often painted onto the rough walls of catacombs. This fresco in the catacombs of Domitilla in Rome dates from the second century.*

about unanimous in ascribing it to him. For centuries it was incomplete, but a full manuscript was discovered in 1875.

Clement chastised the Corinthians for kicking out some of their leaders, whose sermons they found wearisome, to make room for newer preachers—and for providing no retirement benefits to those they expelled. He also said that church services should be held at scheduled times and that planning and order was important—he suggested emulating the discipline of the Roman legions, and he urged loyalty to the empire and recommended praying for its rulers. He sharply rejected erotic art, instructing the Corinthians that morality was more important than aesthetics. And his text indicates that the doctrine of the Trinity, God in three persons, was held by Christians from its earliest days.

Clement also figures in the *Shepherd of Hermas*, in which he appears as a prominent member of the church in Rome. Hermas is a descriptive narrative, a lengthy allegorical work attributed to the brother of Pius I (bishop of Rome from 140 to 155). Because it was written in Greek, it may have been better known among the Eastern Christians than in the Western church. When it appeared is a matter of much debate, with the year 160 given as the outside date, and the latter part of the first century the earliest.

Hermas depicts a series of revelations experienced by a slave who lived in Rome. The "pastor" is an angel, dressed in shepherd's garb, whose mission is to instruct the slave in the Christian way. The angel provides five visions, twelve "mandates," and ten parables or "similitudes," all stressing the importance of repenting from sin and adhering strictly to the Christian moral code and precepts.

Hermas, while popular in the early church, eventually came to be regarded as useful but not inspired. Tertullian, a follower of the rigid Montanist doctrine, rejected it in disgust for what he saw as its wrongheaded belief that Christians could be forgiven if they committed serious sins after baptism. He called it

"The Shepherd of the Adulterers." Nineteenth-century researchers revived scholarly interest in it—pointing out that, whatever its content, it was as much a work of historical importance as the paintings in the catacombs.

As for the *Didache*, it's a handbook of sorts, a manual in Christianity for those who lacked access to copies of the Gospels or Paul's Epistles. It begins by stating the case:

> There are two ways, one of life and one of death, and there is a great difference between the two ways. The way of life is this: First of all, thou shalt love the God that made thee; secondly, thy neighbor as thyself. And all things whatsoever thou wouldst not have befall thyself, neither do thou unto another. . . .
> But the way of death is this: First of all, it is evil and full of a curse; murders, adulteries, lusts, fornications, thefts, idolatries, magical arts, witchcrafts, plunderings, false witnessings, hypocrisies, doubleness of heart, treachery, pride, malice, stubbornness, covetousness, foul-speaking, jealousy, boldness, exaltation, boastfulness.

These words, and the rest of the book's sixteen chapters, were written by the Twelve Apostles themselves, the *Didache* claims. Some historians suggest that it was a product of the first Apostolic Council, held in A.D. 50 (Acts 15:6). Like Clement's epistle, it was lost for many centuries. Rediscovered in a library in Constantinople in 1873, it consists of moral instruction, including guidelines for prayer, worship, baptism, fasting, and the communion service or Eucharist. Abortion opponents cite its explicit—and historically very early—condemnation of the practice: "Do not kill children, either by abortion or after birth." It is also one of the first texts, if not the very first, to add to the Lord's Prayer a doxology: "for thine is the power and the glory until all ages."

None of these three books is read much in modern times. As examples of the earliest Christian literature, however, their value is incalculable. Primitive and problematical they may be, but they open another window, from a perspective outside the New Testament, onto the lives of the first of those who were drawn to the person and teachings of Jesus Christ. ∎

*An early third-century mural of Callistus in Rome's catacombs adds an unusual element to the standard illustration of the Good Shepherd. The shepherd carries a pail of what is thought to be milk and honey—symbols of the Kingdom of Heaven as well as the food given to newly baptized Christians.*

By the time Ignatius met him on the way to Rome, Polycarp had become bishop of Smyrna. After Ignatius was transported out of Smyrna to Troas, farther up the Aegean coast, he wrote letters, not only to the Smyrnaeans as a community, but to Polycarp personally. In his message to Polycarp, Ignatius praised the holiness of Christian marriage and also the life of celibacy that he and Polycarp had chosen. "Your mind is grounded in God as on an immovable rock," he wrote.

Polycarp was among the most beloved of early Christian leaders. According to one of his disciples, Irenaeus, who later became bishop of Lyon in Gaul, a dispute arose among the early churches over whether Christians should celebrate Easter, the feast of Jesus' Resurrection, on the day of the Jewish Passover, or as now, on the Sunday after Passover. Many of the churches of the East, including Asia Minor, opted for celebrating Easter on Passover, in recognition that Jesus was the perfect paschal sacrifice, while the churches of the West kept Easter on the following Sunday, because that was the day on which Jesus rose from the dead. Polycarp was selected unanimously by the churches in Asia Minor to travel to Rome and argue the Eastern position to Rome's bishop, Anicetus. Polycarp and Anicetus never did resolve their differences on the Easter date, but they did agree that they were united in worship of Christ. (See also page 280.)

Around the same time, Polycarp wrote a letter to the Christians of Philippi (to whom Paul had also written), in which he argued, as Ignatius had, against Christians who refused to believe that Jesus had been a real human being, and not a god in disguise. Whoever "does not confess that Jesus Christ has come in

**IGNATIUS ON HYPOCRISY**

*The prince of this world is eager to tear me to pieces, to weaken my will that is fixed on God. Let none of you who are watching the battle abet him. Do not let your lips be for Jesus Christ and your heart for the world.*

## Whispers that the Christians were 'atheists' who refused to worship local gods made the pagans afraid their cities would suffer natural disasters or economic catastrophes.

the flesh is antichrist," Polycarp wrote. That letter, like those of Ignatius, was filled with quotations from the Jewish and Christian Scriptures.

Polycarp headed the Christian church in Smyrna until he was eighty-six years old. As for the Christians themselves, the very fact that they were becoming part of the urban landscape, in the period of quasi-tolerance that Trajan had initiated, started to turn their pagan neighbors actively against them in many places. Whispers that the Christians were "atheists" who refused to worship beloved local deities began to surface everywhere; the pagans feared that if the ancestral gods deserted their cities, they would be prey to natural disasters and economic catastrophes. Every time there was an earthquake in Asia Minor, it seemed, an outburst of local violence against Christians was sure to follow.

So it was not surprising that in 155, during the reign of Hadrian's adopted son Antoninus Pius, who was in turn the adoptive father of the famous emperor Marcus Aurelius, Polycarp found himself dragged in front of a hastily convened Roman tribunal in Smyrna. A pagan mob had for days been calling for Christian

*The agora (market) of the ancient city of Smyrna (top) would have been familiar pastoral turf for its revered bishop, Polycarp. The city was a major commercial hub of Roman Asia Minor, blessed as it was with a magnificent natural harbor. Modern Izmir (the Turkish rendering of Smyrna) still thrives as a result of port activities—second busiest in Turkey after Istanbul.*

blood. They first threw a group of Christians, including a teenage boy, to the wild animals in the Smyrnaean arena. Then someone remembered the old bishop who was in charge of all those Christians. Polycarp! "Down with the atheists! Let Polycarp be found!" the crowd began to chant.

Polycarp was at first not eager for martyrdom, and he let his friends spirit him away to a series of farmhouses outside the city. When he was finally tracked down, he offered no resistance, welcoming his pursuers and ordering that they be given food and drink. He also asked to be allowed to pray before being taken away. When they said he could, he stood and began praying in their presence. When he finished two hours later, those who had come to get him marveled at his constancy in spite of his age, and some even expressed regret over the whole affair, acknowledging that they had not been sent out to capture a desperado, but a godly and venerable old man.

He was taken straight to the stadium, where a Roman proconsul was waiting to try him on capital charges. The crowd was roaring like the very animals who had fed on his fellow Christians a few days earlier. But Polycarp was listening to another voice that seemed to come from heaven. It was saying, "Be brave, Polycarp, and act like a man."

The story of what happened next comes from the oldest surviving account of a Christian martyrdom, written down by one of Polycarp's own community at Smyrna. The proconsul, taking pity on the aged man just as those who arrested him had done, offered the bishop a deal: All he would have to do was say, "Away with the atheists"—just once!—and he could go free.

That was not so bad. Polycarp fixed a stern glance on the yelling crowd, looked up to heaven with a groan, and complied. Then the proconsul asked him to do just one more little thing: revile Christ in the name of Caesar. That

## The flames shot up around him like a veil, but his body would not burn, glowing instead like bread baking, like gold melting in a jeweler's furnace.

the bishop could not do. "For eighty-six years, I have been his servant, and he has done me no wrong," Polycarp declared. "How can I blaspheme my king, who has saved me?"

The proconsul ordered Polycarp to be burned alive right in the arena. As he was tied to the stake above the pyre, he prayed continuously. The fire was lit— and then, his followers remembered, something miraculous happened. The flames shot up around him like a golden veil, but his body would not burn, glowing instead like bread baking or gold melting in a jeweler's furnace. Finally, in exasperation, someone stabbed the old man to death. His spurting blood was said to have put out the fire.

The Christians of Smyrna never forgot Polycarp. They spirited his bones away to a grave that would become a place of honor for those who revered the martyrs—and as the years passed, and the number of Christians doubled every couple of decades, there would be much more hostility and many more martyrs, until eventually, the forces of imperial Rome itself would be arrayed in all their might to stamp out the new religion once and for all. Because of course, the Christian faith did not die with Polycarp. He had already personally passed it on—this faith that he had received from the apostle John himself at the end of the first century—to Irenaeus and the other great Christians of the end of the second century.

Some forty-five years before Polycarp's martyrdom, the emperor Trajan, writing to his loyal administrator Pliny, had hoped that offering suspected Christians an opportunity to recant at trial—such a reasonable thing to do—would quietly

**IGNATIUS ON FELLOWSHIP**

*Be zealous, therefore, to assemble more frequently to render thanks and praise to God. For, when you meet together frequently, the powers of Satan are destroyed and danger from him is dissolved in the harmony of your faith.*

*The roar from the throng at the stadium in Smyrna is deafening. They want the old bishop dead. The kindling is lit. But, as the Christians in the city would recall, it wasn't the fire that would kill him. Miraculously, as if to preserve his body, the blaze fails to incinerate him, and his life is finally ended by the slash of a sword.*

eradicate the new and dangerous cult without much bloodshed. For Pliny had written so confidently: "From this one can easily conclude, what a number of people may be reformed, if they are given a chance for repentance." Now, both Pliny and Trajan were dead, and the "great number" had never materialized. What was materializing instead were greater and greater numbers of new Christians.

# As Christians move across Rome's empire, some take on the forbidding lands to the East

**Syriac Christianity sends its missionaries into the war-torn states of Mesopotamia, where a composite book of the Gospels is written, as well as one of the first hymnals**

The triumph of Christianity in its first three centuries was a triumph over the Roman Empire, which lay generally to the west of its birthplace in Jerusalem. To the east of Jerusalem lay another empire, Persia, against which the Romans and their forerunners, the Greeks, engaged in intermittent war for eleven centuries, five of them before Christ and six after. Not until the twentieth century would the Christians progress in the East as they did in the West, but it was not for lack of trying.

Between the two empires stretched a wide and lush plain, bounded by two great rivers, the Tigris on the east and the Euphrates on the west, rising in the Armenian mountains south of the Black Sea and moving southeastward in a "V," finally joining for the last seventy-five miles and flowing into the Persian Gulf. The plain is called Mesopotamia (literally in Greek, "between the rivers") and for eleven hundred years it was disputed territory, occupied now by Persians, now by Greeks or Romans, a perpetual battleground.

At the dawn of the Christian era, Mesopotamia and the mountainous country to the north and east accommodated three buffer-state kingdoms: Osrhoene (pronounced as *Os-ro-AYE-nee*), Adiabene, and Armenia. The first two would soon vanish from history, but the third, Armenia, would endure as a nation for the next two thousand years, tough, implacable, resolutely Christian, and right into the twentieth century paying for its faith in blood, oppression, and sorrow.

Yet it was to Osrhoene that the faith came first—came, it was said, in the form of a letter signed by Jesus of Nazareth himself, a reply to an appeal from King Abgar the Black of Osrhoene's Arab dynasty. Abgar was ill. Would Jesus come and cure him? In the letter, Jesus ostensibly commends Abgar's faith, but says he can do nothing until he has been "taken up," after which he'll send a disciple.[1] And the fourth-century church historian Eusebius tells that after Jesus' death and resurrection, the apostle Thomas sent to Osrhoene a disciple named Addai—in Greek, Thaddaeus, one of the "seventy" commissioned by Jesus in Luke 10:1.

A history entitled *The Doctrine of Addai*, written about 400, details Addai's ministry in Osrhoene's capital, Edessa, a city known to Abraham by its ancient name, Orhay. Alexander the Great's successors renamed Osrhoene as Edessa (it's now Urfa in Turkey), and not far from it, an entire Roman legion had been annihilated when one of King Abgar's predecessors led it into a Persian trap. The Romans never again fully trusted either Osrhoene or the Arabs.

*The Doctrine* tells of Addai healing the ailing Abgar, converting him to Christianity, and making Osrhoene the first Christian kingdom. It records that many were persuaded, not coerced, into the faith by the signs and miracles wrought by Addai and his disciples, and these erected a church, later destroyed in a flood. Addai, it continues, died peacefully, was buried with high honors and succeeded by his presbyter Aggai, the royal robe-maker whose preaching greatly furthered the success of the mission. But then disaster struck. When King Abgar's

*The marketplace in today's Urfa, Turkey, the modern name of ancient Edessa, where the Christians made some of their first forays into the East.*

unbelieving son succeeded him, he ordered Aggai to quit preaching and go back to making robes; Aggai refused, and was executed.

How much of all this, asks the historian Samuel Hugh Moffett, can be taken as reliable history? In his book, *A History of Christianity in Asia*, he makes an assessment. That a first-century mission was launched by the Christians to Edessa under a missionary named Addai he considers probable; that it was sent by Thomas, possible; but that its king became Christian, highly improbable, though a successor king of Osrhoene a century later may very well have become the first Christian king.

---

1. For the text of the letter, see Volume I of this series, *The Veil Is Torn*, p. 230. That Jesus ever wrote such a letter, or anything else for that matter, is accepted by virtually no modern historian, yet the letter enjoyed great celebrity in ancient and medieval Christianity. The historian J. B. Segal in his book *Edessa 'The Blessed City,'* writes that it was translated into every medieval Christian language, engraved on many church archways and on the city gate of Philippi in Greece, and included in an old Saxon devotional book just beneath the Lord's Prayer and the Apostles' Creed. The book is preserved in the British Museum. The church in the sixth century declared the letter spurious. With the letter in its early appearances was an alleged "portrait" of Jesus, painted in Jerusalem by an artist named Hannan. No trace of any such portrait survives.

Light was shed on Osrhoene's early Christianity many centuries later from an unexpected source. For years, scholars had possessed small portions of a mysterious collection of Jewish-Christian hymns called *The Odes of Solomon*, believed to have been composed in Edessa at a very early date, but too fragmentary for conclusive research. Then in 1909, a British scholar, A. Rendel Harris, decided to examine a bundle of old manuscripts that had lain for years on an office shelf. They turned out to be an almost complete set of the *Odes*. Arguably the first Christian hymnbook, they disclose a portrait of the Christian East whose imagery is already qualitatively different from that of the West. Ode 19, for instance, begins:

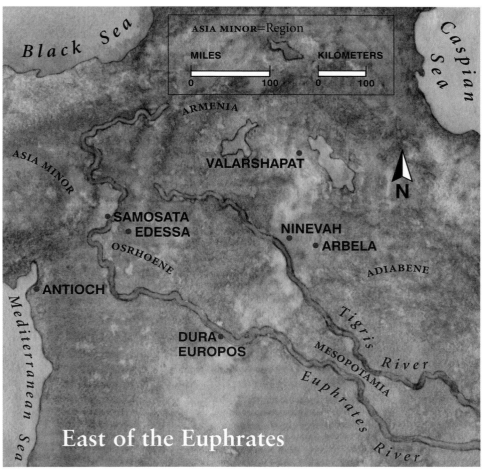

East of the Euphrates

> A cup of milk was offered me
> And I drank it in the sweetness of the Lord's kindness.
> The Son is the cup,
> And the Father is he who is milked;
> And the Holy Spirit is she who milked him.[2]

The *Odes* describe an early morning worship service, with the people stretching out their arms in the form of a cross, as did many early Christians. Though the Jewish influence in the *Odes* is plain, there is a strong emphasis on love as distinct from law, and at one point, they portray a Messiah who embraces the Gentiles "because they have praised me." Finally, while a hymnbook is not a theological treatise, the verses clearly follow Paul and John in affirming a belief in a pre-existing Christ. Thus Ode 41:

> The Son of the Most High appeared
> In the perfection of his Father.
> And light dawned from the Word
> That was before time in him.
> The Messiah in truth is one,
> And he was known before the foundations of the world,
> That he might give life to persons forever
> By the truth of his name.

---

2. In the Eastern Church, the Holy Spirit was often referred to with a feminine pronoun because the Greek word for "Spirit" is feminine. The translation here is *The Odes of Solomon* by James Hamilton Charlesworth of Duke University.

*The very Oriental demeanor of the kingdoms near the Tigris and Euphrates rivers explains the exotic appeal these lands held for Romans. This mosaic of a wealthy family found in a tomb at Edessa in Osrhoene shows them garbed in Persian-looking slippers, trousers and headgear. The unique dress of the area is also evident in the darkstone sculpture of King Antiochus IV of Commagene just to the north of Osrhoene. His rule (A.D. 38–72) followed a pattern common to others in the region repeatedly annexed, then reestablished by the Romans, until the emperor Claudius put an end to the fickle seesaw history by destroying Commagene because of its perceived friendship with Rome's archnemesis, the Parthians.*

After A.D. 113, the history of Osrhoene and Edessa becomes far more specific, because the Roman Emperor Trajan focused western attention on Mesopotamia with a military offensive. He drove through to the Persian Gulf, claiming the whole region for Rome, including the Persian capital, Ctesiphon, on the Tigris. In 117, however, there came a major reversal. Trajan suffered a stroke and died. His successor, Hadrian, aware that Rome had no hope of sustaining an army big enough to control the whole region, pulled back to the Euphrates, leaving Osrhoene, for the moment, a client kingdom of Persia.

Thereafter, much more is known of Christian history in Edessa. Over the next half century two men appear who would shape Christianity in the East for years to come. Both were converts, both born and raised in the buffer states, both would write voluminously and attract a huge following, and both would be challenged as heretics in the West. But the differences between them were much wider than the similarities. In fact, in theology and temperament, each seemed the polar opposite of the other.

The older of the two was Tatian, born about 110 of pagan parents, probably in Adiabene's capital city of Arbela, east of the Tigris. He was converted to Christianity as a young man and became a student of the eloquent Christian evangelist Justin in Rome. When Justin was martyred, Tatian returned to his native land and found it flooded with assorted stories of Jesus' life, many dubious or obviously untrue. He therefore produced a book combining the accounts of all four gospels into one, which he called the *Diatessaron* (pronounced as *Di-a-TESS-a-ron*). It was written in Syriac, the working language of both Syria and Mesopotamia, a version of Jesus' language, Aramaic. Tatian's *Diatessaron* became the first "gospel" read in the Mesopotamian church.

Though he was an eminent and respected New Testament scholar, Tatian's other teachings were much more controversial. He set up a school or community in or near Arbela, whose graduates founded a strict sect called the Encratites, which forbade the eating of meat and the drinking of wine, and pronounced sex evil, even within marriage. These teachings were condemned first in the West, later in the East, as false.

They were in notable contrast with the other highly respected Christian authority in Mesopotamia, Bardaisan (pronounced as *Bar-DAY-san*), known in the West as Bardesanes (pronounced as *Bar-de-SAN-ees*). The son of wealthy parents believed to have fled from the Persian court during a succession dispute, he was raised in prestige and luxury at Edessa, and schooled with Osrhoene's crown prince. Bardaisan shone both mentally and physically, becoming an authority on Persian philosophy and a superb archer in a city renowned for its skill with the bow. Colorful stories were told of his aptitude. Once, during the visit of a Roman emperor, Bardaisan had a youth hold up a shield. Firing arrow after arrow, Bardaisan created a portrait of the youth in the shield. The story survives in the Roman account of the visit.

One day, Bardaisan happened to pass Edessa's Christian church and heard Hystaspes, bishop of Edessa, preaching inside. He became fascinated with the ideas Hystaspes expressed and was soon baptized. Like many converts, he became an outspoken champion of his new faith, distinguishing himself in confrontational dialogues with the city's dominant pagans, and he was made a deacon in the church.

But like Tatian's, Bardaisan's writings got him into trouble and were finally condemned even by his mentor Hystaspes. Striving to make one great world religion (as would others for the next two thousand years), he sought to find common ground between Christianity, astrology, Persian philosophy, and cosmology, and wound up publishing wild speculations of a thirty-person Trinity and a theology in which the Father marries the (feminine) Spirit to produce a Son—through, but not out of, the Virgin Mary.

All of this was denounced as false by later Christian writers. Curiously, however, little of it appears in Bardaisan's one surviving work, *The Book of the Laws of Countries*, which chiefly depicts Jesus as bestowing freedom upon the human race. Bardaisan died in 222, and like Tatian, was followed by a sect, the Bardaisanites, which lasted by some accounts for another four hundred years.

*The ruins of one of the many watchtowers built at Samosata (present-day Samsat) stands guard on the west bank of the Euphrates. The city was located at a strategic crossing of the river and therefore on an important east-west trade route carrying spices and silk on to Rome.*

Unlike Tatian's Encratites, however, the Bardaisanites did not condemn sex—far from it, they believed sex "purifying."

Christian progress in the second buffer state, Adiabene, is much sketchier, though it was without doubt taking place. Adiabene lay east of Osrhoene and beyond the Tigris, its capital city of Arbela (now Arbil in Iraq) the reputed site of Tatian's community and school. A sixth-century document called *The Chronicle of Arbela* speaks of Christian merchants introducing the faith there in the first century and reports the martyrdom of Simeon, second bishop of Arbela, in 123. A Persian account dated eleven years later records a barbarian invasion from the Caucasus being halted with the help of an Adiabene satrap named Rakbakt, described as a Christian convert.

Christian accounts mention two original missionaries, one named Mari, the other Pkidha. They also mention a bishop, Semsoun, put to death later by the Zoroastrians, though many scholars dispute this martyrdom. This would be the first Christian encounter with Persia's great religion whose practice survives to this day in India, where the Zoroastrians are known as the Parsees. Under Persia's Parthian kings, Zoroastrianism was a particularly tolerant religion. A century later, however, with the fall of the Parthian dynasty, that was to change radically.

For one accomplishment, the Edessan courtier Bardaisan might very well take credit. His childhood friend became Abgar VIII, king of Osrhoene, known in the Roman records as "a holy man," and very probably a Christian, who is credited with prohibiting the bloody rite of castration that characterized Osrhoene's ancient pagan religion.[3] The evidence for his Christianity is good, says historian Moffett, and this would reliably make him the first Christian king. The Romans honored Abgar VIII with a state visit to Rome and conferred upon him a Roman name.

He died in 212, and the Romans invited his son and successor, Abgar IX, for another state visit. However, he was arrested on his arrival, deposed, and imprisoned in chains. That was the end of the Osrhoene kingdom. The Romans made it a colony, demonstrating that they still didn't trust Arabs. Whom they *did* trust were the people of Mesopotamia's third buffer state, the Armenians, whose story, one of the most stirring in Christian history, will begin in the next volume. ∎

---

3. In the rites of the mother-goddess Tar'atha, men and women would be driven into a frenzy by the music of pipes and flutes, at the height of which men would castrate themselves.

# CHAPTER 3

# *The man who taught them how to fight back*

**The Christians suffered false charges in silence until the deft convert Justin gave them skill with words, then paid for it with his life**

Marcus Cornelius Fronto was not a man whose views could be taken lightly. Lawyer, senator, friend of Caesar, tutor of the future emperor Marcus Aurelius—when he described the Christian sect, what he said was regarded as authoritative by those who mattered. And to Fronto, the Christians were repulsive.

He sketched their customary ritual. On an appointed day, he said, they gather at a banquet with people of either sex and every age, most of them relatives. "There, after full feasting, when the blood is heated and drink has inflamed the passions of incestuous lust, a dog, which had been tied to a lamp, is tempted by a morsel thrown beyond the range of its tether. It bounds forward with a rush, the light is upset and extinguished, and in the shameless dark, lustful embraces are exchanged. All alike, if not in act, yet by complicity, are involved in incest, as anything that occurs by the act of individuals results from the common intention."

What lent credence to Fronto's description were the things other Romans could see and hear of these Christians. Though they lived in the midst of other people, they were indeed a community unto themselves. Their central rite, which they called a "thanksgiving"—the Greek word for it was *Eucharist*—was veiled

in secrecy. It was a meal of some kind which only full members could attend. The most appalling stories were told about it. They actually consumed, it was said, the body and blood of their founder.

This would be the man Jesus, whom they call "Christ." He was crucified at Jerusalem back in the days of Tiberius on some sort of sedition charge. There was talk of their "reenacting" his crucifixion at each session. So, like the disgusting Druids, for all anyone knew, these Christians might well be practicing human sacrifice. They apparently also practiced cannibalism, and to this must be added incest, for they spoke of "loving" their brothers and sisters, with everything that implied.

Yet they could not be called crafty or deceptive. In fact, they were gullible fools. The worshipers of "that crucified sophist" Jesus, wrote the pagan writer Lucian, could easily be bilked by a few confidence men. They set so little store

by their possessions that "if any charlatan and trickster, able to profit by it, came among them, he quickly acquired sudden wealth by imposing upon these simple folk."

Finally and beyond all that, their community even within itself appeared to lack all proper respect for things like title, social status, education, gender. They did not seem to realize that any society must be structured. They treated one another as equals, sometimes even their slaves. It was shocking. Small wonder Christianity held such appeal to the lower classes and, of course, to silly women. Small wonder, too, that responsible people of rank, senators and statesmen, saw their ideas as a threat. They were. How long could Rome last if fantasies like this took hold?

Apart from this implicit threat to the social order, however, it's improbable that the Roman aristocracy, the great patrician families, much cared about the

*This substantial marble altar, in Pompeii, Italy, stands in a temple dedicated to the cult of the Emperor Vespasian (A.D. 69–79). Since public policy decreed Rome was ascendant by the will of its gods, acceptance of the divinity of the emperor was used as a test of loyalty to the state. Refusal to acknowledge that divinity brought automatic conviction and sentence.*

perceived excesses of Christian worship. Even Fronto's celebrated depiction of them, says his biographer Edward Champlin, was probably no more than a passing reference used to illustrate the "superstitions" imported by the bizarre mix of races flooding into Rome as the empire grew. Along with the grotesque sorceries of these Christians, there were the depraved sacrifices of the Druids brought from Gaul[1] as well as the wine-crazed contortions of the worshipers of Bacchus from Greece (likewise prohibited and likewise practiced), the legalistic gymnastics of the Jews, and the stargazing lunacies of the Chaldean astrologers.

However, the really grave offense of the Christians, the one for which they would be expelled, enslaved, and executed, was their atheism—that is, their effrontery in denying Rome's twelve gods, within the very walls of the city. Did the Roman leadership, drawn from the patrician class and later the army, actually believe in these gods, these stern personifications of sterner virtues, their auguries, and demanding rituals? Probably not, but they very much believed in what they represented. Patrician philosophers of the first century B.C. like Varro and the more famous Cicero would have thought such a question naive. After years of study, Varro deemed civic gods and goddesses worthy of compulsory devotion not because they existed, but rather because they reinforced civic values. As Cicero averred: "Without piety, good faith and justice cannot exist, and all society is subverted."

This was not cynicism. The Romans believed that their city was ascendant by divine will, and that its rule was for the good of all. They were not conquering the world; they were liberating it. So perhaps it was not such a leap for the Senate, the upper legislative house of Roman patrician families, to make Julius Caesar a god in 42 B.C., the year after his death. He was already worshiped in the East, after all, and had not the very heavens saluted him with a blazing comet (later known as Halley's) during his funeral rites? Temples were built and a priesthood enlisted. Even legal oaths, it was decreed, could be taken by the "genius," or immortal guiding spirit, of Caesar.

Julius's successor, Caesar Augustus, was declared a god, but only in the provinces. The Romans were grateful to him for his having ended a half century of civil war and inaugurating the *Pax Romana*, the Roman Peace, a new era of prosperity. Ironically, the first Caesar to assert unqualified divinity for himself was the degenerate Gaius, nicknamed Caligula.

Degenerate or not, this emperor-god, too, was supported by Rome's upper classes. Though unconvinced by imperial "deification," they saw the oath to divine emperors as a loyalty test to Rome itself, and it was therefore enforced on

---

1. The Romans had a deep-seated aversion to human sacrifice, something practiced by two of the toughest opponents they faced in their rise to world power: the Gauls and the Carthaginians. When Julius Caesar ordered a temple to the Egyptian deities Isis and Serapis torn down, a secret temple to the Cappadocian goddess Ma-Bellona was found beneath it with pots full of human flesh. Despite legal prohibitions, however, the practice continued, even in Rome.

pain of death.[2] Since Roman religion buttressed the state, foreign religions were regarded as undermining it, particularly those with secret rites whose deity was a jealous god that forbade oaths to Rome's own deities.

Christians, therefore, could be charged with atheism at any time. However, a crackdown was most likely during plagues, famines, or a military defeat on the empire's frontiers. At such times, most Romans would make offerings to propitiate their gods. Christians not only refused to participate, but some seemed to welcome any catastrophe as a sign of their Messiah's imminent return. The response to their recalcitrance was often mob fury. "Let these nonbelievers themselves become a sacrifice to the gods in the public arena," people raged. So informers would denounce their neighbors and bring them before the magistrates. The accused would be asked to burn a pinch of incense to the divine emperor, or sometimes to take an oath on his "genius." Refusal brought instant conviction and sentence. Some were asked *"Christianus es?"* ("Are you a Christian?"). An affirmative answer amounted to a guilty plea.[3]

## A crackdown was most likely during plagues, famines, or a military defeat, when Romans would make offerings to their gods but Christians would not participate.

Not until 250, under Decius, did the empire as a whole attack the Christians systematically. The earlier sporadic persecutions were nonetheless terrifying. Christians could live in undisturbed peace for years, then suddenly be confronted with sheer horror. The threat of arrest was always there. After all, though they might meet in secret, they lived for the most part in full view of their neighbors in the empire's most populous cities. It was there, of course, that the first evangelists could find the biggest audiences. By A.D. 80 or 90 there were already Gentile Christians living in Rome, and by the middle of the second century their numbers approached thirty thousand, enough to support an impressive professional staff of 150 presbyters or priests, plus deacons and full-time "visitors." They could hardly be called an underground church.

As city folk, they were mostly artisans, tent-makers, cloth-dealers, laborers, slaves and servants, potters, plasterers, masons, and tavern keepers. They also included people of wealth and station; their early writings reveal a sophistication found only among the educated classes. Their preaching in the marketplaces,

---

2. The Jews were usually exempted from the requirements to sacrifice to Rome's gods, partly because they were allies before they became subjects, and partly because their worship was ancient, and the Romans were wedded to tradition, even other people's. Since the earliest Christians were nearly all Jews, they at first enjoyed the same privilege. Once they were differentiated, however, the Christians came under attack—frequently from the Jews, who saw them as pirating their Scriptures and traditions.

3. Informing on people was a profession in imperial Rome, though a despised one. The government paid these *delatores* a share of the estate confiscated from the miscreant convicted by their sworn testimony; the rest of the property went to the emperors, who could always use the money. Informers were paid in various ways. If the punishment were merely a fine, the informer might collect half. Under some emperors, there was a fee schedule, the amount varying with the seriousness of the offense. Informers grew so rapidly in numbers that various emperors attempted to restrict them, or banish the worst among them. False accusers were punished, often with the very penalties that their victims would have merited if convicted.

their mixed-gender services, their care for the sick, all in the tightly packed living conditions of Rome, inevitably drew attention, much of it scornful. Their children were taunted by other children. Christians were ridiculed in graffiti like the one still there on the Palatine Hill, showing a man standing before a crucified donkey, over the words, "Alexamenos worships his god."

The rumors of their sexual excesses lay in sharp contrast to the facts. Many took Paul's advice and became celibates, vowing they would never marry. Divorce was disapproved among the Christians. So was the remarriage of widows. Some observers, like the second-century pagan physician Galen, wrote admiringly of them: "They include not only men, but also women who refrain from cohabiting all their lives; and they also number individuals who, in self-discipline and self-control, have attained a pitch not inferior to that of genuine philosophers." Fidelity and chastity in marriage were still ideals in imperial Rome, respected if not observed, but Christians practiced them so conspicuously and universally they became hallmarks of their faith.

They similarly distinguished themselves by their support for the needy, the sick, for widows and orphans. They consistently networked. The wealthier employed the needy, preferred their brethren in business, and opened their houses as meeting places, adorning the walls with frescoes and the floors with

## Most Christians refused to attend the gladiatorial games, to use imperial coins proclaiming the emperor a god, or if they were teachers to retell the bawdy deeds of pagan deities.

mosaics showing communion loaves, chalices, praying figures, and such symbols of Christ as lambs and fish.[4] The Christians were their own mutual-aid society that transcended class.

They distanced themselves from their neighbors in other ways. Most refused to attend the gladiatorial games, or use imperial coins that proclaimed the emperor a god, or teach school, lest the syllabus require retelling the bawdy shenanigans of pagan deities. They shunned the theater for the same reason, along with sculpture or painting, and they denounced rampant homosexuality within the public baths. A Christian had to be careful in businesses where contracts were sealed with oaths to deified emperors.

Where they refused to do things everybody else was doing, they also took part in activities that excluded others. They attended worship services or study groups in the evenings that sometimes lasted till dawn. So they were a strange people, and since most of them were converts, they stood in marked contrast not only to their neighbors but also to their former selves. As one of them wrote:

---

4. Portraits of Christ were few in Roman houses, and those that survive mostly show him as an idealized, beardless youth like the god Apollo. "We do not know of his external appearance," wrote Augustine in the fifth century. In early representations, Christ is portrayed as a beardless youth. Not until later did the depiction of a bearded, long-nosed, individualized Savior become the unmistakable convention.

One of the oldest known representations of Christ is actually a derisive graffito on the wall of a former guardroom on the Palatine Hill in Rome. Dating from about A.D. 200, it depicts a figure nailed upon a cross with another looking on, one hand upheld in a gesture of worship. To add offense, the crucified figure was drawn with what appears to be the head of an ass. A crude inscription reads: "Alexamenos worships his god."

We who formerly delighted in fornication now embrace chastity alone; we who formerly used magical arts, dedicated ourselves to the good and unbegotten God; we who valued above all things the acquisition of wealth and possessions, now bring what we have into common stock and share with everyone who is in need; we who hated and destroyed one another and, on account of their different customs would not live with men of a different race, now, since the coming of Christ, live on excellent terms with them and pray for our enemies.

The author of those words was Justin, a newcomer to Rome, a Christian convert from the East, who arrived in the city about the year 150 and was destined to make a profound difference to the attitude of the Christian community there. For until Justin, the Christians generally suffered in silence the abuse that was so widely heaped upon them. Or they would merely complain like the bishop of Antioch: "Godless mouths falsely accuse us, the godly who are called Christians, saying that our wives are the common property of all and indulge in promiscuous intercourse; that further we have intercourse with our own sisters; and that—most godless and cruel of all—we taste human flesh."

But Justin did not merely complain; Justin fought. He was a lethal debater, and with devastating artistry on public platforms everywhere, he preached the Christian message and declared the Christian case. In the end, he would pay for his eloquence with his life, but some listened, and the seed took root.

Born about the year 100 of pagan parents in the Roman colonial city of Flavia Neapolis in Palestine (ancient Shechem in Samaria), Justin was to live under three emperors—Trajan, Hadrian, and Antoninus Pius—and to die under a fourth, Marcus Aurelius. The son of well-to-do farmers originally from Italy or Greece, he demonstrated from his youth a love of philosophy, and a zest for

*Philosophy lay at the heart of learning in the ancient world and had an important place in Roman life as a framework for argument and debate. Justin saw in this an opportunity to persuade Romans that the search for Truth at the heart of the Stoic and Platonist philosophies was something they shared with the Hebrew prophets—and by extension Christianity. A Roman sarcophagus (left), now held by the Vatican museums, was decorated with this relief of three philosophers in conversation. This depiction of a typical philosopher (center) dates from the first century B.C. or the first century A.D. The second-or third-century A.D. mosaic of a philosopher (right) is held by the the Rheienisches Landesmuseum in Trier, Germany.*

debate: not in the tendentious style of the Roman schools, but rather debate as the means to know Truth, which to Justin meant to know God.

So by arguing he searched, and his search is recounted in one of his three surviving works, *The Dialogue with Trypho.* "I put myself first into the hands of a Stoic," he writes, seeking through the austere, impersonal, morally principled philosophy of Stoicism an avenue to Truth. But after studying with him for some time, "I got no further with respect to God, for he did not know himself, and he was continually saying that this learning was not necessary."

Next he sought out a Peripatetic, a disciple of Aristotelian philosophy (so named because of Aristotle's habit of walking about as he taught), but his new teacher's preoccupation with tuition fees persuaded him he was not a philosopher at all. Still, Justin was not discouraged. Philosophy continued to sound for him "a special note" of "supreme excellence." He then approached a Pythagorean "of great reputation" who told him he must first learn music, astronomy, and mathematics. But just at this point a Platonist philosopher arrived in Flavia Neapolis and took him as a student. Plato enchanted him. "I was quite enraptured with the perception of immaterial things, and the contemplation of ideas added wings to my intelligence," and at last he found himself on the brink of knowing "the Good." Then it happened. He met an elderly man who was Christian.

Well-schooled in philosophy, the old Christian deftly laid bare a major weakness in the approach of Plato's followers. The soul, they held, could achieve union with God only in dreams which the dreamer could not remember later. "What's the use of that?" asked the old man. There could be none, and he cited the axiom that neither God nor Nature ever did anything without purpose. So the Platonic union with God must be false.

## Justin watched Christians die in the arena, and when he saw 'they were afraid neither of death nor of anything else ordinarily looked upon as terrible,' his faith was born.

If man were to come to know God, the Christian argued, it must be through something God himself does, not man. But did God so intervene in the Nature he had created? The old man directed his student to the Jewish Scriptures. Justin plunged into them, devouring them so diligently he could recite them chapter and verse for the rest of his life. But these alone did not bring him to conversion. Could the righteous God he found there be somehow represented on Earth by these dreadful Christians about whom he had heard such repellent stories? Not very likely.

Then, about the year 130, he saw a horrible but amazing sight that changed his mind. In the arena, he watched Christians die. "I saw that they were afraid neither of death nor of anything else ordinarily looked upon as terrible," he wrote. The sight gave birth to his faith. "I concluded that it was impossible that they could be living in wickedness and pleasure." For if such were the goals of the Christians, why would they not perpetuate their pleasures and escape death by offering the required sacrifice to the gods? He believed, and became Christian.

But Flavia Neapolis held little challenge for this eager young convert. He moved to Ephesus, the capital and Christian center of the province of Asia, where John the Apostle was said to have written the Fourth Gospel. Far from abandoning philosophy, Justin saw in it an opportunity for Christian evangelism, and took full advantage of the spirit of free inquiry that prevailed wherever Greek influence had been felt. He opened a Christian philosophical school and strove to reconcile with Christianity the two philosophies he saw as closest to it. God, he concluded, had not confined to the Jews his intervention into the lives of his human creatures. He had influenced the Greeks as well. Thus, while the Hebrew prophets had begun to discern the Truth, so too did Stoicism and Platonism.[5] Meanwhile, instead of fleeing from conflict with the pagan world, he

---

5. The idea of Plato being a "pagan prophet" probably started with Justin. Plato wrote the following account of creation, so reminiscent of the opening verses of both Genesis and John's Gospel: "He was good: and in the good no jealousy in any matter can ever arise. So being without jealousy, he desired that all things should come as near as possible like himself . . . the god took over all that is visible—not at rest, but in discordant and unordered motion—and brought it from disorder into order, since he judged that order was in every way better."

sought out opportunities to confront it, contradicting the theories of his pagan peers so effectively that they became worried and jealous.

A record of one debate appears in *The Dialogue with Trypho*. Trypho was a Hellenized Jew with whom Justin conducted a polite public debate at Ephesus in 135. For Justin, it was the combative opening bell.

When Trypho introduces himself and requests a discussion of philosophy, Justin strikes immediately to the flaw the old man had shown him in philosophy. Why philosophy? he asks. Had not Plato himself observed that every philosophical proof must be stronger than the thing which is proved through it, because the latter is inevitably dependent on the former? How, therefore, could human reason

## To Justin's dismay Marcion, the bishop's son, taught that the God of the Jews was 'fickle, capricious, ignorant, despotic, and cruel,' inferior to the 'Supreme God, Jesus' Father.

lead to a true perception of God, if God, the Creator of the human mind, must be superior to it? "How could you get as much out of philosophy as you could from your own [Jewish] lawgivers and prophets?" he demands. For while through reason we could not find God, through the prophets and through Christ God had found us and redeemed us.

The fight was over in the first round, but Trypho no doubt knew that Justin's real target in this discourse was not philosophy at all, but the currently dangerous teachings of one Marcion, a bishop's son, expelled from his own congregation, it was said, for immorality, who taught that the God of the Jews was "fickle, capricious, ignorant, despotic, and cruel" and inferior to the "Supreme God" who was Jesus' Father. Justin knew that the validity of Jesus much depended on the validity of the Jewish prophets who came before him. So he spoke as a friend and strong supporter of the Jewish tradition.

Confronted with pagan religions, however, Justin was not at all conciliatory. Plato must have been influenced by Christ in some fashion, he declared, even though Christ came later, and the Jewish prophets were Christ's forerunners too, but the pagan gods were demons—particularly those enshrined in myths that resembled the story of Jesus. Put into the heads of ancient poets, they allowed opponents of Christianity to argue that Christ was the mere embellishment of a myth.

Justin's reputation as a skilled defender of the faith soon spread to the Christians at Rome, who badly needed his help. Senior people in the imperial bureaucracy were once again becoming belligerent and menacing.

The emperor Hadrian's twenty-one year-reign ended just three years after Justin's debate with Trypho. Like his predecessor Trajan, Hadrian was wise, superstitious, statesmanlike, and no more ruthless than he needed to be. Unlike Trajan, he pronounced no oppressive measures against the Christians.

In fact, he sent a directive to the governor of Asia, known as the "Rescript of Hadrian," ordering instead a crackdown on false informers. All charges against Christians must be thoroughly investigated, he ruled, and false accusations must entail punishment.

However, it was during Hadrian's reign that Telesphorus, listed by Catholic Christians as the seventh bishop of Rome after Peter, was arrested and executed. No record remains of either the charges or the manner of his execution, though one ancient account says his evangelical preaching was so successful that the numbers

# Ancient Israel's last president

## The giant Kochba's nine-fingered army defies Rome until his temper foils him

*An aerial view of Betar, in the Judean hills, the remains of the headquarters for the rebellion against Rome by Simon Bar Kochba, self-proclaimed "President over Israel."*

He was so powerfully built, it was said, that he could snatch from the air huge stones hurled against him by Roman catapults and then fling the boulders back at his attackers. According to another tale, he found the strongest and fiercest men for his rebel army by proclaiming that only those who severed one of their own fingers were eligible—and thousands, eager to serve at his command, willingly passed the painful test. He and his nine-fingered men led a highly successful revolt against the Romans for nearly four years, setting up efficient Jewish administrative centers deep within the Roman empire, and even minting coins proclaiming independence for the Jewish state. He fell from grace, taking the Jews with him, because he killed a holy man in a fit of temper, and he died in the coils of a giant snake.

That's some of the mix of fact and legend surrounding Simon Bar Kochba—also known as Simon Bar Koziva, Shimeon Bar Koshba, or Shimeon Ben Kosiba. He is credited with leading the spectacular second revolt of the Jews against Rome, beginning in A.D. 132, and continuing to 135. Much of his history is uncertain, if not clearly mythical, and until the middle of the twentieth century, there was considerable doubt about whether he had ever lived at all.

Yet live he did, as was revealed by astonishing discoveries in caves near the Dead Sea in the 1950s, when archaeologists came upon some thirty-five documents dating from Bar Kochba's time, including a number of letters, written by Bar Kochba himself, describing himself as "President over Israel."

The contents of the letters are unremarkable, dealing with such things as the ownership of a cow and the shipment of wheat; none mentions any specific battle, and they are all undated. But when Yigael Yadin, the archaeologist whose expedition turned up the letters, presented photos of them to Israeli Prime Minister David Ben-Gurion in 1960, members of the Knesset and the cabinet who were present were at first struck dumb. Then, Yadin recalled, "the silence was shattered by spontaneous cries of astonishment and joy. That evening the national radio interrupted its scheduled program to broadcast news of the discovery. Next day, the newspapers came out with banner headlines over the announcement. This was not just another archaeological discovery. It was the retrieval of a part of the nation's best heritage."

Most contemporary sources now see the Bar Kochba rebellion as having been provoked by unendurable pressure applied to the Jews by the Roman

of his converts alarmed the authorities.[6]

In 135, Hadrian put down the Bar Kochba rebellion (see sidebar) and outlawed circumcision, an essential part of God's covenant with the Jews given to Abraham (Gen. 17:12). Hadrian refrained from deifying himself, but instead declared his beloved and beautiful pageboy Antinous a god, an action appalling to both Christian and Jew. Hadrian died miserably in 138 of an unidentified but chronically debilitating disease, after three attempted suicides. His successor

emperor Hadrian. When he took power in A.D. 117, Hadrian seemed to sympathize with Judaism, and was even said to have promised the Jews that they could rebuild the Jerusalem temple leveled by Roman forces in A.D. 70—probably for political reasons and possibly under the influence of the Jew-baiting Roman historian Tacitus. However, Hadrian changed his mind, enacted a law against castration that forbade circumcision as well, began deporting Jews, and started construction of a new city, Aelia Capitolina, on the old Jerusalem site, with a temple to the pagan god Jupiter where the Jewish temple had once stood.

The rebellion simmered for years, erupting full-force in 132, when Bar Kochba organized a guerrilla army that may have numbered as many as 100,000 men, and began seizing towns and territory. Eventually, the rebels held some fifty strongholds in Palestine, along with 985 towns and villages—including, according to some but not all accounts, Jerusalem itself.

In this, Bar Kochba was aided by the much-admired Rabbi Akiva, who became his armor bearer and proclaimed him the Messiah. Bar Kochba fought the Romans for three-and-a-half years and, according to the Jewish Talmud, became so convinced of his own powers that he arrogantly ordered God to stay out of his affairs, demanding, "Lord of the Universe, neither help nor hinder us."

Bar Kochba had strong religious support from the sage Eleazar, his uncle, who sat in sackcloth and prayed continually. When the Romans learned of Eleazar's role in boosting the rebels' morale, they dispatched an agent to the city of Betar. There, the agent publicly approached Eleazar and pretended to whisper something in his ear. Bar Kochba's men, of course, seized the agent, who falsely told them that Eleazar was about to hand the city over to Rome. Enraged, Bar Kochba confronted Eleazar, dismissed the holy man's denial of the accusation, and kicked him so hard that Eleazar died.

Betar fell to the Romans shortly afterwards, and the rebellion ended with the slaughter of an estimated 580,000 Jews. The blood that flowed was said to be so heavy that it rose to

the level of the horses' nostrils, and coursed from Betar into the Mediterranean Sea with so much force that it carried boulders along with it. For their part, the Romans lost so many of their own that when the emperor reported his victory to the Senate, he omitted the traditional, "I and the army are well."

Bar Kochba was killed—beheaded by the Romans in some accounts, strangled by a giant snake in others. With the now leaderless revolt put down, Hadrian plowed Jerusalem under and clamped down even more tightly on Judaism, barring Jews from the entire region of the Holy City, forbidding not only circumcision, but the study of the Torah, the keeping of the Sabbath, and even the making of any Jewish calendar.

Bar Kochba's defeat "marked the end of Jewish hopes for an independent state for almost 2,000 years," writes Rabbi David E. Lipman in his essay *The Bar Kochba Revolt*. "We didn't have our own country again until May 14, 1948"—when the modern state of Israel was proclaimed in the Middle East.

The rebel leader's followers had changed his actual name, Bar Kosiba, to Bar Kochba, meaning "son of a star," underlining their conviction that he was the Messiah. But in the Jewish tradition he is denied such a title, for the Messiah is still to come. ∎

*In 1982 the remains of a group of Bar Kochba's rebels were reburied with full military honors at Masada, Israel. Bar Kochba's defeat meant the end of Jewish hopes for an independent homeland for almost two thousand years—until May 14, 1948, when the modern state of Israel was proclaimed.*

and adopted son, Antoninus Pius,[7] proved actively tolerant of Christians. Upon his accession he revoked all Hadrian's outstanding death sentences, repealed on behalf of the Jews the edict against circumcision, and directed local authorities in Asia to treat Christians with tolerance.

However, many of the new emperor's senior administrators did not share his benign attitude towards Christianity, thanks especially to Fronto's monstrous depictions of Christian rituals. By 150, the attitude to Christianity had hardened among Fronto and his colleagues because of rumors that the sect's orgiastic activities were growing even worse.

This was easily explained. After the execution of Bishop Telesphorus by Hadrian, the Roman church was rapidly infiltrated by Gnostic teachers whose belief in the meaninglessness of the material world led them in either of two, opposite, directions: asceticism or debauchery. That is, either they rejected the lures of sex as unreal and therefore worthless, or surrendered to them because they were unreal and therefore harmless. It was the latter group that caused the scandal, perhaps occasioning Fronto's much published fulmination against the Christians, known as *Fronto's Oration*, probably during his consulship in 143. It runs deeply into the lurid:

> They recognize one another by secret marks and signs, and they enjoy mutual love almost before they meet. Here and there among them is spread a certain cult of lust, and they promiscuously call one another brother and sister, so that their frequent fornication becomes, by the use of a sacred name, incest.
>
> Thus, their vain and insane superstition glories in its crime. Unless there were a foundation of truth, wise rumor would not speak of these wicked matters, rightly suppressed. I hear that they worship the head of a most disgusting animal, consecrated by some stupid conviction or other: Their religion was born worthy of such customs! Others say they worship the genitals of their leader and priest, and, so to speak, adore their own source. This may be erroneous, but certainly the suspicion would arise in their secret nocturnal rites. And anyone who tells of a man paying the supreme penalty for his crime, and the deadly wood of the cross in their ceremonies, attributes suitable altars to those depraved criminals. They worship what they deserve.
>
> The story of their initiating novices is as detestable as it is notorious. An infant, concealed in meal so as to deceive the unwary, is placed before the one who is in charge of the rites. This infant, hidden under the meal, is struck by the novice, who thinks he is striking harmless blows, but kills him with blind and hidden wounds. Horrible to relate, they drink his blood, eagerly distribute the members of his body, and are united by this sacrifice and pledged to common silence by this awareness of guilt.

*The use of coded signs, like this first-century inscription showing early Christian symbols of fish and an anchor, led anti-Christians such as Fronto to claim that they were a subversive and secretive cult with much to hide.*

---

6. Telesphorus, the bishop of Rome martyred about 138, is acclaimed in early Christian legend for inaugurating the tradition of the Christmas Eve midnight service, though Christians did not settle on December 25 as the date to observe Christ's birth for another two hundred years.

7. Reportedly, Antoninus received the additional tag Pius after the emperor Hadrian saw him helping his extremely aged father-in-law and Marcus Aurelius's father, Marcus Annus Verus, up the Senate stairs. This would have reverberated with associations to "pious Aeneas," Rome's mythic Trojan founder.

# Snapshots in stone of city life in Rome

**Sales gimmicks like live monkeys and display counters show that some things haven't changed**

Snapshots in stone: Sturdy bas-relief sculpture, with its carved figures rising slightly from a stone surface, provides vivid glimpses of life in the streets of Ancient Rome. The play of light and shadow on the flat background adds depth and realism to human forms, and the technique was widely used by the Romans to illustrate social or historical events, especially in commemoration of an individual's death. Quite lifelike figures adorned funerary *stele* (commemorative stone tablets) and the marble caskets known as sarcophagi. Many well preserved examples still survive. A butcher prepares the day's cuts for sale (1). Meanwhile, an enterprising vendor uses two monkeys (left) to attract customers to her stall (2). Boots are fashioned as they would be for centuries afterwards in a cobbler's shop (3). Except for the togas, the exchanges depicted in these memorial carvings might occur in contemporary stores—as in the cases of the cutlery merchant (4), and the silversmith assisting a shopper with a selection from racks of his wares (5). ■

This diatribe, coming as it did from a source so close to the empire's highest authority, left the Christians horrified. Thus the urgent call from Rome for the help of the man they heard so much about at Ephesus.

Justin's arrival in the capital can be reconstructed. He would have landed at the port of Ostia and, full of expectation and foreboding, walked the fourteen miles to the city. He would at last behold the great sights of a place whose magnificence he had heard described all his life. He knew, too, that Rome was the home of a moral turpitude into which one could gradually and unconsciously slide and never return. Either way, Rome was the nexus of the greatest empire mankind had ever known, a metropolis more dominant in its day than would be Louis XIV's Paris, Queen Victoria's London, or the Moscow of the czars and the commissars. It was home to the best and the brightest of all the world's talents, and its citizenry gloried in their dominance.

There before him were the city's celebrated seven hills, dotted with the brightly colored palaces of the imperial family and the mansions of the two or three thousand members of the patrician class. He would perhaps pause and confer a few coins on the beggars who frequented the twin-door Ostian Gate, which took him through the six-hundred-year-old Servian Wall. Now appeared before him the Tomb of Cestus, a massive, marble-faced pyramid more than a century old, and beyond it the crowded, narrow, but mathematically aligned streets of the city, redesigned by Nero after the Great Fire of A.D. 64, which he had blamed on the Christians.

Passing beneath row after row of six- or seven-story tenements, homes for most of the city's million inhabitants, one quickly learned to avoid the garbage heaved out the upper-story windows. So many slaves and freedmen, drawn from all over Italy, Greece, and Gaul, had poured into Rome that a new wall would soon be built to let the city expand. In the meantime, even unlit cellars, garrets, and the tiny spaces under stairways were rented out. In defiance of building codes, apartments were expanded to dangerous heights, propped against each other with buttresses extending across streets that did not prevent the frequent thunderous collapse of brick, wood, and mortar into piles of rubble and screaming victims. Despite the lessons of the Great Fire, such buildings were still subject to frequent conflagrations. With charcoal braziers heating most apartments, sparks could alight on furniture or fabric, and fire easily spread along narrow streets crowded with tradesmen's wares, pedestrians, and litters bearing the wealthy.

The firefighting corps by now consisted of seven thousand freedmen quartered in twenty-one stations throughout the city and trained in the use of pumps and vinegar-soaked blankets to douse flames. These crews doubled as the city's night watch, aiming to catch thieves in the act as well as to douse fires before they spread. To patrol the daytime streets, a police department of three thousand men was organized on military lines.

Rome's great buildings and monuments would have deeply stirred Justin. In the city center—a hollow between its seven hills—Augustus had begun erecting what became the most palatial metropolis the world would ever know. "I found Rome a city of brick and left it one of marble," Augustus declared. He and his successors built or rebuilt the Forum, the Senate, the Hall of Records, temples to Venus and Peace, Pompey's Theater, the Coliseum, the Circus Maximus, the bronze-roofed Forum of Trajan, and the huge public baths. These were all relatively new works, and more were going up every day.

This, then, was the mighty city whose senior authorities frowned fiercely upon its tiny Christian minority. Why, these officials continually asked themselves, do people join this sect? With all that Rome had to offer, what was the

appeal of this crucified Jew? Why were so many abandoning the gods of a city that had accomplished more than any other in human history?

Did not Venus, the goddess of lust, for instance, offer them all the possible rewards of sexual satisfaction? But these rewards, many found, were momentary, enjoyable and then gone, and constantly requiring the ever more perverse to sustain such joys as she provided. What of Apollo, what of Mercury, what of Diana, goddess of the hunt? But the enchanting stories of these assorted beings, fascinating though they still were to children, had long ago paled, and anyway who could actually believe them? The gods, like humanity itself, seemed chained to a great wheel from which there was no escape.

The twentieth-century philosopher Mircea Eliade would call this futility "the Myth of the Eternal Return." Ancient polytheism, he said, suffered two disastrous blows. The first came with Abraham and his monotheism, the second with Christ, who promised a personal relationship with God, forgiveness for sins, and a concept of history in which individual choices could change the world. It was a message that for more and more people would prove irresistible.

Not, though, in the early second century, says the historian W. H. C. Frend, when the Christian numbers grew chiefly from within. The reason was not mysterious. It was the campaign of vilification waged relentlessly against them. Though the charges were grossly untrue, the Christians themselves, by their reluctance to respond, seemed to confirm them. Had not

Christ himself commanded them to "turn the other cheek" (Luke 6:29)? And anyway, what did these ravings matter, many Christians reasoned, because Jesus would soon return.

But Jesus did not return, and as that hope grew fainter, members of a younger Christian generation—sometimes raised in the faith from infancy, sometimes converted from the pagan world—sought to fight back, to engage their enemies in dialogue, in public debate, even in name-calling and counter-accusation. These became known as "apologists." The term's English meaning has come to be reversed over the years. It now refers to those who ask for pardon. But the Christians of the second-century Age of the Apologist were not seeking pardon; they were explaining, driving home a point. And first and most forceful among them was Justin.

*In Justin's time all roads led to Rome. At its heart, cupped between seven hills, was the great Forum, the center of political, religious, and economic life (as in the artist's reconstruction, left). At the height of its power, Rome was the most impressive metropolis ever constructed, then or since. Even in ruins (above), the Forum retains much of its grandeur—and remains a magnet for tourists, just as it was eighteen centuries ago.*

When Justin arrived in Rome, his first assignment was to rebut the attack made by Fronto. He did this with a document that came to be known as *The First Apology*. It petitions Antoninus and his adopted sons, Marcus Aurelius and Lucius Verus, to make a proper investigation rather than condemn the Christians on the basis of gossip. "We demand that the accusations against them [the Christians] be probed, and if these be shown to be true, they be punished," wrote Justin, "as any guilty persons should be. If, however, no one has any way of proving these accusations, sane reason does not allow that you, because of a mischievous rumor, do an injustice to innocent men."

*Those who followed Christ, Justin wrote in his appeal to the emperor, found their lives inexplicably transformed, their former burning love of evil turned to good.*

Why, he asked, was officialdom's crackdown focused only on Christians? Why not Gnostics like the followers of Simon Magus? Why not those who preach outright blasphemy like the Marcionites? "You neither molest nor execute them, at least not for their beliefs. . . . Those who follow those teachings are not checked by you; on the contrary, you bestow rewards and honors on them."

As to the charge that Christians were not loyal subjects of the emperor, this was far from the truth. "When you hear that we look forward to a kingdom, you rashly assume that we speak of a human kingdom, whereas we mean a kingdom which is with God. We, more than all other men, are truly your helpers and allies in fostering peace. As we have been instructed by him, we, before all others, try everywhere to pay your appointed officials the ordinary and special taxes." It was true, he said, "that we do not worship with many sacrifices and floral offerings the things men have made, lifeless things set in temples, and called gods." But that was because Christians worshiped only the true God. "In other things we joyfully obey you, acknowledging you as the kings and rulers of men, and praying that you may be found to have, besides royal power, sound judgment."

No matter what had been falsely said about them, those who followed Christ's teaching turned away from evil actions, he said. For example, they cherished marital fidelity. "Not only he who actually does commit adultery, but also he who wishes to do so, is repudiated by God, since not only our actions, but even our inner thoughts, are manifest to Him." Even divorce was frowned upon. "All who contract a second marriage according to the human law are sinners in the eyes of our Master."

For the fact is, he said, that Christ came to call to repentance not the just or the pure, but the impious, the incontinent, and the unjust. Those who followed Christ found their lives inexplicably transformed, their former burning love of evil turned to good. "We who delighted in war, in the slaughter of one another, and in every other kind of iniquity have in every part of the world converted our weapons of war into implements of peace—our swords into plowshares, our spears into

**JUSTIN ON HIS CONVERSION**

*Indeed, when I myself reveled in the teachings of Plato, and heard the Christians misrepresented and watched them stand fearless in the face of death and of everything that was considered dreadful, I realized the impossibility of their living in sinful pleasure.*

*Justin set up a school at Rome, in an apartment above the Timiotinean baths, where he taught philosophy for his living and preached Christianity gratis. He doubtless also took his message into the public baths, which were often a venue for debate and discussion.*

# In the Christians' first big schism, they and the Jews part company

## With the Temple and Jerusalem gone, rabbinical Judaism rises into being, and a struggle with Christianity begins that will rage on for centuries

Nearly a thousand years before Western and Eastern Christians parted in bitterness, fifteen centuries before Roman Catholics and Protestants divided, and even longer before the Protestants themselves splintered into countless denominations, the first and most painful division of them all rocked Christianity to its core. It would fiercely separate the Christians and their earliest brothers, the Jews.

The Jews and Christians had, after all, sprung from the same root, as third-generation Hebrew Christian writer Jakob Jocz observes in his book-length study of the controversy, *The Jewish People and Jesus Christ*. Jocz, a prominent twentieth-century Messianic Jewish theologian, writes: "The parting of the roads between the Messianic movement and Judaism began upon Jewish soil as a result of a religious controversy between Jews and Jews." Put simply, the first Christians were Jews, as was Jesus himself.

Jesus was born into a Jewish family, growing up with Jewish faith and life and customs, studying the Hebrew Bible, observing Jewish Law, and accepting it as divinely appointed. His disciples were Jewish, his ministry was carried out almost exclusively among the Jews, and the first church in Jerusalem was a Jewish church. Jesus was welcomed in the Jewish synagogues, where he worshiped and preached. The eager crowds that surrounded him were overwhelmingly Jewish. The devoted multitude following him, as he made his way to the cross, was largely faithful Jews, weeping in sorrow. Many Jewish people showed themselves deeply devoted to him.

What happened? The Jews were his blood relatives, his family in the strictest sense of the word, and it was to them, he said, that he had been sent. But he would come to be seen by his own people as an enemy, his name a curse, his teachings reviled or, worse, utterly ignored.

One common view explains Jesus' persecution in political terms—he was a rabble-rouser, a threat to Rome as much as to Judaism. But Jocz notes that Jesus remained aloof from political issues, except for his startling advice that a man should render unto Caesar—that is, the government—what the government was owed; debt to God was a separate issue.

Another popular explanation blames the division between Christians and Jews on the apostle Paul. Jesus' message was welcomed by Jews of his time, this claim goes, but Paul turned it into something else,

something that Jesus never intended and the Jews could no longer accept.

That theory, however, ignores significant facts: chief among them the Crucifixion itself, which took place long before Paul's arrival on the scene, as well as the heavy persecution of the Christians immediately following Jesus' death. Jewish leaders were already working hard to root them out, rounding them up and killing them, with the as-yet-unconverted Saul leading the charge.

Such persecution was inevitable, Jocz declares, because Jesus' claim to be the Messiah demanded a response. Either he was right, and the only response was to submit to him, or he was wrong and a blasphemer. The Jews declared him wrong.

According to Jocz, Christianity begins with humanity in crisis, helpless to act on its own behalf, while central to Judaism is the assertion of human strength. It's a basic difference in the understanding of mankind's deepest problem, Jocz says, and the terrible division was therefore inevitable.

But the Christians were only part of the Jews' dilemma. "Without their religion, the Jews had no history, and without their history no religion," writes the scholar Alfred Edersheim in *The Life and Times of Jesus the Messiah*. How could a religion rooted in a specific geographical location and structure, Jerusalem and the Temple—both now destroyed—survive with its heart, so to speak, ripped out? This they answered by addressing two vexing problems.

First, they quickly dealt with the troublesome presence of those Christians who continued to attend Jewish religious observances, and to argue forcefully there for the new faith. In about A.D. 85, the *Birkat ha-minim* was added to the twelfth of eighteen benedictions recited daily in the synagogues. In its earliest form, the *Birkat ha-minim* was a single sentence calling down a specific curse upon Christians: "[M]ay the Nazarenes and the *minim* (heretics) perish as in a moment, and be blotted out from the book of life, and with the righteous may they not be inscribed."

Though by medieval times the text would be softened and directed against undefined "slanderers," its initial impact was profound, John writes: "The Jews . . . agreed that if any one should confess him [Jesus] to be Christ, he was to be put out of the synagogue" (John 9:22 RSV). The separation, of course, had been a two-way street from the beginning, with many of the earliest Christians distancing themselves from the Jews.

Their second task was to refashion out of a

Temple-based, sacrificially centered faith one that could survive its grievous loss. A pattern, of course, had already been set in the synagogues of the Diaspora, functioning far from Jerusalem. But these had always been subsidiary to the Temple and the Holy City.

The *Mishna*, a collection of oral traditions and teachings of the rabbis, emerged in about A.D. 200 in Palestine under Rabbi Judah (called "The Prince"), and helped resolve the dilemma. In the *Mishna*, the core of what would become the *Talmud* in the fifth and sixth centuries, Judaism shifts its focus from the Temple to the synagogue and, therefore to the dispersed nation of Israel itself.

Similarly, Johanan Ben Zakkai, a first-century scholar of the *Torah* or written Law, taught that study of the *Torah*, wherever undertaken, was as valuable and important as sacrifices in the Temple had been. Another scholar, Gamaliel of Jamniah, head of the Sanhedrin after Jerusalem was destroyed, established uniform rites of worship and a standardized calendar for religious observances, which were to take place thenceforth in synagogues, no matter where they were.

By the end of the first century, Christians were actively competing with Jews for Gentile converts, each side hurling increasingly vehement abuse against the other. The pagan philosopher Celsus, who was opposed to them both, recorded the Jewish explanation of Jesus. He was born, they said, the illegitimate child of a Jewish peasant woman and a Roman soldier named Panthera, the woman having been divorced by her husband, a carpenter, for adultery.

When grown, Jesus emigrated to Egypt, worked as a laborer, learned magic, and returned to his own country, cocky, conceited, and proclaiming himself to be God. His supposed miracles were never authenticated, his prophecies were proved false, and in the end God abandoned him and let him die on the cross. His disciples stole his body and pretended he had risen from the dead. Such was the Jewish story.

Moreover, observes the historian W. H. C. Frend in his *Martyrdom and Persecution in the Early Church*, the Jews had "all the advantages of wealth, lawful status, a coherent religious sense, and revolutionary appeal to dissatisfied provincials." However, "these were nullified by one fact. Judaism remained a national cult, protected indeed by its claim to antiquity, but repellent to most non-Jews."

Nevertheless, Judaism endured, and in the two millennia that followed, Christianity and Judaism would grow independently, acknowledging and bewailing but often nevertheless exacerbating the deep wounds separating the two great faiths. ∎

*This reconstruction of the interior of a third-century synagogue at Dura Europos, Syria, displayed at the National Museum in Damascus, was built on a prominent escarpment above the river Euphrates. Dura Europos, a remote Roman outpost, was destroyed in A.D. 256, the town literally disappeared for more than sixteen hundred years. It was rediscovered during the First World War and excavations began in 1928 (see also p. 264.) The walls of the synagogue are adorned with episodes from the Torah, even though Jewish law forbids the representation of living creatures. Thus did Roman culture influence the synagogue, just as it did the Christians.*

*Justin debates Crescens, a distinguished Cynic philosopher, humiliated by Justin in public encounters. Crescens tried and failed to have Justin arrested as a Christian. According to Tatian, one of Justin's pupils, Justin foiled the attempt by showing Crescens to be "immoral, greedy, gluttonous, and insincere in debate."*

farmers' tools—and we cultivate piety, justice, brotherly charity, faith, and hope."

How officialdom reacted to Justin's petition is not known. Antoninus Pius called off the persecution of Christians, however, and some historians suspect that Justin's appeal to Rome's deep respect for justice had produced the inquiry he sought, and the new Antoninus policy was the outcome. Far more significantly, however, Justin had demonstrated an aggressive new fearlessness in the Christian community, a willingness to beard the imperial lion in its den. Close behind him, other apologists would follow his example.

As he had at Ephesus, he set up a school at Rome. It was in his apartment, above the Timiotinean baths where he taught philosophy for his living and preached Christianity gratis. As John the Apostle had back in Ephesus, he doubtless took his message into the baths themselves. Why should such a superb opportunity for debate, discussion, and the proclamation of the faith be a field abandoned to the enemy? From his apartment, too, he poured forth his letters and papers in defense and furtherance of the Christian gospel.

Here again, Justin rapidly gained note as a sharp debater, and eagerly threw himself into confrontations with those who opposed Christianity. As well as friends, this made him enemies, one in particular. The man's name was Crescens, a distinguished Cynic philosopher, humiliated by Justin in public encounters. Even under Antoninus Pius, mortifying such a highly placed representative of authority was dangerous. When Antoninus died in 161, it became lethal.

Crescens had tried before and failed to have Justin arrested as a Christian, bringing the same charge against him that had successfully produced the execution of Ptolemaeus (see sidebar, p. 89). According to one of Justin's pupils, a man

**JUSTIN ON THE SOUL**
*The soul can with difficulty be recalled to those good things from which it has fallen, and is with difficulty dragged away from those evils to which it has become accustomed.*

*When a cataclysmic plague arrived, the emperor ordered Romans to begin sacrifices to appease the gods. But the Christians refused, and the response was public outrage.*

named Tatian, Justin had foiled the attempt by showing Crescens himself to be "immoral, greedy, gluttonous, and insincere in debate," though Tatian's view of the case may not be unbiased.[8]

Justin greeted the new emperor, Marcus Aurelius, with his *Second Apology*, this more urgent than the first and more specific on the lapses in Rome's sense of justice. The Ptolemaeus case is cited and Crescens unflatteringly mentioned. Finally, the *Second Apology* is diplomatically imbued with the language of the Stoics, for the new emperor was known to be one of those. In it, Justin again asked that the Christians be tried for specific crimes, rather than for their beliefs. Whether Marcus ever saw this document is not known. What *is* known is that

8. Tatian may have been grinding his own ax against Crescens who had, he claimed, also plotted against him. A native of Adiabene, Tatian was attracted to Christianity, like Justin, from Greek philosophy. Unlike Justin, he condemned Greek civilization as wholly demonic. He urged on all Christians so puritanical an ethic that he was opposed by most prominent Christian teachers of his time. Practicing what he preached, he moved to Syria and founded an ascetic order (see also p. 62).

some time after it was published, Justin was arrested. The informer, said the Christians, was Crescens, and the occasion was a cataclysmic plague.

Having already devastated the eastern provinces, it reached Rome itself in 166, and the emperor delayed his departure for the Danube frontier because he considered the plague a greater danger than the barbarians. He ordered preparations begun for sacrifices to appease the gods, preparations in which all Romans were expected to participate. The Christians once again refused, some seeing the plague as a sure sign that the End Times had arrived. The response was public outrage. People whose families were dying around them viewed the Christians as the cause. How could these fanatics let little children die, they asked, through their insane loyalty to this crucified Jew? Starting in the eastern provinces, mob vengeance broke out, the martyrdoms began and then spread west.

The prime target in Rome this time was not the bishop. It was that glib-tongued smart-aleck Justin (as his enemies no doubt saw him), so fast with an answer, so quick to put people down. Let's have him to the arena. Justin was arrested along with six of his pupils, one of them a woman. Tatian, who wasn't among the arrested, named Crescens as the accuser, but many historians doubt this.

Justin scarcely needed an accuser; his Christian convictions had been everywhere published.[9] In any event, informers were no longer hard to find. Marcus Aurelius had already reinstated them as legitimate servants of the empire. The judge would be Junius Rusticus, chief magistrate of Rome and a confidant of Marcus.

A brief transcript of the trial was preserved by the Christians. Short as it is, it may represent all there was to report of the proceeding, since Christians were usually willing to convict themselves. Thus Rusticus asked: "What are the doctrines that you practice?"

"I have tried to become acquainted with all doctrines," replied Justin, "but I have committed myself to the true doctrines of the Christians, even though they may not please those who hold false beliefs."

To the prefect, such a response bordered on outright defiance. "Are these the doctrines that you prefer?" he asked, providing Justin with an opportunity to equivocate.

Justin rejected it. "Yes," he replied, he believed with all Christians in the God "whom alone we hold to

*The Emperor Antoninus Pius revoked all outstanding death sentences imposed by his predecessor, Hadrian, and directed local authorities in Asia to treat Christians with tolerance. This bust is in the British Museum.*

9. Of the many volumes he wrote, only one survives apart from his *Apologies*—his *Dialogue with Trypho,* in which he tells of his spiritual journey to Christianity.

be craftsman of the whole world," and in Jesus Christ his Son, also God, who "came down to mankind as a herald of salvation," as foretold by the Hebrew prophets. The language of what would become known as the Apostles' Creed was already taking shape.

But Rusticus had heard enough—enough to convict, anyway—and he cut Justin short. Still, there was a chance he might implicate others. "Where do you meet?" he asked.

Justin saw the peril and answered evasively. "Wherever it is each one's preference or opportunity," he replied, adding derisively, "In any case, do you suppose we can all meet in the same place?"

Impatiently, Rusticus repeated the question. Justin explained that he held classes in his apartment above the baths, where he had lived his entire time in Rome.

Rusticus gave up. Justin would implicate himself, but not others. "You do admit, then, that you are a Christian," Rusticus said.

# When Christianity breaks a marriage

## Christ had warned it sometimes would and in this case a teacher lost his life

People believed he had come to bring peace on Earth, said Jesus Christ, but in fact he would not bring peace, but division, splitting even families and households (Luke 12:51–53). That prophecy would be fulfilled all over the world for the next two thousand years, as in the case of one well-born Roman woman in the mid-second century.

In his work called the *Second Apology*, Justin tells her story without identifying her. She and her husband had lived dissolute lives, he says, until she "came to the knowledge of the teachings of Christ," gave up drunken orgies and promiscuity with the household servants, pleaded with her husband to do the same, and warned him of the "punishment and eternal fire that will come upon those who do not live temperately and conform to right reason."

Ignoring her pleas, the husband persisted in his degenerate conduct until the woman concluded it was wrong to continue living with such a man. Her Christian friends objected, saying she should stay with him in the hope he would change. Soon after, however, he left for Alexandria, where his reputation grew even worse, and the woman gave him a bill of divorcement and left him. She feared, says Justin, that "by continuing in wedlock and by sharing his board and bed, she might become a partaker in his lawlessness and impiety." Furious, the husband returned and publicly, formally declared her a Christian, a capital offense. The wife petitioned the emperor for time to set her affairs in order before answering the charge. He agreed.

For the moment thwarted, the husband turned his anger upon her Christian teacher, one Ptolemaeus (pronounced *Tol-e-MAY-us*), already in jail for reasons undisclosed. The husband knew a centurion at the prison who confronted the teacher with the fatal question: "*Christianus es?*" ("Are you a Christian?") As "a lover of truth and not of a deceitful or false disposition," according to Justin, who doubtless knew him, Ptolemaeus thereupon confessed. His sentence was prolonged until he could finally appear before the city prefect Urbicius, who again posed the question and gained the same answer. He was promptly handed over for execution.

However, this peremptory procedure exasperated Lucius, another Christian who had watched the hearing. "Why have you punished this man?" shouted Lucius. "He is not an adulterer, nor a fornicator, nor a murderer, nor a thief, nor a robber, nor has he been convicted of committing any crime at all. He has simply confessed to the name Christian." What a far cry from the policy of the tolerant Emperor Antoninus Pius, he said. What of Caesar's tradition of justice? What of "the sacred Senate?"

Thereupon Urbicius put the same fateful question to Lucius, who replied affirmatively and was ordered executed with Ptolemaeus. Lucius thanked the prefect. Now, he said, he would be "liberated from such wicked rulers and go to the good Father and King." A third Christian suffered the same fate.

Justin cited the case in a formal petition to the emperor, protesting a miscarriage of Roman justice and predicting he, too, would suffer the same fate. A few years later he did. No reply to his petition is known. Neither is the fate of the Christian woman. ∎

*While Roman law made it technically illegal to be a Christian, this did not sit well with some of the empire's legal authorities. Although they did not hesitate to convict people of doing something, or refusing to do something, they believed it unjust to convict somebody for being something. Accordingly Christians were subjected, often under duress, to one of two tests. They were required to either burn incense to the god Caesar, as in this painting, or swear by the emperor's "genius," meaning his divine spirit. When Christians refused to do this they could be convicted of defying an imperial order and sentenced, frequently to death.*

"Yes I am," replied Justin, assuring his doom.

Rusticus now turned to a man named Chariton, who quickly incriminated himself. His sister, Charito, was given a chance to blame her friends for deceiving her. Had she been duped into taking part in the rumored promiscuity of the Christians? She had not been deceived, and there was no promiscuity, she said. "Rather, I have become God's servant and a Christian, and by his power I have kept myself pure and unstained by the taints of the flesh." She, too, was convicted. After her, Hierax, Paeon, Evelpistus, and Valerian all readily confessed themselves Christians since childhood.

Rusticus did not immediately pass sentence. He sent all seven back to prison, giving them time to reconsider their confessions. There they were probably visited by other Christians, for the persecutions at this stage were still highly selective.

How long the reprieve lasted is not recorded, but Rusticus was not known as a patient man. He again called the prisoners before him, this time threatening them with scourging or beheading. "Do you suppose," he asked Justin incredulously, "that you will really ascend into Heaven?"

"I do not merely suppose it," he replied. "I know it certainly."

He then gave all seven one last chance. "Since this then is your statement, impious ones, let us proceed to the issue that is before us: Agree together to sacrifice to the gods, lest you be miserably destroyed. For what person of intelligence would choose to relinquish this sweetest light and prefer death to it?"

Justin took up the challenge and brazenly defied him. "And what person of sound mind," he responded, "would choose to turn from piety to impiety, from light to darkness, and from the living God to soul-destroying demons?"

"Unless you sacrifice, I shall begin the tortures," Rusticus warned.

"This we long for," came the reply, "and this will grant us great freedom at the terrible tribunal of Christ, when each of us shall receive according to his deeds. And so do what you will. We are Christians and do not sacrifice to idols."

Rusticus ordered them lashed, no light penalty: One danger of a Roman flogging was that the prisoner might die under it, cheating the executioner, whose work often followed. (Whether Charito was flogged with the men is not recorded.) Would they now make the required sacrifice? One by one they answered that they would not. Thereupon Rusticus passed the sentence. "I decree," he intoned, "that those who have defied the imperial edicts and have refused to sacrifice to the gods are to be beheaded with the sword." In the account preserved by the Christians, Rusticus is described as "a terrible man, a plague, and filled with all impiety." The Roman mob no doubt took a very different view, denouncing him for irresolute vacillation. Why did he give them opportunity to recant? And why just the sword? Why not the arena?

No description of the executions survives. The date is set as approximately 165.

In the annals of the Christians, Justin is remembered as "Justin Martyr." Martyrs he and his students certainly were, and as martyrs they would want to be remembered. But Justin did something more. "How deeply he touched us," writes the historian Henri Daniel-Rops in *The Church of the Apostles and Martyrs*, "this man who groped in the dark so long for the Way, the Truth and the Life."

But in Christ, Justin found all three, and in so doing he made it possible to see the whole course of Christian thought as thoroughly within the tradition founded by Plato. He fused the heritage of Greece with that of the Jews, and thereby helped to lay the foundations for what would one day be known as Western culture.

Moreover, while Christians would argue for centuries over whether and when they should take up arms to defend the Truth, Justin unequivocally showed them they need have no qualms whatever about defending it with words. Words were weapons too, and Christians should learn to use them with all the skill God had conferred upon them.

**JUSTIN ON TRUTH**

*I am proud to say that I strove with all my might to be known as a Christian, not because the teachings of Plato are different from those of Christ, but because they are not in every way similar. Indeed, all writers had a dim glimpse of the truth.*

# Their willingness to die hideously—this fact, beyond all others, drew converts to Christ

**The stalwart deaths of Crispus and Papylus, whose calm defiance infuriated their judge, typify the figure of the martyr that inspires and shapes the faith's opening centuries**

The amphitheater was packed that day in the city of Pergamum, north of Ephesus, near the Aegean's east coast. Once the seat of the Attalid kings, the Greek-speaking metropolis was now reduced to provincial status and overseen by a Roman proconsul named Optimus. Before him stood two men, charged with the crime of being Christian.

There is a Greek account, and a Latin, of the events that ensued—the Latin, probably an encapsulation of the Greek with a few details added. The chief controversy involves *when* it happened rather than *what* happened, whether in the mid-second century under Emperor Marcus Aurelius, or in the mid-third under Emperor Decius. Expert opinion favors the former.

From his official seat in the central balcony of the amphitheater, Optimus addressed the first prisoner, a rugged but elderly man. "What is your name?" he asked. "My first and most distinctive name is that of Christian," replied the old man firmly. "But if you want my name in the world, it is Carpus." (The Latin account names him as Bishop Carpus of Gordos, a city about two hundred miles to the east).

Optimus became grave. "You're surely aware," he said, "of the emperor's decrees to venerate the gods who govern all things. So I suggest you right now offer sacrifice." Offering sacrifice, meaning symbolically burning incense to the emperor as to a god, or swearing by the emperor's "genius" or spirit, was the legal expedient developed to solve the Christian problem. Charging people with simply *being* something offended the Romans' acute sense of justice. Charging them with *doing* something, or refusing to do it, that was a different matter.

But Christians everywhere, many of them anyway, were refusing to perform this simple sacrificial rite. That amounted to deliberate defiance of imperial authority, in effect treason, and the Romans well knew how to deal with treason. Yet the Christians' reason for refusal was, for them, equally compelling. Had not Jesus, when challenged by the high priest, described himself with the unmentionable name of God, thereby assuring his Crucifixion? There comes a time, that is, when a man must speak the truth, even at the cost of his life.

Such a moment had now come for Carpus. "I am a Christian," he declared, "and I venerate Christ, the Son of God, who has come in these latter times for our redemption."[1] Christians must worship God, "in truth," he said, because people take on

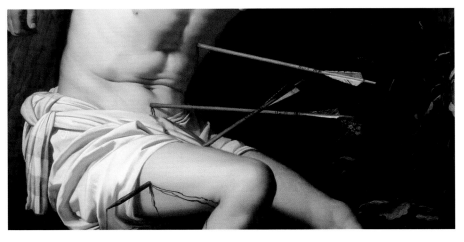

*Details from The Martyrdom of St. Sebastian by Gerrit van Honthorst, seventeenth century.*

the image of what they worship. The images which the Roman world worshiped were the concoctions of the devil, and those who worshiped them would take on that diabolic image. "Wherefore, proconsul, know you that I shall not offer sacrifice to them."

Optimus by now was furious. "Sacrifice to the gods!" he commanded. "Do not play the fool."

Such an order from a proconsul was intended to terrify. Quaking dread was the expected response. But Carpus, says the Greek account, just smiled and "gently replied, 'May the gods be destroyed, who have not made heaven and earth.'" Livid, Optimus stormed, "You *must* offer sacrifice! These are the emperor's orders!"

"The living," answered Carpus, "do not offer sacrifice to the dead."

"Do you think the gods are dead?" demanded Optimus.

Carpus replied that they were not only dead; they had never lived. The

*Detail from The Martyrdom of St. Ignatius, by Francesco Fracanzano, seventeenth century.*

only power they possessed was the one conferred upon them by the people who worship them. Take that away, "and you will discover that they are nothing, made of earth's substance, and eventually they will be destroyed by time itself. Whereas our God, who has created the ages, is timeless and abides eternal and immortal, ever the same."

Optimus was exasperated. "By allowing you to babble on so much, I have led you to blaspheme the gods, and the august emperors. We must let this go no further." He ordered Carpus "scraped." The old man was led before the crowd, now outraged by his defiant smile and screaming for him to suffer. He was "hung up," says the Greek account, while two men, each armed with metal claws, tore and lacerated his flesh, Carpus meanwhile shouting, "I am a Christian! I am a Christian!" until his voice gave out.

A certain Papylus was now brought forward, a leading citizen of Thyatira, a town that would become familiar to generations of Bible-reading Christians as the home of Lydia, Paul's first convert at Philippi, and one of the seven churches listed in the Book of Revelation. Was he a senator? demanded Optimus. He was not, said Papylus. Did he have children? Many children, he said.

---

1. The translation is taken from *The Acts of the Christian Martyrs* by Herbert Musurillo.

Detail from *The Martyrdom of St. Lawrence, by Palma Giovane, six-teenth to seventeenth century.*

"He means," shouted someone in the crowd, "he has children in virtue of the faith which the Christians repose in him."

He had "children in the Lord in every province and city," said Papylus, and no, he would not sacrifice. "I have served God from my youth, and I have never offered sacrifice to idols. I am a Christian and you cannot hear any more from me than this, for there is nothing greater or nobler."

Papylus was then hung up and "scraped," uttering not a sound, says the account, and this no doubt enraged the crowd even further. Optimus ordered him burned. He was thereupon nailed to a stake. But as the wood was brought forward for the fire, he died where he was. "He prayed in peace," says the account, "and gave up his soul."

One final vengeance awaited the crowd, because Carpus was still alive. Bleeding from innumerable wounds and barely able to speak, he nevertheless still brazenly smiled. So he was pinned down and nailed to a stake, then raised for the shrieking crowd to behold. As the fire was lit at his feet, he delivered one last taunt, a burst of derisive laughter at the entire enraged assembly. "What are you laughing at?" said a bystander. The faint reply was heard and recorded: "Blessed are you . . . Lord Jesus Christ . . . Son of God . . . Because you thought me, a sin-ner . . . worthy to share this . . . with you." With those words uttered, says the account, "he gave up the spirit."

But the story was still not over. A woman named Agathonike was standing nearby, her young son beside her. She suddenly saw the glory of the Lord, she said, calling to her from heaven. She broke free and rushed towards the flames that were consuming Carpus. "Have pity on your son!" people in the crowd shouted to her. "He has God who can take pity on him," she called, taking off her cloak and flinging herself on the fire. "God has providence over all."

Then something astonishing happened. The temper of the crowd appeared at that instant to have changed. Stunned into silence by what the woman had done, they seemed to suddenly revise their view of the whole event. "This is a terrible sentence!" they began to shout. "These are terrible decrees!"

That transformation from outright hatred of Christians, to silent reconsideration of them, to the perception of injustice against them, and finally to acceptance, if not of their faith at least of their integrity, would gradually take place all over the empire during the next two centuries. What pivotally influenced that change has never been doubted. It was the startling testimony of those who refused on pain of death to renounce their faith. They would be known thereafter in Christian hymnology as "the noble army of martyrs."

Until the empire-wide crackdown on Christianity by Decius in the mid-third century, outbreaks of persecution were sporadic, brief, and unpredictable. Apart from the highly profiled martyrdoms at Lyon, Carthage, Rome, and Alexandria, similar, less publicized cases kept occurring all over the empire. History records with little dramatic detail the martyrdom of Sagans, bishop of Laodicea, and Thraseas, bishop of Eumenia, together with his fellow Eumenians, Gaius and Alexander. The proconsul Sergius Paulus is remembered for creating martyrs in the largely Christian town of Sagaris in Laodicea. In a violent outbreak at Philadelphia, 110 miles southeast of Pergamum, eleven men were arrested, tortured, then sent down to Smyrna to be torn to pieces by animals at the provincial games. One of them, Germanicus, had to tug on a reluctant animal before it would eat him, a display that incensed the crowd. Elsewhere, Proconsul Arrius Antoninus, reputedly a bloodthirsty persecutor, was visited by a large crowd of Christians who offered themselves to him. He executed a few, but then contemptuously informed the rest that if they wished to die, they could easily find a rope or a cliff.

From Athens comes the report of a bishop named Publius, put to death along with most of the local Christian community. Even in immediate postbiblical times, Symeon ben Clopas, who had been a young cousin of Jesus and was now an aged bishop of Jerusalem, was "tortured in various manners," writes the historian Hegesippus, and eventually martyred as a Jewish heretic.

Wrote the pagan scholar Lucian: "The poor wretches have convinced themselves that they are going to be immortal and live for all time. So they despise death and willingly give themselves into custody, most of them. Furthermore, their first lawgiver persuaded them that they are all brothers, after they have transgressed by denying the gods, worshiping that crucified sophist himself, and living under his laws." The persecution was not centrally orchestrated, but local

*Detail from* The Martyrdom of a Saint, *by Francesco Granacci, fifteenth to sixteenth century.*

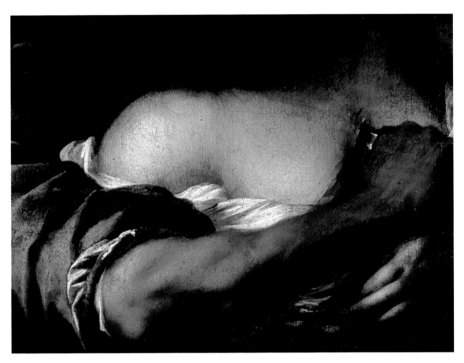

*Detail from The Death of St. Agnes, by Francesco del Cairo, seventeenth century.*

and spontaneous. Some provinces like Spain and Britain were little touched by it, but especially in the east, it was a dangerous time to be a Christian.

Almost always, the pogrom came in response to popular wrath against the Christians, whose repudiation of the gods was blamed for every flood, famine, fire, or plague. "Rid the earth of the likes of these! They don't deserve to live," one mob at Rome had shouted. "Christians shared with murderers and informers the lowest depths of unpopularity," writes the historian W. H. C. Frend in his exhaustive study, *Martyrdom and Persecution in the Early Church*. Tertullian, the outspoken evangelist and apologist from Carthage, recounts the way Christians were alluded to in street gossip: "It's surprising that a wise man like Lucius Titius has suddenly become Christian. . . . Such a good man, that Seius Gaius, except that he's a Christian . . ." and with a sneer, "The smart set, now they're becoming Christians!" The Roman Caecilius, a literary invention of the Christian apologist Municius Felix, writes of the Christians:

> Fellows who gather together they illustrate the dregs of the populace and credulous women with the instability natural to their sex . . . a secret tribe that shuns the light, silent in the open, but talkative in hid corners; they despise temples as if they were tombs; they spit upon the gods; they jeer at our sacred rites; they despise titles and robes and honor.

Rome's officialdom, however, was always loath to act in response to mob fervor, because it invited anarchy. A complaint process was developed under which accusers could levy charges of Christianity against other citizens. If the charge was proved—usually because the accused refused to make the requisite sacrifice or take the oath—the penalty involved the man's whole family. Not only would he pay with his life or be sent to die working in the mines, but his estate would be seized and his wife and children left impoverished. Since the informant shared in the man's estate, the process led to horrendous abuse. The emperor Hadrian sought to prevent this by subjecting the informant to the same penalties if the charge was not upheld. However, Hadrian's successors repealed that reform, and the abuse was resumed.

Once the law had formally spoken, the authorities were free to use the punishment as a means of satiating the blood lust of the mob, and the descriptions of what followed would challenge belief, were they not so unanimously and widely attested to. "Here we are touching one of the most obvious symptoms heralding the moral disintegration of Roman society and its future decadence," writes historian Henri Daniel-Rops in *The Church of Apostles and Martyrs*. "This civilization was prepared to debase mankind, and itself, in spectacles of unbelievable bestiality."

As the crowds screamed and jeered, the victims were hanged by their hands and lashed. Vinegar or salt was rubbed into their wounds. They were nailed to crosses and crucified. Nails were driven between their eyes. They were branded with red-hot metal. Their limbs were hacked off, their bodies torn to shreds. They were tied to posts and burned alive.

The greatest crowd-pleaser, however, was provided by wild animals. Lions, tigers, panthers, wild bulls, and bears were carefully starved, or taught to savor human flesh, or antagonized into a frenzy, then turned loose on a prisoner tied to a stake or bound up and pushed forward on a cart into the faces of the snarling beasts. Usually the animal would leap upon the victim and begin tearing chunks of flesh from an arm or a thigh. But the behavior of such creatures is never predictable. Sometimes they would refuse to attack the victim. In one celebrated case, a wild cat lay down at a woman-martyr's feet, much to the disgust of the crowd and the awe of her Christian companions.

"A certain taste for blood had always existed at Rome," notes Daniel-Rops. "The people were fairly accustomed to taking the sight of it for granted. After all, their religion, whose ceremonies had the appearance of veritable butcheries, would not have predisposed the Romans to any refinement of sensibilities. The custom of carrying out capital punishment in public encouraged the mob to enjoy degrading spectacles. It was quite common for a slave to be beaten to death. The public's taste for blood was systematically used by the government for the 'distraction of the mob.' . . . Collective degradation was henceforth a government affair."

That those who bravely endured such an ordeal should be revered by their comrades in the faith was certainly understandable. Few were men and women of great distinction. Nearly all were simple working people—tradesmen, small merchants, mothers of families; many were slaves. Their bodies, or what was left of them, were carefully gathered up by their fellow Christians—sometimes officials had to be bribed to release them—and reverently buried. Commemorations of their deeds on the anniversaries of their deaths began early on to take place at their tombs, and churches were eventually built atop many of them.

What harried the Christians was the uncertainty. Bloody pogroms developed in some cities, not in others. Some individuals were singled out, some not, and often without regard to their status in the Christian community. It was soon concluded,

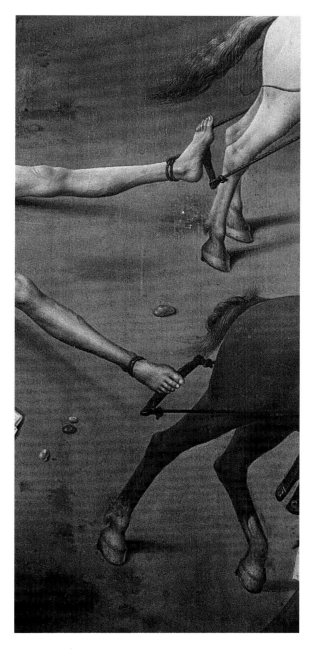

*Detail from The Martyrdom of St. Hippolytus by Dirck Bouts, fifteenth century.*

*Detail from The Martyrdom of St. Cecilia, by Orazio Riminaldi, sixteenth to seventeenth century.*

therefore, that it must be God who did the selecting, choosing some and not others for the "honor" of sharing in Christ's own fate. Martyrs came to be seen as a class apart, those who had come the closest to the imitation of Christ. As they awaited death, their dreams were accepted as prophetic. They were considered to have a special power to forgive other people's sins.

The word "martyr" derives from the Greek word for "witness," and the martyr was seen as bearing witness by his sacrifice to the sacrifice made by Christ. But Paul took this idea even further. Not only did the martyr witness to Christ's martyrdom, he actually fulfilled or completed it. Thus in Paul's memorable words: "Now I rejoice in what was suffered for you, and I fill up in my flesh what is still lacking in regard to Christ's afflictions, for the sake of his body, which is the church" (Col. 1:24). The author of the Epistle to the Hebrews sees Christians as "surrounded by such a great cloud of witnesses" that they should "throw off everything that hinders and the sin that so easily besets us" (Heb. 12:1). "I saw thrones on which were seated those who had been given authority to judge," says the writer of the Book of Revelation. "And I saw the souls of those who had been beheaded because of their witness for Jesus and because of the word of God. They had not worshiped the beast or his image" (Rev. 20:4). Apart from stirring the hearts of the faithful, however, martyrdom also posed ecclesiastical problems. Who exactly was a martyr? If a man was imprisoned rather than executed, was he a martyr? No, the Christians decided, to be a martyr, one must die. Those who suffered without dying were termed "confessors." What if a man or woman perished in serving Christ—a missionary who drowned, say, or a soldier killed in a just war? It was decided these may be considered heroes of the faith, but not martyrs. For a martyrdom, the death must be caused by a Christian's refusal to deny Christ.[2]

Moreover, while the Christian must expect martyrdom, he must not court it. At Carthage, Tertullian pleaded with the Roman governor to stop the persecutions. "He who does not avoid persecution, but out of daring presents himself for capture, becomes an accomplice in the crime of persecution," writes Clement of Alexandria. Death must not be sought, he adds, because those who court martyrdom are not really martyrs at all. They are calling attention to themselves rather than to Christ. But the state's authority is beneath that of God, he says, and the state must be defied when it ventures into outright idolatry.

What, one wonders, were the effects of such exhibitions on the people who attended them? Watching the grisly gladiatorial performances could profoundly affect individuals. In his *Confessions* (written in about A.D. 400), Augustine describes a student friend, Alypius, whose companions cajoled him into attending a

---

2. "The term martyr is hopelessly overworked and abused," writes Lacey Baldwin Smith in *Fools, Martyrs, Traitors*. "The hero is not a martyr. There is a profound difference between a willingness to take a risk, even to court destruction, and the deliberate walking into the torture chamber or the fire." Unlike heroes who affirm a society, martyrs tend to be "offspring of a society in conflict with itself" who "violate the most revered and treasured abstractions that shape a society." Neither can a martyr be "a blind victim of happenstance. Choice—sometimes desired, sometimes enforced—and premeditation are all important." Finally, "the death must be part of some long-term enterprise." The martyr dies for an overwhelming cause.

gladiatorial show in Rome over his initial protests:

"The whole place was seething with savage enthusiasm, but he shut the doors of his eyes and forbade his soul to go out into a scene of such evil. . . . (Finally) he was overcome by curiosity and opened his eyes . . . (and) he then received in his soul a worse wound than that man, whom he had wanted to see, had received in his body. . . . He saw the blood and he gulped down savagery. Far from turning away, he fixed his eyes on it. Without knowing what was happening, he drank in madness, he was delighted with the guilty contest, drunk with the lust of blood. . . . He looked, he shouted, he raved with excitement. He took away with him a madness which would goad him to come back again, and he would not only come with those who first got him there; he would go ahead of them and he would drag others with him."

Joyce E. Salisbury, in her splendid book on the martyrdom of Perpetua at Carthage, *Perpetua's Passion,* observes that the later amphitheaters offered superb acoustics. Spectators were given an intimate relationship with what was transpiring in the arena. It became a shared experience, reinforced by the ceremonial meal before the show began. So much so that Tertullian warned his fellow Carthaginian Christians to stay away from the amphitheater shows. This shared experience was real, he said. It bonded people, and they need not be bonded with those who collectively enjoyed human suffering.

Imperial officialdom had a different view of these "circuses," where gladiators routinely butchered each other and the torture-death of Christians was only one highlight of the program. Gladiatorial shows "inspired the audience to noble wounds and to despise death," wrote Pliny the Younger. There was "no better schooling against pain and death" than watching criminals die, wrote Livy. It taught them not to be afraid of blood and thus made them better soldiers.

Not everyone shared this positive viewpoint. The Christians, who often died fearlessly and courageously, striking awe and respect into many who watched them suffer, also caused some to have second thoughts. That response gradually

*An angel bestows the martyr's crown on St. Cecilia. Detail from the painting by Orazio Riminaldi.*

gained ground until the Christians prevailed and such public exhibitions were prohibited.

But not permanently. One of the most chilling stories of martyrdom describes groups of Christian men being lined up before their tormentor and being asked to renounce Jesus Christ. As each refused, a three-inch nail was hammered into the top of his head while the others watched. That report came neither from the second century nor the third, but from the twenty-first. The scene was a Christian village in southern Sudan under persecution by a militant Muslim government.[3]

The total number of Christians who perished under Roman persecution in the first three centuries is not known, but probably comes to several thousand. The real Age of Christian Martyrdom lay far ahead. At the close of the twentieth century, organizers of the International Day of Prayer estimated that two hundred million Christians were facing active persecution. A report from the Christian History Institute put the number of twentieth-century Christians killed for their faith at twenty-six million. ■

3. From a letter written by Dennis Bennett, executive director of the relief group Servant's Heart, to some members of the United States Senate, March 4, 2002.

# CHAPTER 4

# *The noble emperor who scorned the Christians*

## Last of the great pagans, Marcus saw the empire as doomed after a barbarian breakout wreaked havoc and forewarned of what was to come

The imperial messengers galloped south and west from the Danube frontier, over the Julian Alps and into the Po River Valley, changing horses at the post stations and then rushing into the towns, warning the magistrates to bring their people in from the suburbs and nearby farms to within the walls, neglected though the walls were. Farther from the main highways, more distant freeholders and small plantation owners first learned of the collapse of the frontier when they saw the smoke plumes rising from their neighbors' homesteads. Then they pushed carts, hurriedly filled with their valuables, toward the doubtful safety of the nearest Roman garrison.

The year was A.D. 170. For the first time in a full century, war had come to Italian soil. But now the combatants weren't civilized Roman legions, fighting among themselves to support their candidate for emperor. Rather, the enemy was the fierce, bestial savage, laying waste all in his path. Not for almost four hundred years had the barbarians reached Italy. Now they were back.

Along the frontier, a line of watchtowers and legionary fortresses, known as the *limes*,[1] stood guard against the dark German forests of the north and the

---

1. The *limes* (pronounced LEE-maze, the plural *limites*) was originally a country trail, then the trail running along a boundary, finally the word for the boundary or frontier itself.

Out of the forests of the north and through the Alps poured 100,000 barbarians
bent on destruction and slaughter. Roman garrisons were overrun and towns
and villages destroyed as the invaders cut a hundred-mile swath across
northern Italy from the Alps to the sea. The year was A.D. 170, and the historian Ammianus described the sudden incursion as "the united madness of the
different tribes."

sunny vineyards and olive groves of the Mediterranean. But in a surprising end-run, the barbarians had dodged around the defenders, and as many as one hundred thousand Marcomanni, Sarmatians, and Quadi—cruel and hungry, hairy and painted, dressed in reeking animal skins—had poured through the Danube defenses. Like ants, they swarmed over the Alpine passes and into the plush northeastern Italian plain, burning, raping, and killing, sacking the city of Opitergium and besieging the Adriatic port of Aquileia.

The historians of the day recorded surprisingly little of these traumatic events. The barbarians remained in control of northeastern Italy for over a year, and heroic efforts had to be made to maintain communications between the frontier and Rome. Yet there are few accounts of it. Fifty thousand crack troops were stationed on the upper and middle Danube, six legions in all, including two new ones, the Second and Third Italica, raised specifically for a campaign to discipline the unruly Germans. But these legionaries could do little more than limit the barbarian forays across the river, cutting off and punishing any isolated raiding parties that they caught.

The waste and slaughter of the breakthrough must have been immense: a hundred-mile swath cut across northern Italy from the Alps to the sea. It was such a prodigious calamity that the historian Ammianus described it as "the united madness of the different tribes." And the reliable Cassius Dio noted with awe, "Among the barbarian corpses were found even women's bodies in armor." The presence of women suggested to some that the barbarians had come, not simply to raid, but to occupy territory—Roman territory.

No one lounging comfortably in a Roman bath wanted to think about that very much, because it suggested the unthinkable: the fall of the empire, the end of the world.

A year later, with no new crops planted to feed them and legions prodding them from behind, the barbarians started moving back across the Julian Alps. Then, as the horde reached the Danube and began the return crossing—within

*Emperor Marcus Aurelius, though a studious jurist, philosopher, and orator, is best known as a man who spent the crucial years of his reign in an armed camp waging war on the northern barbarians who threatened the empire. Detail from the great equestrian statue of Marcus in Rome.*

range of the Roman troops still on the frontier—the Roman commander united all his forces to strike them, turning retreat into rout, drowning thousands, and recovering almost all their booty.

Leading those Roman forces was their supreme commander, Imperator Caesar Marcus Aurelius Antoninus Augustus, known to history as Marcus Aurelius, first citizen of the empire, one of the finest jurists, philosophers, and orators of his age, the greatest and the last of the "Good Emperors of pagan Rome." The barbarian breakthrough was the beginning of a war that would absorb the rest of Marcus's life.

Marcus Aurelius enjoyed the supreme blessing and curse of being the best of men, fully in command of his civilization, at just the moment when the world was threatening to disintegrate, when all the anarchic forces without and sophisticated vices within began conspiring to topple an empire that seemed to its inhabitants civilization itself.[2]

For the average Roman citizen or freeman—the Gallic wine merchant, the Iberian rancher, the British tin miner, the Greek stone mason—such a fall was simply unimaginable. Just twenty-three years earlier, the empire had celebrated

*'The people that once bestowed commands, consulships, legions, and all else,' lamented the poet Juvenal, 'now long eagerly for just two things—bread and circuses.'*

the nine-hundredth anniversary of the founding of Rome. Nine hundred years! And over three hundred years had passed since Rome had crushed Carthage and won undisputed control of the Mediterranean. *Mare Nostrum*, they called it, meaning "Our Sea." Now, hard white marble adorned the temples, baths, and arenas of a thousand cities from Egypt to Britain, Armenia to Portugal. What Rome hadn't absorbed wasn't worth conquering or was just too far away.

But Marcus's philosophy had taught him that nothing human endures—except duty. And through the eyes of duty, he could see how fragile was this whole extraordinary edifice of empire.

There were a half-dozen external threats, but most ominous was the pressure on the limes, the two-thousand-mile fortified frontier running from the German Alps north down the Rhine to the North Sea, and east down the Danube to the Black. The tribes across the limes were restless, being pushed by the even wilder Germanic and Turkic hordes behind them, a barbarian avalanche that began high in Central Asia.

Still, as Marcus looked north and east from his camp on the Danube, he knew that the tide could be held back, but only if Rome kept its integrity and remained true to the principles of virtue through which it had become great. And that was the real worry.

---

2. In the second century, historians recognized three "civilizations"—those of Rome, China, and Persia, beyond which lived hundreds of "barbarian" peoples. More recently, Mesoamerican civilizations have been recognized as well. Each would no doubt have considered a successful barbarian invasion as the end of the world.

*The remnant of a Roman road sign (above) still marks the limes, the northern frontier of the Roman empire and a fortification line stretching across Europe, up the Rhine and down the Danube to modern Romania and the Black Sea. The foundations of the Roman fort of Abusina (right) stand on the limes at what is now the town of Eining, Germany.*

Centuries earlier, the citizen-militia had been replaced by a professional army, increasingly recruited outside the Italian heartland. Then the very success of the empire, bringing with it a flood of cheap imports like Egyptian grain, had eviscerated the dutiful citizen farmers and artisans. Some rose into the bureaucratic ranks, the patricians and *equites* (knights) growing obscenely wealthy in the imperial service. But many Roman citizens simply lived off the free grain ration and lolled at the public baths or the games.

"The people that once bestowed commands, consulships, legions, and all else," lamented the dyspeptic poet Juvenal, "now disturb themselves no more, and long eagerly for just two things—bread and circuses!" And their supposed betters, the gentry, were if anything worse. As the wealth and personal retinue of noble Romans burgeoned, so did their sloth, luxury, and licentiousness. Too many young aristocrats preferred fine wines and witty mistresses to forced marches and camp life. Too many young wives preferred to have lovers rather than children—birth control, abortion, and the exposure (abandonment in open fields) of infants were commonplace. The latest celebrity actor and the all-star gladiator were far more entertaining than strategy and politics. Ease and indolence do not make for big families, and by the mid-second century the workforce had shrunk, and the government had to conscript labor to transport essential supplies into the city.

Beyond this, something even more serious was eating the heart of the empire—not vice, but what seemed to Marcus a dangerous insanity. Something slavish, yet somehow attractive to patricians, plebian citizens, freedmen, and slaves alike. A dream, but a subversive dream, voiding honest citizens' oaths to the gods and their emperor. It was called Christianity. Most Christians professed their loyalty to the empire, confident it could be "saved," though only if it abandoned paganism and became Christian. Events would one day vindicate their view, for they correctly envisioned the course that the empire was indeed destined to take. Though it would perish in the West, it would survive in the East as a

Christian empire for another thirteen centuries.[3]

However, other Christians spoke of the empire as the sum of all evils—"the harlot of the Seven Hills," as one of their writings called Rome (Rev. 17). To Marcus, such people were blind. Did they not realize that the only alternative to Rome's peace and prosperity was the war and anarchy stirring beyond the limes? They claimed to love humanity. Could they not see that humanity had never before succeeded as it had succeeded in Rome?

To Marcus, the empire was surely the gift of the gods, but it was a gift conferred through centuries of strife and struggle. In his epic poem of Rome's founding, the *Aeneid*, the first-century poet Virgil quipped, "Such hard toil it was to found the Roman people." Toil indeed, much of it organizational. For Rome's legions had conquered the world more through discipline and technology than through raw courage. Its cities had been created and linked by civil engineering, methodical administration and, at least initially, religious piety.

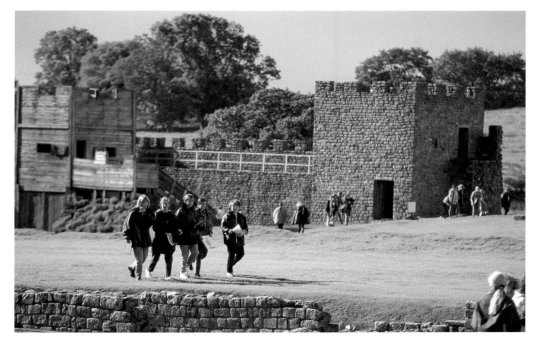

*Vindolanda was a Roman strong-point built as part of Hadrian's Wall in Northumberland, England. The wall, never entirely successful, was designed to prevent the Pictish tribesmen of Scotland from raiding into Roman Britain. Today its reconstructed replica is a "destination site" for visiting tourists and schoolchildren.*

Many cities were in fact founded as army camps. Between roughly 200 B.C. and A.D. 100, wherever the legions crossed into hostile territory, they completed their daily twenty-mile march by mid-afternoon. Then, while auxiliaries (non-Roman light infantry and cavalry) stood guard, legionaries took up their picks and shovels. Military surveyors had already laid out the stakes marking the new camp or *castra*: a square, four hundred yards on a side, quartered by two streets, the commanders' tents at the center, with bivouacs marked out for the legion's sixty centuries (companies). Fortification was the first task: a deep ditch dug, and its dirt and sod piled up in a tall rampart. Next came the tents and latrines; then supper

---

3. The devotees of traditional Roman religion did not refer to themselves as "pagans," of course. That was a term later applied to them by Christians. The word *paganus* originally indicated a villager, rustic, or yokel. Christianity first spread through the urban centers. The last holdouts of the "old gods" in the sixth through tenth centuries were neither in the cities nor on the large plantations, but out in the wilds, in the hinterland.

and a night's sleep, in as much security as might be expected in enemy territory.

Certainly, in Rome's march across Italy and Sicily, Gaul, Spain, North Africa, the Balkans, Anatolia, and Syria, there had been fighting—terrifying ambushes, battles, and sieges. But the steady advance of these fortified Roman *castra* across a land always gave conquest the air of inevitability.

Once the battles had been fought and the military campaigns turned from conquest to pacification, the most strategic sites in the new territories were

# The few, the proud, the Roman Legions are the schools and builders of the empire

## Discipline: If a man sleeps on guard duty, his buddies must beat him to death

*The centurion (left) from an historical reenactment is accompanied by a standard bearer carrying a vexillum, or banner identifying a vexillation or battlegroup.*

Century

Legionnaires

Cohort

First Cohort *(First cohort has ten centuries)*

Contubernium

**ROMAN LEGION**

Eight Legionnaires = One Contubernium
Ten Contubernia = One Century

Six Centuries = One Cohort
Ten Cohorts = One Legion

It has been said that the fate of a civilization depends on finding something to challenge ambitious young men, born without privilege. If such spirited youth are not somehow brought into the system, they fester as malcontents and outlaws. Rome knew how to handle them. By the second century, its twenty-seven to thirty legions were recruiting almost ten thousand young provincials yearly into their ranks. The rustic young men would be taught how to bathe, how to wield the *gladium* or short sword, how to throw the *pilum* or barbed javelin, and mainly how to accept without question the Legion's discipline. (The penalty for sleeping on sentry duty, for example, was to be beaten to death by one's tent-mates or *contubernium*.) After twenty-five years of service, the provincial legionary would retire a Roman citizen, with rudimentary Latin, a full purse and the deed to a farm. Orderly, the legions certainly were. A contubernium of eight shared a tent, a mule and sets of cooking and excavating tools. Ten *contuberia* made up a century of eighty, commanded by a centurion (equivalent roughly to a captain, today). Six centuries (480 men) formed a cohort, with its head centurion (or *pilus prior*), standard bearers and horn blowers to maintain cohesion. (The elite First Cohort would have five double-centuries of 160, for a total of 800, including most of the legion's clerks and specialized artisans.) Ten cohorts would make up a legion of roughly 5,500 soldiers; but it would fight as a unit only in a major campaign. ■

selected for permanent *castra*, with tall wooden palisades, huts, and even public baths. Then a second army of eagle-eyed Roman merchants flocked in, to provide for the troops and scout out local entrepreneurial opportunities—slaves, crafts and jewelry, agricultural produce, and metals. The army pacified, but the merchants romanized.

The camp was transformed into a city. Slaves built new walls, typically eight hundred yards on a side, stone-faced, and filled with a Roman innovation, concrete.

(Top) The testudo or "turtle," a fighting formation creating a protective shell of shields, used to close on the walls of a besieged city. Unlike the Germans, the Romans never had enough iron; their shields were made of oxhide-covered wood, their body armor usually bronze, their helmets often iron. The short sword or gladium was designed, not for slashing, but for stabbing. (Left) An actor portrays a centurion in a Guatemala passion play. (Inset) Another actor plays a centurion on a movie set at Avignon, France.

The main streets were widened, lengthened, and resurfaced with stone. New streets were added, dividing the city into blocks called *insulae* (literally islands). Each block was eighty yards square and was bisected by an alley. Sites were marked out for forums—colonnaded public squares surrounded by temples, courts, schoolrooms, public recital halls, and libraries. Other sites were reserved for public toilets, markets, arenas and theaters, and especially for the centers of social life—the public baths.

Retiring legionaries were granted deeds for lots inside and farmland outside the new cities. Developers arrived with their craftsmen and slaves, buying up blocks and filling them with private houses and four-story apartment buildings, wood-framed, concrete-walled, and stuccoed. The ground floor fronts of these buildings held shops, often belonging to family chains—wine and snack shops, bakers, butchers, olive oil and charcoal dealers, potters, weavers and leather-workers, tinsmiths, coppersmiths and ironmongers, carpenters, masons, and stonecutters. Wholesale warehouses rose near the gates for grain, wine, oil, and cement. Pottery works, making drain pipe and roof tiles, set up under the walls.

## Water was channeled into the city by mighty aqueducts, fed by lakes and rivers up to sixty miles away. Arched structures carried the water over intervening ravines and river valleys.

Meanwhile, more teams of slaves and (if the local tribes were subdued) legionaries built the highways, linking these new cities with the rest of the empire. Drainage ditches were cut and curb stones set, twenty feet apart for major roads, twelve for feeder routes. The soil between the curbs was then dug out several feet deep, and that ditch filled with layers of rock, stone, and gravel, cambered to let the rain run off. Important roads were eventually surfaced with smooth, cut stone, mortared in the gaps. But most level stretches remained packed gravel, their maintenance the responsibility of the nearest municipality that collected the road tolls.

The first purpose of the Roman roads was strategic, to permit rapid movement of the legions. So they took the shortest, straightest route, embankments raising them above marshy ground, but with little concern for the steep grades to be climbed by merchant wagons (though for important routes, short tunnels cut through ridge lines). Permanent bridges replaced boat bridges; stone and concrete piers were sunk into the riverbeds, connected by wooden or stone arches.

Thanks to these roads, a legion could easily average twenty miles a day, marching from Rome to Cologne on the Lower Rhine, over the Alps, in sixty-seven days; from Rome to Antioch in Syria in 124 days. Forced marches were much faster.

Post houses were built at twelve- to twenty-mile intervals for imperial messengers to change horses. Even in winter, express messengers could ride from the Lower Rhine to Rome, thirteen hundred miles, in nine days, though a routine

dispatch might take a month. As political, commercial, and tourist travel grew in the provinces, these post houses were joined by public *mansiones* (hotels) and private taverns. Such sites, in turn, might grow into towns.

Early in the lives of these new cities, while their populations were small, work began on permanent water supplies. This required the engineering and organizational skills that underpinned Rome's greatness. Water was channeled into the city by mighty aqueducts, fed by lakes and rivers up to sixty miles away. Multi-arched bridge-like structures carried the water over intervening ravines and river valleys, soaring high above the ground, while intervening hills were penetrated by tunnels. Where the aqueducts entered the cities, they spilled into large, brick-lined cisterns. From there, lead pipes, running under the sidewalks, carried the water to public fountains (for most Romans, the city's more than six hundred public fountains were the source of their drinking and cooking water), to wealthier homes and to the marble-lined public toilets and baths.[4]

Some Christians shunned the baths because of their reputation for salaciousness and immodesty. The rich had their own baths, but the public baths were more than swimming pools. They were vital gathering places for gossip, discussion, and the exchange of ideas, open throughout the empire to all classes

*The ruins of the Roman city of Volubilis near Meknes, Morocco, were laid out on classic military lines. Many cities were in fact founded as army camps or castra. Between 200 B.C. and A.D. 100, the steady advance of Roman conquest was closely followed by economic development and urbanization. Inset is a relief representing the boundary markers used by Roman army engineers to lay out streets.*

---

4. The theory has often been advanced that the decline and degeneracy of the Roman population was the result of lead poisoning of its water supplies via its lead pipes. Though the vast majority of the population remained rural, it was the urban dwellers who ran the empire, and they might conceivably have been affected by the lead. The agricultural slaves and tenant farmers were almost entirely uninvolved in imperial life.

# Water, the essential need, where the Romans excelled

## The Roman baths, where people talked, dined, and debated, were made possible by feats of engineering that continue to amaze

The twentieth-century essayist G. K. Chesterton once remarked that anyone called upon to defend a preference for civilization over barbarism would be hard-pressed to point to any single reason for his preference—warm houses, postal delivery, and public transportation might all figure into a fragmentary answer. Yet the word "civilization" is derived from the Latin for city and citizenship, implying that it blossoms only when many people can live together in close proximity. And that inevitably requires public sanitation, one of civilization's most important fruits.

In the case of Roman civilization, sanitation was not only a necessary precondition of tightly packed communities. The public baths or *thermae* themselves were the venues for leisurely political debate, artistic musings and entrepreneurial negotiations. Romans bathed not only to get clean (and in winter, warm), but also to meet with friends and fellow citizens.

The rituals of bathing differed from province to province, but generally the bather would first have his skin rubbed with oil in the *unctuarium* and exercise in a *palestra* or courtyard. He would then relax and chat with friends in the *trepidarium* or warm room, while being served snacks and drinks by public slave-attendants, and then move on to the hot and steamy *caldarium*. Here he sat, perspiring and scraping his skin with a *strigil*, the curved metal knife that served ancient skin-care needs in place of soap. Finally came a soak in the *calidarium* (hot bath) and a quick dip in the *frigidarium* (cold bath).

After swimming, the bather might stroll with friends in the public gardens, decorated with mosaics and marble sculptures, or perhaps watch an athletic event in a theater-like rotunda, listen to a poetry recital in an attached theatre, or have a meal in the restaurant. Visitors might book a room at the baths.

For Christians, the baths posed problems. Some shunned them as homosexual brothels. Others saw them as an opportunity to preach the Gospel.

The largest Roman bath was built by Diocletian in A.D. 305, covering an area of 130,000 square yards and capable of serving over 6,000 bathers at a time (though later converted into a church by Michelangelo). Others were almost as large, and the thermae were the most impressive buildings in every provincial town.

Such baths required the logistics of a functioning empire. Cool running water was brought in from miles away by aqueducts large enough to drive a wagon through. A constant supply of charcoal or wood was needed to feed the hypocaust or underfloor furnace, which heated the floors, walls and pools. ∎

The thermae or public baths, like these (left) built by the emperor Caracalla (A.D. 212-217), were a visible advertisement of the grandeur and luxury of the empire. Wherever its citizens traveled, they could cleanse their pores in a steamy caldarium, like the one (above) at Leptis Magna in Libya. The water for the baths, fountains, and other public sanitation services was brought to the empire's cities from upland lakes, often as much as sixty miles away, by massive aqueducts, like the Claudian near Rome (below).

The thermae were heated by hypocausts that ducted their hot air under marble floors, raised up on pillars (far left). These became so hot that bathers had to wear special sandals to protect their feet. Earthenware piping also carried hot air up through the walls, as here (right) at Ostia's Casa del Triclinio. Since it took three days to heat up a thermae, they were kept permanently hot. A city's water supply for the baths, public fountains, and toilets was deposited by the aqueducts into large concrete cisterns, and then flowed from there to the baths, public fountains, toilets, and private homes in large lead pipes like these (left) bearing the name Aureli Caesar for Marcus Aurelius. In times of drought, public officials would cut off the flow to private homes using curiously modern-looking valves (inset right).

including women (in their own pools), children, and even slaves and foreigners upon payment of a few cents.[5] They were comfortably furnished and decorated by the city's wealthy families. Not only the water, but the walls and floors were heated. This feature alone accounted for the centrality of the baths for people whose own homes were so inadequately heated they wore overcoats indoors for much of the year. People could, and did, spend hours every day in them. Exercise courts, lecture halls, and shops sprang up around them, offering massages or beauty treatments.[6]

Sewage disposal was a marvel of Roman ingenuity. The toilets, baths, and private houses were connected by clay pipes to sewers under the sidewalks, and

*The family was the cornerstone of Roman life, and its duties and obligations extended to dependent relatives and household slaves. Important families also had a small army of "clients"—lower-ranked business and political dependents who provided services but could also call on the head of the house for favors. Taken from a funeral plaque found at Erdek, Turkey, this frieze shows a Roman-style family banquet.*

these, in turn, joined two or more tile-lined mains, often six feet in diameter. Supplemented by storm drains on each street, they were big enough to allow the maintenance workers (sometimes prisoners condemned to death) to row small boats through the pipes as the sewage flowed under the city walls and out to the nearest river. Household waste was less efficiently handled. Though some went into toilets flushing down the sewer lines beneath each street, some had to be hauled off in carts, and some, as recorded in surviving records of lawsuits, was unceremoniously dumped from windows.

---

5. In smaller towns, the baths would reserve different hours for men and women; in larger cities, men and women would use different facilities. By Marcus Aurelius's time, however, sexual morality had slipped so much that he had to issue a decree forbidding mixed bathing.

6. The public baths built in Rome by the emperor Caracalla (A.D. 212–217) were so immense that twenty centuries later, the ruins of one of the larger rooms were being used for summer productions of opera.

Within a century of being founded, these new cities might have reached their stable size—perhaps twenty-five to fifty thousand people within the two-mile circuit of their walls—and they had all the conveniences of life. Their streets bustled. Their citizens gossiped, arranged business deals, and lounged in the baths. On feast days, marble temples sheltered their sacrifices. Local aristocrats sponsored public games in tall stone arenas and plays in their theaters. Legal actions were heard in local courts, and the births of citizens registered by public scribes.

What the local farms or mines couldn't provide—iron, marble, lead, or wine—was imported, while local surpluses were exported by a network of entrepreneurs extending back to Rome itself.

*A substantial home in the resort town of Herculaneum, on the Bay of Naples, laid out in typical style with the rooms arranged around a central garden. It was common for a wealthy Roman family to have a home in town and another on the family's rural estates.*

Not all the empire's cities had grown up in this orderly fashion. In the more populous and civilized East—Greece, Asia Minor, Syria, Palestine, Egypt—the empire took the cities as it found them, adding a few baths and temples, and otherwise simply providing the *Pax Romana* (Roman Peace) that knitted them into the imperial economy. But by the time the empire reached its natural limits at the end of the first century A.D., Gaul alone had sixty municipalities. Spain, Britain, fertile North Africa, Sicily, the Balkans, and Italy itself were laced with highways and jeweled with stone walls and marble temples.

Home to perhaps fifty million people, the empire has been called a federation of cities. Yet it was Roman. Provincials could win Roman citizenship and its legal advantages by military or civic service. And everyone paid the taxes needed to support the army, the government, and the slothful city of Rome—the last at a cost of perhaps ten percent of the empire's gross domestic product.

Most of the population remained agricultural; farm technology was ox-and-plow, and farm workers were tenants or plantation slaves. Since the transportation system could only soften the local impact of drought and famine, these could still be devastating. But in the Mediterranean, shipping supplied the needs of Rome itself. In the second century, imperial largesse gave Roman plebeians—poor citizens, descendants of the long-gone independent farmers—not only freedom from taxes, but a daily grain ration. So between mid-March and mid-November, grain ships as large as twelve hundred tons plied from Egypt and North Africa to the nearby ports of Ostia and Puteoli.

Though the whole Mediterranean shore was Roman, shipping still needed navy galleys to protect it from freebooters, especially near Albania, Sardinia, and the Greek islands. The navy also protected the Channel crossing to Britain and the sea lanes to the allied Greek cities on the Black Sea. Shallow-draft squadrons patrolled the Rhine and Danube.

Rome itself, with its population of about one million, was a drain on the imperial economy, but it provided the empire with its leaders. By Marcus's time, recruitment for the army had become ninety-five-percent provincial, but officers and provincial administrators were the sons of the Roman nobility, who began apprenticing at age fourteen. For Rome's was a family culture, and the family extended far beyond husband, wife, and children. It included adopted children, poor relations, and the often well-educated, well-treated household slaves.

Each great family had a cloud of clients as well—lower-ranked citizens providing personal and political services, plus African, Spanish, or Greek artisans. The most economically important clients were freed slaves or their descendants, often wealthy entrepreneurs in their own right but still financially bound to their former masters. Many managed the family's plantations and trading ventures far out in the provinces.[7] These reported to the father, the *paterfamilias*, who must not run these enterprises himself, common trade being beneath his dignity. Even dirt-poor plebeians, ousted from the ancestral farms in earlier generations, felt it more dignified to live on the dole, than to lower themselves to the trades.

The paterfamilias was also the family's jurist. When a youth "donned the toga" of an adult at fourteen, he was still totally subject to his father's will. He could choose neither his career nor his wife, for a marriage was an alliance and could significantly alter, for good or ill, the family's status. Adoptions were customary, both to give gifted children better prospects and to help great families find worthy heirs.

The paterfamilias had the power of life and death over the household's women and children. A father who caught his daughter in adultery, even with a citizen, could legally kill the lover, provided he also killed the girl. Yet despite this dolorous patriarchal authority, the Roman treatment of women was curiously lenient, even indulgent. Women, freed from their fathers by marriage, could own property and inherit apart from their husbands. Marcus enacted a reform, permitting them to bequeath their wealth to their children, overriding other family claimants. Though women were barred from public office, the clever and dedicated wielded great political influence. In fact, for nearly a quarter of the third century, women largely ran the Roman empire (see Chapter 8). Wealthy widows were very free—so free they gained a reputation for profligacy.

The nobility often paid dearly for their ascendancy. In both Rome and the provincial cities, they were obliged to sponsor public spectacles like games, plays, religious feasts, even the construction of public buildings. Many, particularly in the provinces, were slowly ruined by these massive expenses, either slipping into poverty or becoming paid bureaucrats in the imperial service.

At Rome, the power of the great families, whose members were identified by

---

7. Eventually, the Christians would draw a distinction between the office or function a man filled and the man himself, something that would have been incomprehensible to a Roman. That's why Rome, despite all of its administrative competence, never conceived of the limited liability corporation. People did business, not companies.

## LIST OF ROMAN EMPERORS

- Julius Caesar 48–44 B.C.
- Augustus 43 B.C.–A.D. 14
- Tiberius 14–37
- Gaius (Caligula) 37–41
- Claudius 41–54
- Nero 54–68
- Galba–Otho–Vitellius 68–69
- Vespasian 69–79
- Titus 79–81
- Domitian 81–96
- Nerva 96–98
- Trajan 98–117
- Hadrian 117–138
- Antoninus Pius 138–161
- Lucius Verus 161–169
- Marcus Aurelius 161–180

Continued on page 224

the colored borders on their white togas, was exercised through the ancient six-hundred-member Senate and the two consuls it elected yearly. But the Senate's power had been diluted since the days of the republic. Now the emperor controlled the army, appointed the governors for the frontier provinces, and could elevate worthy knights, foreign noblemen, and wealthy freedmen to senatorial rank. Though incredibly small, given the size of the empire, the senatorial class was the indispensable talent pool from which the emperor drew his military commanders and civil administrators.

The emperor himself was viewed as the father of the empire, the *pater patriae*. Though his real power depended on the loyalty of the army, he ruled by the legal fiction that he was both elected by the Senate and the natural or adopted heir of Caesar Augustus. Adoption into the imperial family as *Imperator Caesar Divi Filius*—"son of the deified Caesar"—often came after the untimely death of his predecessor.

By A.D. 161, Rome's 913th year and the empire's 192nd, Antoninus Pius had ruled this sprawling monument to human industry, ingenuity, and ambition for twenty-three peaceful years. For thirteen of those years, his carefully tutored and adopted son, Marcus Aurelius, had ruled with him. With characteristic genius, some said, Rome solved the problem of succession that dogged hereditary monarchies. The sitting emperor simply adopted the most promising successor. However, since Antoninus and his three predecessors had all died without natural heirs, they had little choice but to adopt, not out of genius, but necessity.

Marcus was one of the most promising ever. Though many facts of his life are obscure, his assessment of himself and the people around him are preserved in his book, *Meditations*, written in the last decade of his life as he campaigned on the Danube front. He was born on April 26, 121, the son of Annius Verus, a descendant of a noble Italian family that had made its fortune in Spain, and of Domitia Lucilla, an extremely wealthy Roman heiress.[8] When Marcus was three, his father died, and the boy was adopted by his paternal grandfather, who had the same name.

Almost nothing is known of his grandfather, except that he served the third of three terms as consul, a stellar distinction, when Marcus was five. Thus Marcus opens the *Meditations*:

> From my grandfather Verus: the lessons of noble character and even temper.
> From my father's reputation and my memory of him: modesty and manliness.
> From my mother: piety and bountifulness, to keep myself not only from doing evil, but even from dwelling on evil thoughts.

Wealth and privilege did not spoil the young Marcus. He was "a solemn child from earliest infancy," says an ancient biographer, and he was not robust; he endured chest and stomach ills his entire life. His early education was the best available, a combination of oratory and philosophy, studies in political discourse and moral perfection.

> From my [childhood] tutor: not to become a partisan of . . . the races or gladiators; to bear pain and be content with little, to work with my own hands, to mind my own business, and be slow to listen to slander.
> From [my teacher] Diognetus . . . to write philosophic dialogues in my boyhood, and to aspire to the camp-bed and the skin coverlet and other things which are part of Greek training.

In his young adulthood, Marcus's teachers in Stoic philosophy were Apollonius of Chalcedon and Quintus Junius Rusticus, grandson of one of the "Stoic martyrs" who died resisting Domitian's tyranny—and who himself sentenced Justin Martyr to death for being Christian. But his most influential oratory teacher was Marcus Cornelius Fronto, leader of the literary movement of the day, later consul (and author of the bitter denunciation of Christianity described in the preceding chapter).

> From Rusticus: to realize the need for reform and treatment of character . . . to be accessible and easy to reconcile with those who provoke or offend. . . .
> From Apollonius: moral freedom, not to expose oneself to the insecurity of fortune, to look (only) to reason, to be always the same, in sharp attacks of pain, in the loss of a child, in long illness. . . .
> From Fronto: to observe how vile a thing is the malice, caprice and hypocrisy of absolutism.

---

8. Marcus Aurelius's mother had inherited, among other things, vast brickworks outside Rome, where there had been an almost unbroken building boom since the Great Fire of 64.

*The much-imitated victory statue of Marcus Aurelius is perhaps the only surviving example of the many equestrian statues that once adorned Rome. The reason for its survival was that the rider was misidentified as Constantine, the great Christian emperor, and the statue was moved to the protection of the Basilica of San Giovanni in Laterano. The statue dates from Marcus's lifetime. Its original position is uncertain. In the sixteenth century, Michelangelo moved it from the basilica to the Capitoline Hill to decorate the newly designed Piazza del Campidoglio. It was removed in 1980 because pollution was destroying it. After careful treatment and restoration, including the application of gold plating, it is now displayed in the atrium of the Capitoline Museum, with a replica placed in the center of the piazza.*

A bust of the young Marcus shows a beardless youth, chin firm, lips full and slightly parted, eyes wide apart and deep-set, head covered in thick curls worn long over the forehead and ears: truly a solemn young man. Later busts and imperial coinage would show him prematurely aged, heavily bearded and weary.

Marcus attracted the attention of his uncle, the emperor Hadrian, very early. Cassius Dio reports that Marcus, "while still a boy, so pleased his many powerful and wealthy relations, that they all loved him." When Marcus was sixteen, Hadrian adopted Antoninus Pius as son and heir, on condition that Antoninus himself adopt Marcus and a younger cousin, Lucius Verus, as his heirs. Their contemporaries speculated that Antoninus's adoption was primarily a device to give Marcus time to come fully of age. Thus began Marcus's life in the imperial household, an honor he did not cherish; in fact he listed the dangers it posed to anyone seeking virtue. "Do not be drenched in the purple dye," he warned himself. Only an emperor was permitted the royal purple.

Still, duty was duty, and it came early. He was made consul at the unprecedented age of eighteen, and began attending imperial councils. At twenty-two, he became consul for the second time, a staggering distinction for one so young. By then, too, he was married to his cousin, Antoninus's fifteen-year-old natural daughter, Faustina, and became for life what the Romans called uxorious, or excessively fond of his wife.

> From the gods . . . that I preserved the flower of my youth and did not play the man before my time, but even delayed a little longer . . . that my wife is what she is, so obedient, so warm-hearted and so artless . . . for these things require the gods to help and Fortune's hand.

At twenty-six, he was made Caesar, or junior emperor, and that year, Faustina bore him the first of what would be at least fourteen children, including two sets of twins. Only five would see adulthood, one of them the future emperor Commodus. Letters to and from his long-time teacher Fronto revealed his continuing deep grief at the deaths of his "chicks."

As co-emperor, Marcus could divide his time between his administrative duties and his beloved philosophy. But his leisure carried a price. Moorish brigands were raiding into Mauretania and Spain, the Germans were restless on the Rhine-Danube frontier, Egypt was troubled, and the empire of Parthian Persia, based on the Iranian plateau, was again eyeing the Roman ally, Armenia. In his day, Hadrian had traveled continuously from Britain to Mesopotamia and back again, overseeing the borders. But Antoninus indulged his own passion for peace by never leaving Rome and its temples. Worse yet, he neglected Marcus's advanced education and the empire's security by never sending his adopted son to the frontiers.

> From my father by adoption: gentleness and unshaken resolution in judgment. . . readiness to hear those who had anything to contribute to the public advantage; the desire to award every man according to desert.

The Pantheon (left) is one of the great spiritual buildings of the world and an architectural marvel. Built between 125 and 118 B.C. as a Roman temple, it was later consecrated as a Catholic Church. The dome has a span of 142 feet and for over 1,500 years (until Brunelleschi's dome at the Florence cathedral in 1436) was the largest in the world. (Inset) A lararium at Pompeii. Located in every Roman home, these small shrines were dedicated to the Lares, guardian spirits of house and field, in which their images were kept and worshiped. The Christian insistence that there is only one God, of course, struck pagan traditionalists as mere "atheism."

In 161, after a brief illness, the aged Antoninus Pius died, mumbling angrily to himself about a "foreign king" playing him false, meaning the Parthian king of Persia. Now thirty-nine, Marcus was effectively ruler of the world. Yet surprisingly, he refused to accept the Senate's election as Imperator and *Pontifex Maximus*—supreme priest—unless his adopted younger brother Lucius Verus was made co-emperor. Marcus had an unfeigned distaste for power, and only his training and Stoic philosophy impelled him to accept the office.

In accordance with a growing custom, the Senate elected Antoninus to divinity, his body was burned on a funeral pyre, an eagle was released to symbolize the ascent of his spirit to the gods, and a college of priests was chosen from the family's closest friends to administer to the new cult of the *Divus Antoninus*. By now, deifying a newly deceased emperor had become a practical necessity. It conveyed the message: Rome is eternal. The empire never imposed this religion on its provincial cities; it didn't need to. Worship of the *Divi Augustus* was the provinces' most immediate bond to the capital.

The roots of Rome's religion ran deep. From prehistoric times, the family worshiped its divine ancestors along with the sacred hearth, the holy fire at the center of the household. In the early days, the Roman was a farmer, and the family's properties were marked by the ancestral tombs and sacred boundary stones. The family calendar was marked by rituals like feasts at the ancestral tombs, pouring milk and honey to the dead to keep them content in the underworld. The newborn child was formally introduced to the sacred hearth nine days after birth, the paterfamilias picking up the baby in front of the fire to acknowledge paternity. There were rites of purification and invocation (calling on a god), public processions marking sacred spaces, and ancient prayers promising an eventual, if vague, victory over death.

Gradually the great families and their clients coalesced into clans, and at the heart of each coalition was a calendar of feasts and rituals, honoring gods like father Jupiter, mother Juno, messenger Mercury, warrior Mars, smithy Vulcan. A Roman aristocrat was a priest, and a citizen was anyone admitted to the rites of Rome's gods and the divine founders. All associations—political and social— were bound by oaths and defined first by their feasts, sacrifices, priesthood, and prayers. Ritual permeated everything. Three gods guarded the entrances to homes: Forculus the door, Cardea the hinges, and Limentius the threshold, and the devout greeted each in turn. Yet it was a religion without doctrines or creeds. As long as the rituals were observed, it didn't much matter whether they represented some truth. The rite was what counted; that's what held things together. Christianity was to reverse that order. The rite would be an expression of the doctrine.

With the fall of the republic and the gradual disappearance of independent citizen-farmers in the last two centuries before Christ, however, a great change began. The wealthy bought up the small farms and soon only they still revered the family gods. This left the plebeian citizens, the freedmen and the slaves, depending upon the distant civic gods and austere public sacrifices. The loss was real; most of the mysticism was gone from life.

Instead, there were the games, held forty times a year. For most, the games became the substitute for family piety, as they mutated from public sacrifices into orgiastic baths of human and animal blood. Blood-spattered gladiators became popular heroes. In the barbarian breakthrough of 170, Marcus had to draft gladiators into the army. Vainly, he offered ballet as a substitute, but his popularity plunged. The people wanted blood, not art. They also wanted magic, and an explosion of interest in astrology, Egyptian gods, and Asian mysticisms descended upon the city. Rome became a smorgasbord of different cults.

Officialdom struggled to control all this. When, in 186 B.C., the wine-soaked orgies of the god Bacchus got out of hand, 3,500 devotees were put to death. But Bacchus was an ancient god, one imprudent to neglect. So a century later, a toned-down version of the "Bacchanals" became acceptable. Likewise, the Egyptian cult

*A relief from the Arch of Marcus Aurelius in Rome (A.D. 176–180), showing the emperor leading a public sacrifice in his role as Pontifex Maximus, the chief priest of the empire.*

# 'By far the nastiest sports event ever invented'

## Thus does one historian describe the gladiatorial shows that over the years claimed the lives of tens of thousands, many of them Christians, to thrill the crowds with the sight of blood

The first-century entertainment industry knew all about advertising, and the colorfully painted signs on the walls and rock faces of one city promised a great show. Thirty pairs of fierce gladiators would battle in the arena. Crucifixions would amuse those having no other plans during the noon break in the games, and there would be awnings to shield the spectators, if not the agonized victims, from the midday sun. Whether that show was ever held, nobody knows, for the city was Pompeii in Italy and the year was A.D. 79, when Mount Vesuvius blew apart and freeze-framed city life in mid-process. The ads for the big show lay buried under volcanic rubble along with much of the citizenry until they were uncovered seventeen centuries later.

As the time for such a show—known in Latin as a *munus*—grew near in any large Roman city, programs were circulated. On the evening before the munus, the organizer threw a feast for the gladiators, inviting everyone else to come and witness what would be, for many contestants, the last meal.

"The curious circulated round the tables with unwholesome joy," writes the French scholar Jerome Carcopino. "Some of the (gladiators), brutalized or fatalistic, abandoned themselves to the pleasures of the moment and ate gluttonously. Others, anxious to increase their chances by taking thought for their health, resisted the temptations of the generous fare and ate with moderation. The most wretched, haunted by a presentiment of approaching death, their throats and bellies already paralyzed by fear, gave way to lamentation."

The next day's events began with a festive parade of dignitaries, musicians, armor-bearers, and horses. The events themselves would be accompanied by organ music, much as organ music would accompany some sports events in the twenty-first century. After preliminary contests with blunt weapons, a blast of the war trumpet summoned horsemen for the first real fight.

The slaughter that was about to occur, before an attentive audience of both sexes and all ages and occupations, was "by far the nastiest blood sport ever invented," writes historian Michael Grant in his *Gladiators*. "No amount of explanation can mitigate the savagery."

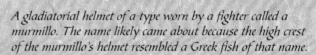

*A gladiatorial helmet of a type worn by a fighter called a murmillo. The name likely came about because the high crest of the murmillo's helmet resembled a Greek fish of that name.*

Gladiators almost always dueled one-on-one. No particular time limit was set, nor were scores kept. Referees beat the reluctant with sticks to get them going. They stabbed each other, ducked, and stabbed again. Finally, one of the two was either dead or so grievously wounded that he could no longer fight. If he remained alive, the audience decided his fate.

One who had fought bravely, or who was a popular champion, might be spared and carried from the arena to be treated by physicians. (Galen of Pergamum, one of the best-known doctors in history, attended to injured gladiators before he was appointed personal physician to Marcus Aurelius.) But when the audience found the loser cowardly, they signaled their disgust with thumbs up (not down, despite the movie epics). At major *munera*, the six virgins who tended the sacred flame in the Temple of Vesta gave the signal. The victor then bloodily dispatched his opponent.

The toll was astounding. "For century after century, tens of thousands, throughout the empire, did not leave the amphitheaters alive," says historian Grant.

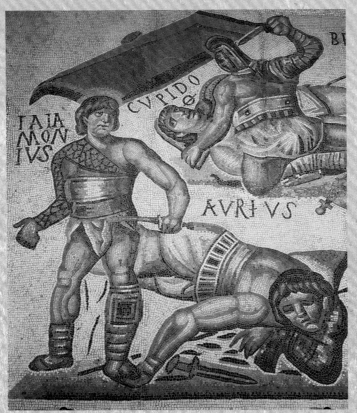

Christians were often among the unfortunates condemned to the arena, but most who ended their lives as gladiators were slaves or common criminals. Some were professionals, earning acclaim from men, and close attention from admiring women. Occasionally, an enthusiastic member of the nobility might enter the fray. Otherwise, gladiators held the lowest social standing, forbidden even honorable burial.

Fighters were assigned to categories and fitted out with appropriate weapons and armor. Among them were lance-bearing horsemen, or *equites*, in tunics with shields and visored helmets; bare-torsoed *murmillo*, with brimmed helmets and short swords; the all-but-naked *retiarius*, wielding a net and a long-handled trident, his opponent, the helmeted *secutor*, holding a short-handled blade.

Best-known of all gladiators was Spartacus, a prisoner of war forced to enter a gladiatorial school in 73 B.C. He led seventy others in a revolt in the town of Capua, twenty miles north of Naples. They assembled a rebellion of forty thousand men, but after two victorious years, Spartacus died in battle, and six thousand of his followers were crucified along the roadside between Capua and Rome.

Even so, the Romans were fascinated and attracted by gladiators. Thomas Wiedemann, in his book *Emperors and Gladiators*, portrays them as "like highwaymen." They "symbolized the rejection of a normal, lawful, civilized life-style," he writes, and their outlaw chic prompted highborn men to emulate them, and highborn women to seek sex with them.

The rise of Christianity is generally credited for the eventual abolition of the Roman gladiatorial games. Prohibited in 325, they finally vanished early in the next century. ■

*For all their sophistication, Romans reveled in the incredible butchery of the arena (above). Most of those who fought and died in dozens of venues around the empire were slaves or common criminals, many were Christians, and a few were professionals who could earn wealth and fame as a result of their success. But even for the most successful, gladiatorial combat forever condemned them to the lowest social standing and eventually an anonymous burial. As incomprehensible as the savage action on the field might be, the food vendors and music accompanying the games would instantly be recognizable to sports fans of the twenty-first century. Organ music, horns, and trumpets were popular (below). As happens at ball parks and hockey arenas today, music would be used to involve the crowd in the highs and lows of the action taking place before them.*

of Isis, suspiciously attractive to the poor, was suppressed for over a century, before a tamer version was given a temple in Rome. Chaldean astrologers were expelled five times before they gained respectability.

Meanwhile, some of the aristocracy—those drawn to something beyond their own pleasures, anyway—committed themselves to "reason and duty," as defined by one (or an eclectic mix) of the established schools of philosophy, particularly Platonism, Aristotelianism, Epicureanism, and Stoicism. Apart from atheistic Epicureanism, these all proposed some version of a single, impersonal, purely rational god, or Divine Reason—and even the Epicureans were willing, somewhat cynically, to engage in the public sacrifices. By Marcus's time, Stoicism was favored. "Be content to make a very small step forward and reflect that even this is no trifle," he writes. Founded by the Greek Zeno, the four-hundred-year-old Stoic school believed in a world that was in some way the life of a single, passionless deity. The good life, therefore, was a dispassionate one, a life of *apathia*, acting only according to reason and out of duty.

Hence, Marcus took very seriously the duties that Rome's traditional religion imposed upon him as Pontifex Maximus. For major feasts, the emperor would lead the prayers and sacrifices—such as opening the jugular of a young white bull and catching its warm blood in a silver basin. Most of Rome's two hundred such festivals did not require his personal attention, but he emphasized the priestly roles of all those in authority, from the paterfamilias, who was pontifex of the family, to the *decurion*, as pontifex of the provincial city, to the elected presidents of the trade fraternities into which the city's artisans were organized, each of whom was pontifex of his *collegia*.

A priesthood conferred status, binding important families to public service, and therefore officialdom had a vested interest in the whole elaborate paraphernalia of pagan worship. Stirring a renewed interest in it was a means of encouraging a renewed public piety, a rebirth of public virtue, and a renewed public commitment to the empire itself. A major obstacle to this pagan rejuvenation, however, was Christianity. The Christians volubly denounced the entire pagan system as foolish superstition at best, demonic at worst. Almost a century earlier, Trajan had said that hunting Christians was "not in accordance with the spirit of the age." But the age had changed. Trajan had reigned in an era of peace and prosperity. Now would begin the reign of Marcus, who faced ominous threats from the north, the west, and the east. The need was now urgent for the divine intervention of its gods.

Rome's difficulties began almost immediately upon the accession of Marcus and Lucius Verus. In late 161, the "foreign king" against whom Antoninus had muttered angrily on his deathbed, the Parthian Vologases III, invaded Rome's ally Armenia, and installed a cousin on its throne. The nearest provincial governor, Severianus, had invaded Persian territory with a single legion. Caught on the upper Euphrates, it was slaughtered, and Severianus committed suicide. Why had he embarked on such a foolish single-legion attack? Because, Rome later learned in disgust, a seer, one Alexander of Abonutichus, had told him that his horoscope assured him of a great victory. So much for astrology.[9] By now Rome had a war on its hands.

*A bust of Lucius Verus. Marcus sent his cousin to the eastern front in the hope that the playboy and dilettante would develop character "through the fear inspired by warfare."*

The situation was sufficiently serious to merit an emperor's intervention, and after deliberation, Marcus sent young Lucius to the eastern front. This might, he knew, solve more than the Persian problem. Lucius was, frankly, a dilettante, a playboy, an embarrassment to the new administration. "And so," says an ancient biographer, "at least his immorality could not be carried on in the city . . . and he might return a reformed character through the fear inspired by warfare." For the four years of the ensuing war, Marcus remained in Rome, fretting anxiously, spending long days reviewing legal cases as the empire's last court of appeal, and watching his son, Antoninus, grow ill and die at the age of four.

Lucius's generals—particularly the Syrian Avidius Cassius—acquitted themselves well in the Parthian War, putting a client king of Rome back on Armenia's throne, temporarily occupying Persian Mesopotamia, burning Vologases' palace at Ctesiphon, and forcing a peace treaty. So on his return in 166, Lucius was granted a formal triumph, a parade through Rome with wagonloads of booty, complete with shuffling prisoners and swaggering veterans of the victorious eastern army. If the war had sobered him, it wasn't evident. Marcus spent five days living in Lucius's villa, apparently to provide him with a sober example. Yet while Marcus diligently pursued his judicial responsibilities, Lucius partied.

Unfortunately, in addition to their booty, those veterans brought back the most severe plague recorded in antiquity, perhaps typhus, bubonic, or smallpox.

## Such a great pestilence so devastated all Italy that everywhere estates, fields and towns were left deserted, uncultivated and uninhabited, and relapsed into ruins and woodland.

The accounts of it are sparse but chilling. "Such great pestilence devastated all Italy, that everywhere estates, fields, and towns were left deserted, without cultivators or inhabitants, and relapsed into ruins and woodland," says one account. It was probably an exaggeration, but only slightly. By 167, the pestilence had become most severe where the populace was most dense, notably in Rome itself and the camps of the army. The dead were carried away daily in carts, a scene that would be repeated again in the fourteenth and seventeenth centuries, always with the implication that the end of the world was at hand.

The plague would continue for most of the next decade and delay for another four years Marcus's long-planned conquest of Germany. Its chief victim was the army, the institution that more than any other embodied the organizational and technological genius that was Rome. Since Augustus's day, it had normally numbered twenty-eight legions—sometimes more, as when Marcus raised two for Germany; sometimes less, as when Severianus lost one in the East. In Augustus's

9. The astrologer Alexander of Abonutichus was father-in-law of the respected senator Mummius Sisenna Rutilianus, proconsul of Asia. In other words, this was advice a politic legion commander could not prudently ignore. Twelve years later, Alexander's astrological perceptions would be heeded again. The result would prove even more catastrophic, as Marcus was destined to discover.

time, the legions were stationed evenly about the empire. But now, the Rhine-Danube limes had drawn half of them—four on the Rhine, four in Bavaria and Austria, and six on the lower Danube. Britain needed another three—normally two, but there had been a rebellion early in Marcus's reign that left Spain and Africa with three and the unstable East with just eight. Almost two dozen provinces without legions relied on noncitizen provincial regiments to suppress increasingly troublesome brigands.

Rome cared well for its soldiers. When legionaries retired after twenty-five years' service, they were reckoned among the wealthier non-noble Romans. Their salary—three hundred denarii a year—was only five percent of that of a junior procurator who served as a provincial governor. But they received the same or more after an important victory, or at the succession of an emperor, gifts they frequently salted away until retirement when they often received a gift of land as well.

Those twenty-eight legions provided the empire's mobile reserve. Yet with half their 140,000 infantry manning the stockades and patrols on the German frontier, little was left for the unexpected. Reinforcing different sectors consisted less in moving whole legions, and more in detaching small battle-groups, called *vexillationes*,

*Though it ran along the northern frontier, the River Danube was a major artery of the empire. Overlooking the junction with the March River (top photo), a Celtic settlement on the distant hill guarded an important crossing point on what was known as the the Amber Road, along which precious amber flowed to Rome from the Baltic. Trajan's Table (lower photo), on the bank of the Danube near modern Kladnovo, Yugoslavia, commemorates a Roman bridge, long vanished, which crossed the river at this point to connect with newly conquered land in the territory of the Dacians.*

from as far away as Syria. Though new legions (like Marcus's Second and Third Italica) were traditionally raised in Italy, once they were stationed on a frontier, each five-thousand-man formation drew its three hundred yearly recruits (plus auxiliaries) from its resident province, which became its home. So, if three cohorts were detached from a Syrian legion and marched off to the Danube— twelve hundred miles in two months—they would expect to march home again when the campaign was over.

In the first century, the empire had reached its natural limits: to the south, the Sahara and Arabian Deserts; to the east, the ancient empire of Persia, now under the control of a Persian people known as the Parthians, with the buffer states of Mesopotamia and Armenia endlessly disputed; in the northeast, the lower Danube; in the northwest, the upper Danube, the Rhine, and Britain; in the west, the Atlantic. Only on the Danube and Rhine was there a large, threatening population, yet paradoxically, one too primitive to be conquered.

Rome had repeatedly tried to pacify Germany. In his day, Augustus had sent three legions under Verus to the apparently tranquil Weser Valley, only to lose them all in an ambush by the (as the Romans saw them) treacherous German allies. His successor, Tiberius, made a more modest effort with yet more modest results. Later still, Trajan had taken a half step, occupying Dacia, modern Romania, and thereby creating a great Romanian salient jutting two hundred miles north from the Danube; but that only subdued the tribes of the Dacian confederation, leaving the Marcomanni, the Quadi, and the Iazyge still pressing the limes. Now, sixty years later, Marcus would try again.

However, the central problem in conquering Germany was that there

*As shown (below) in this reconstruction at Roggendorf, Austria, of a typical Celtic house of the first century B.C., such structures were made from wooden planks and wickerwork, with the roof being of thick thatch in the shape of a dome. The photo (inset) shows the remains of an ancient wall that surrounded a Celtic oppida, a regional military and administrative center at Finsterlohr, Germany. By the fifth century B.C. the Celts were building large settlements, which developed into fortresses serving the surrounding region. Protected by substantial fortifications, they enclosed a space covering twenty to several hundred acres and could provide shelter for thousands of people.*

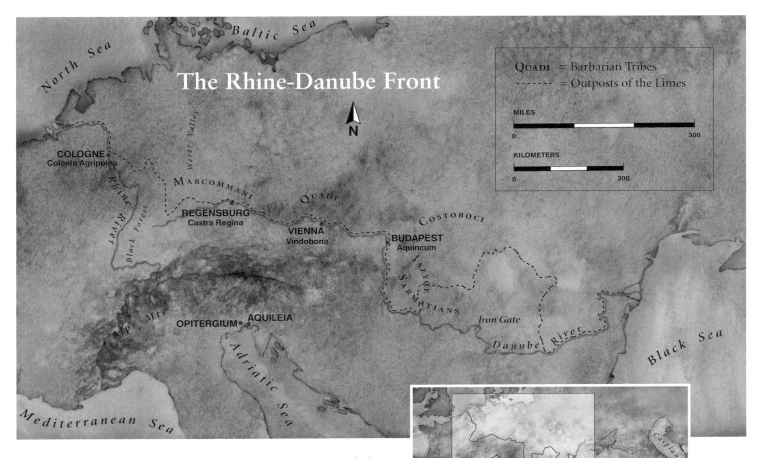

## The Rhine-Danube Front

QUADI = Barbarian Tribes
------- = Outposts of the Limes

MILES
0                    300

KILOMETERS
0            300

North Sea

Baltic Sea

COLOGNE
Colonia Agrippina

Rhine River

Black Forest

Weser Valley

MARCOMMANI

REGENSBURG
Castra Regina

QUADI

VIENNA
Vindobona

BUDAPEST
Aquincum

COSTOBOCI

IAZYGE SARMATIANS

Alps Mts

OPITERGIUM    AQUILEIA

Adriatic Sea

Iron Gate

Danube River

Black Sea

Mediterranean Sea

Caspian Sea

Black Sea

Mediterranean Sea

was nothing to conquer. Julius Caesar had conquered the Gauls in 60 B.C., and Claudius finally conquered the Britons in A.D. 50, but both Gaul and Britain had settled farming villages and market centers. The Germans planted their scant crops in forest clearings, and otherwise hunted game and raided their neighbors. When legions pushed across the frontier, the barbarians melted into the forest. Nor could trade goods pacify them; they had nothing to trade except slaves and few homes to hold Roman luxuries. All the Germans had was a growing population and a hunger for cleared, arable land.

Ten legions might do the job, by pushing clear through Germany to the Baltic and exterminating anyone unwilling to be enslaved. However, Rome had problems enough keeping its twenty-eight legions properly manned. Its total military establishment, perhaps five hundred thousand men, represented one percent of the empire's total population. But most of that population consisted of agricultural people, often slaves, uninvolved in public life. Further, even before the plague, Marcus had difficulty finding competent commanders and administrators for the legions and provinces he already had. The fundamental obstacle was demographic: hopeless slaves don't breed, and pampered aristocrats won't.

Still, Marcus's Stoic sense of duty demanded he do what he could. After a year presiding at special religious rituals for the plague, he and Lucius headed for the Danube in 168. It was Marcus's first trip outside Italy, and what he found was appalling. Plague was still rampant among the legions. They would eventually

# The Christians of the imperiled Twelfth Legion prayed, and then...

## The Twelfth was said to be riddled with Christians—was the storm that saved them sent by God? They called it a miracle, but officialdom could hardly agree

Wounded and exhausted, the Roman soldiers had run out of water after a long and unsuccessful campaign. The Germanic barbarians known as the Quadi vastly outnumbered and surrounded them. So confident of victory were the Quadi that they stopped fighting altogether, posting guards to watch the Romans collapse in the withering heat.

Parched with thirst, too weak to fight, unable to retreat, the Romans stood unmoving as the sun beat down upon them.

Suddenly, out of nowhere, dark clouds formed above the battlefield, and a cool, heavy rain showered down upon them. At the same time, thunder, hailstones, and lightning over the Quadi encampment filled the barbarians with terror. As the downpour continued, the Romans turned their faces upwards and drank eagerly, then caught more water in their helmets and shields and gave it to their horses to drink. The confused and frightened Quadi were shortly overrun by the revived Romans.

That much is supported as fact by a wide array of historical evidence. A controversy, however, surrounds the further question of *why* it happened. The legion involved was the Twelfth, the same unit that had been humiliated in A.D. 66 during the early stages of the Jewish War (Chapter 9, *The Veil Is Torn*, this series). In the 106 years that had elapsed since that event, the Twelfth had been moved north to the German frontier, and included in its ranks a notable number of Christians. These, when all else seemed lost, had prayed to God to save the legion, it was said. The thunderstorm followed. It was a miracle, according to the Christians.

Historians recording the events of the storm include the pagan Cassius Dio and the Christians Eusebius, Apollinarius, and Tertullian. What has been repeatedly questioned over the centuries, however, is the miraculous element. Was the rescuing storm God's answer to urgent battlefield prayers sent up by the Twelfth's Christians? By the Christian accounts, the emperor Marcus Aurelius himself, acknowledging the miracle that had won the day for his army, decreed that thenceforth, the praying soldiers would be known as the "Thundering Legion" and that persecuting the Christians within his empire would be forbidden.

Marcus's supposed gratitude and his change of heart toward the Christians are recorded in a letter he was said to have written to the Senate. Its text is appended to Justin's work known as his *First Apology*. However, historians and scholars generally agree that the letter is fanciful, even a forgery. The truth is that Christians continued to be cruelly persecuted after the Roman victory, and while Marcus recognized that something quite unusual had occurred on the battlefield, if he gave credit to any higher power, it was to a god of the Romans.

The event likely occurred in 172. Roman coins minted in 173 indicate that Marcus erected a temple to the god Hermes in gratitude. The celebrated Column of Aurelius, built to commemorate Marcus's victories and still standing in Rome in the twenty-first century, depicts the rainfall that won the battle, pouring from the beard of a grim, half-human deity, perhaps Hermes or the Egyptian god Thoth-Shou.

To those arguments against the Christian view of the providential storm, John Henry Newman, the nineteenth-century Roman Catholic cardinal and scholar, offered a reasoned response in his essay, *The Miracles of Early Ecclesiastical History*. That the unexpected happened on the battlefield is clear, Newman writes—after all, even Marcus recognized its unusual nature, as is recorded on his column. "Under these circumstances, I do not see what remains to be proved. Here is an army in extreme jeopardy, with Christians in it; the enemy is destroyed and they are delivered. And Apollinarius, Tertullian, and Eusebius attest that these Christians in the army prayed, and that the deliverance was felt at the time to be an answer to their prayers; what remains, but to accept their statement?" Pagans may have accounted for the event "by referring it to their own divinities," but that puts no one else under any obligation to take "their hypothetical explanation of it."

He concedes that the events in the battle may not have been miracles "in the philosophical sense of the word." But "the common sense of mankind will call them miraculous; for by a miracle, whatever be its formal definition, is popularly meant an event which impresses upon the mind the immediate presence of the Moral Governor of the world. He may sometimes act through nature, sometimes beyond or against it, but those who admit the fact of such interferences will have little difficulty in admitting also their strictly miraculous character, if the circumstances of the case require it." ∎

Surrounded by their enemies, exhausted and thirsty, soldiers of the Twelfth
Legion are revived by a sudden thunderstorm. When the case was made that the
prayers of the significant number of Christians in the ranks of the Twelfth had
brought on the storm and subsequently routed the barbarians, Marcus scoffed
and attributed the miracle, if it were one, to the god Hermes, to whom he erected
a commemorative temple.

accept even slaves as volunteers. In January 169, the pair headed back to Rome for the winter, to avoid being infected themselves. But on that return trip came another blow. Lucius suffered a stroke and died. Marcus was now alone.

Then tragedy struck again. Marcus's seven-year-old son Annius Verus died from an ear tumor. Still, duty required that he return to the Danube. That's when the disastrous breakthrough occurred. He wintered there in early 170, oversaw one of the largest concentrations of Roman might ever assembled, and presided over the opening of the spring offensive. The historical record of what followed testifies to the scale of the disaster.

It began with an absurdity, or so later generations would see it. The apparently indispensable Alexander of Abonutichus again consulted the stars and advised the army that victory was assured if they threw two lions into the Danube. The lions were procured

from the south and pitched snarling and clawing into the river. Alas, they did not drown. Instead, they swam to the opposite bank, where the barbarians enthusiastically clubbed them to death, apparently mistaking them for some sort of wolf. Though it's unclear how, the legions that followed the lions met with a similar fate. In what is described in one of the records as "the greatest of blows," the army lost twenty thousand men, many or most of them captured. Within months, the Marcomanni horde broke through to the west, and the great disaster of 170 followed. Making things worse, the Costoboci broke through east of Dacia and invaded Greece. Marcus's first watch on the Danube had begun as an infamous calamity.

Diligently, methodically, dispassionately, the student of Stoicism dealt with the problem. The Costoboci, weaker of the two invasions, after rampaging south through Macedonia, were encircled by a Roman force as they approached Athens and were exterminated. Sometime in 172, the Marcomanni, sated by their bloody invasion of Italy and finally driven out by the defenders, now sought to make their way home across the Danube. Marcus caught them at the crossing and wiped them out on the banks of the river. Even this, however, did little to

pacify their cousins on the other side, particularly the troublesome Quadi. So, despite his losses, Marcus took his army over the river, beginning a series of punitive raids. This discouraged renewed invasions, but it did not bring peace, and Marcus would now spend the last eight years of his life discovering that the Danube War was essentially futile.

Large-scale raids could break up the most dangerous tribal concentrations, but anything like peace depended on purchasing the loyalty of the Germanic tribes, whom the Romans found chronically undependable. Toward this unattainable end, however, Marcus tirelessly strove, even negotiating the inclusion of whole barbarian units under their tribal chieftains within the Roman army, and allowing other clans to settle in the provinces, though not in Italy. It was a decision criticized by later historians as accelerating the fall of the empire and plunging western Europe into barbarism. Yet Marcus could reasonably

*This stone relief from the early second century (left) shows a Roman legionary fighting a barbarian. The thousands of Roman troops stationed along the northern frontier could do little more than limit the barbarian forays, cutting off and punishing any isolated raiding parties that they caught. The worship of Mithras (shown below sacrificing a bull) was virtually the official religion of the Roman military. A Persian cult picked up by legionaries and spread through the empire, Mithraism placed its emphasis on discipline, with an accompanying indifference to theology making it the perfect political religion. By Marcus's time it was becoming the empire's most important cult. There were, however, a growing number of Christians in the Legions whose discipline was cited by the Christian bishop Clement of Rome as a model Christians should follow.*

consider the empire secure so long as the army remained loyal, and he had grounds for thinking it would. Those grounds were chiefly religious.

The army's almost official religion was the worship of Mithras, the Unconquered One and Lord of Time, a Persian cult picked up by legionaries and spread through the empire. It dramatized the battle between good and evil, and promised salvation at death from evil, and oblivion to anyone not accepting its discipline. It combined awesome ceremonies—such as baptism in bull's blood—with fellowship. It was welcomed by pragmatic Romans because it combined the rational deism of pagan philosophy with the polytheism of the traditional cults. Mithras was content to be worshiped under the names of Jupiter, Saturn, or Hercules. There was no Mithraic doctrine, no "Book of Mithras," no historical prophet, no dedicated priesthood, and

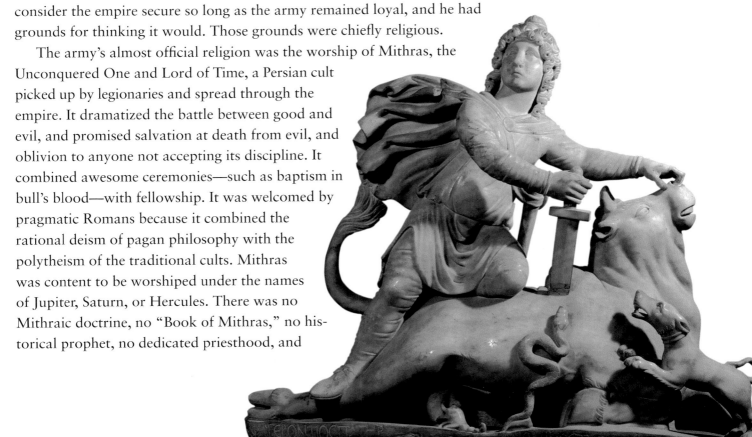

# The two great rivers that divided two rival traditions

**Monuments and structures still standing on the Rhine-Danube frontier recall a conflict Europe has never fully resolved**

Through the heart of what is now modern Europe ran what was once the Rhine-Danube frontier between the Romans and the Germans—the boundary between civilization and barbarism, law and anarchy as Rome's defenders saw it, or between slavery and freedom as the Germans saw it. Today, the proponents of either historical heritage will differ on whether they sympathize with the Marcomanni prisoners or their Roman captors portrayed below on a stone plaque, carved in honor of the Emperor Marcus Aurelius's campaign of the mid-170s. The plaque is now part of Constantine's Arch in Rome, probably incorporated there in Constantine's effort to celebrate and identify himself with the great heroes and figures of Rome's past. Monuments of the Roman Rhine-Danube frontier continue to stand, mute testimony to the tension in the political ideals inherited by modern Europe and only partly reconciled by Christianity. ∎

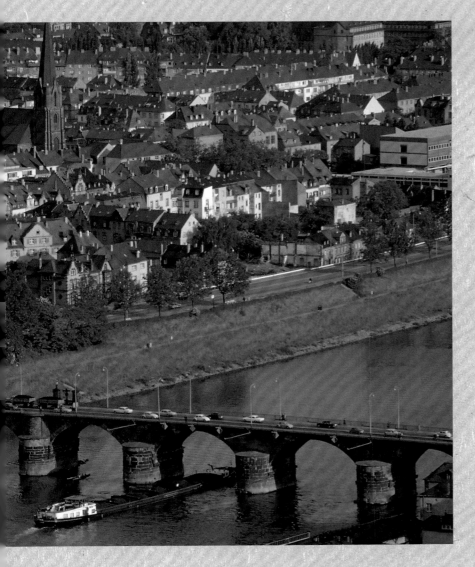

A single Roman tower (above) still stands in Cologne, Germany, one of nineteen that once reinforced the two-and-a-half miles of wall that protected an imperial army camp. At left, modern automobile traffic still uses the Roman bridge over the Rhine at Trier, Germany. Below left, Roman ruins jut from the wall of a home in Regensburg, Germany. Below, Roman columns stand in Buda, on the once-Roman side of the Danube, facing Pest on the side occupied by the Costoboci and their Germanic allies. The two cities together, of course, become modern Budapest.

nothing for women. But Mithraism's emphasis on discipline, together with its indifference to theology, made it the perfect political religion, and by Marcus's time, it was becoming the empire's most important cult.

Marcus's life changed on the Danube. His many and rewarding years of philosophical study were now long behind him. Most of his children had died. His permanent residence was now an armed camp in a climate often inhospitably cold. All was now Stoic duty, whether as commander of the army or as chief jurist of the empire. Wherever his camp was pitched, a river of delegations began to flow toward him. Provincial governors were given wide latitude in preserving the peace, but they naturally referred difficult or interesting cases to him. "Whenever he had leisure from war, he gave judgment," records Cassius Dio. "He engaged in most extensive inquiries and interrogations to determine the just solution . . . often spending eleven or twelve days on a case, judging into the night."

Among the most troublesome cases were those that involved the Christians. That issue had gone beyond annoyance. Such disasters as the massive earthquake in Sardis, numerous local famines, and particularly the catastrophic plague, had evidenced the displeasure of the gods. So, anyway, the people believed. And what

*Exasperated, Marcus issued a decree permitting the torture of Christians to death, and he refused to chastise any excessive provincial zeal in prosecuting them, whatever their rights.*

could displease the gods more than these "godless ones" refusing to sacrifice? Poets and scholars condemned Christianity as superstitious, or given to novelty, or criminally mischievous. The philosopher Celsus revealed in a widely published tract, *True Reason*, that Christians cheered the coming of the end of the world with an eternal fire that would consume everyone except Christians. And had not Marcus's revered teacher Fronto denounced Christians as sexual perverts? Bureaucrats saw a threat to the Roman order they were sworn to defend. As for the people as a whole, their children were dead, their homes destroyed, and they were frequently hungry. What they wanted was vengeance.

Marcus found persecution distasteful, and early in his reign he had decreed that Christians not be hounded for causing natural disasters. However, like most of his class, he tried to reconcile philosophy's hypothesis of a detached, impersonal god—"Divine Reason"—with the ancient pagan rituals, and even his philosophy suggested that the nature gods might be spiritual mediators between mankind and Divine Reason. Thus he sacrificed whole herds of animals in gratitude for his military victories and, passing through Greece in 177, eagerly sought initiation into the ancient Eleusian mysteries of the goddesses Demeter and Persephone.

Such pagan obeisance by the emperor boded ill for the Christians, who recognized the hand of God in much of Stoic philosophy, but only the demonic in paganism. For his part, Marcus, in his writings, only once mentions the Christians. "How wonderful," says the *Meditations*, "is that soul which is

In the wake of the plague, Christians from Lyon to Smyrna found themselves under attack. The lucky ones saw their businesses shut down, while others faced the wrath of the mob and even death at the hands of the authorities.

MANTHA

ready—if it must be at this very moment released from the body—either to be extinguished or scattered or survive. But this readiness must come from a deliberate decision and not out of sheer stubborn discipline like the Christians."

Stubborn obstinacy, that's all he could see in them. Thinking they knew what no one could know—what happens to the soul after death—they formed a disciplined, well-organized faction, withholding the traditional signs of loyalty. All they had to do for loyalty's sake was burn that pinch of incense. Yet they refused. Apparently exasperated, Marcus issued a decree from the Danube that permitted the torture of Christians to death. More important, he refused to chastise provincial governors for excessive zeal in prosecuting the Christians, even when they violated their rights as Roman citizens. When their fate depended on him, Marcus would be lenient; but he would not interfere with noble Romans in their duty.

In an increasingly hostile climate, the simple absence of imperial protection was fatal to many Christians. Following the plague, major pogroms broke out in Smyrna, Lyon, Pontus, Palestine, Athens, and Crete. Particularly in Asia Minor, the mob was often incited by local Jews, eager to distance themselves from the Christians with whom many Romans still confused them. Victims who were Roman citizens might expect beheading; the less privileged were burned, crucified, or thrown to the beasts (see sidebar in preceding chapter).

Anti-Christian polemics like Celsus's *True Reason*, Fronto's denunciation of Christianity, or the works of Lucian of Samosata, were responses to a swelling stream of pro-Christian literature, coming from even relatively minor figures like Justin Martyr's student Tatian, Theophilus of Antioch, Apollinarius of Hierapolis, and Miltiades. The very volume of the writing suggests there was a growing market for popular Christian philosophy. These works were often "open letters" to the emperor, but their readers were literate provincials. Christians saw paganism as far more a liability than an asset to the empire. They advanced themselves as loyal citizens.

*This bas-relief shows Marcus Aurelius surrounded by admirers, of which he deservedly had many. Nevertheless, his final years were filled with frustration and disappointment. He died joyless, cheerless and hopeless, one month before his fifty-ninth birthday.*

As early as Hadrian's reign, Quadratus of Athens wrote a letter to the emperor. Unlike the pagan gods, he argued, Jesus was historical and real, as were his miracles. Though Quadratus apparently delivered his appeal in person, the tolerant Hadrian did not have him arrested. Thirty years later, the Jewish-Christian Bishop Melito of Sardis appealed to Marcus for toleration of Christians. At the same time, he launched a bitter attack against the Jews for inciting anti-Christian violence in Asia. His work would long be cited as the beginning of Christian anti-Semitism.

A few years after that, the Christian Athenagoras took the now-dangerous step of seeking an audience with Marcus while the emperor passed through Athens. Largely ignoring the old anti-Christian slanders of incest and cannibalism, he concentrated instead on answering the charge of atheism. Not once, he said, had Christians joined in any provincial rebellions against the empire, yet they were the only group condemned for their name. "When we assert that he who ordered this universe is the One God, then incomprehensibly the law is brought against us." But this faith may be viewed as the real fulfillment of the promise of pagan philosophy, he said. While in Athens, Marcus endowed chairs of Platonic, Aristotelian, Stoic, and Epicurean philosophy, but he had no time whatever for the Christian Athenagoras.

Even so, people in authority began to listen. They saw that where the outcome of paganism and Stoicism was ultimate futility, the Christians offered the empire hope—hope for a real community of rich and poor, hope for some purpose to history beyond the dreary rise and fall of empires, and above all, hope for something beyond the doors of death. It was an offer increasingly, and paradoxically, attractive to the educated and the privileged.

Marcus's nineteen-year reign, both for himself and his empire, represented a marked decline from initial confidence to closing despair. While he was still a young man, his friend Aelius Aristides had written, "Wars have so far vanished as to be legendary affairs of the past." The cities had nothing to do but to beautify themselves as lasting monuments to Rome and its gods. A generation later, all this was beginning to unravel.

Indeed, Marcus's life had painfully fulfilled what his Stoic philosophy envisioned: cold duty, with no expectation of satisfaction and no consolations of the spirit in his final years. They were filled with disappointment. His most trusted and competent general rebelled and attempted to seize his throne. His own

*Marcus's nineteen-year reign, both for himself and Rome, represented a marked decline from initial confidence to closing despair. At the end, all was starting to unravel.*

beloved wife, Faustina, was implicated in the rebellion. His sole surviving son, heir, and successor, Commodus, was a self-evident disappointment. The danger of the tribes on the Rhine-Danube limes was as ominous as ever. And though plague, earthquakes, and local famines had ignited a popular frenzy against Christianity, it persistently, mystically, kept on growing.

In 175, with no apparent instigation, the skilled commander of the Asian armies, Syrian Senator Avidius Cassius, announced Marcus Aurelius's death and his own assumption of the imperial crown. Cassius was either badly misinformed, or the victim of a plot to make him overplay his hand. When it became clear that Marcus was still very much alive and commanding the Danube armies, Cassius's situation was immediately hopeless. Despite Marcus's promise of clemency, Cassius persisted in his rebellion until he was assassinated by a centurion, ending, it was said, "a dream of empire lasting three months and six days."

Immediately upon Cassius's death, loyal commanders in Asia burned all his records, apparently on Marcus's orders, and the emperor forbade any investigation into the rebellion. The rumor immediately spread that, as Marcus had been more ill than usual, Faustina had assumed he was dying and pushed Cassius into rebellion as a protector for her own underage Commodus.

Be that as it may, later that same year Commodus received the *toga virilis* of manhood. The barbarian Iazyges were defeated, though not humbled, and came to terms, leaving the formidable Quadi neither humbled nor tamed. Marcus's dearest Faustina, possibly pregnant, died unexpectedly at age forty-five during the rigors of Marcus's brief post-rebellion tour of the Asian provinces. She was deified by the Senate, and the Syrian town of Halala where she died was renamed Faustinopolis.

On January 1, 177, Commodus was made Imperator Augustus, co-emperor, though the event could not have brought much joy to his father. As Cassius Dio candidly reported: "One thing most prevented Marcus from being happy, namely, that after rearing and educating his son in the best possible way, he was vastly disappointed in him." One oft-told story of Commodus's youth typifies the general perception of him. He was said to have ordered a slave thrown into the furnace for allowing his bath to go lukewarm.[10]

"Reflect continually that all such things as happen now, also happened before, and on the fact that they will happen again," the Stoic Marcus wrote in his *Meditations*, shortly before his death. Heartbreak was the inevitable price of leadership. "The whole drama . . . which you know from your own personal experience, the whole court of Hadrian, the whole court of Antoninus, and the whole court of Philip, Alexander, and Croesus. All these were similar. Only the actors were different." Joyless, cheerless, hopeless, he dutifully longed for the painless oblivion of death.

Still, by 180, with the Danube war going as well as could be expected, he laid the plan to achieve the greatest goal of his life—the creation of two new provinces, Bohemia and Slovakia, both north of the Danube. The legions were to strike in the spring. But in March, Marcus fell ill, possibly with the plague. Realizing his end was near, he sent for Commodus, now eighteen, and begged him not to neglect the Danube war after his succession. Commodus replied that his first concern was his own health. So Marcus sent his son away, apparently to avoid the contagion. Over the next few days, the emperor stopped eating and drinking, and on March 17, 180, a month before his fifty-ninth birthday, the best

10. Later historians would question how such a moral and insightful a man as Marcus Aurelius could have allowed his dissolute son to succeed him, especially after his four predecessors had all adopted as their heirs the most promising candidate. But in fact, neither Nerva, Trajan, Hadrian nor Antoninus had sons, so adoption was forced upon them.

MANTHA

and most powerful man of his age, Imperator Caesar Marcus Aurelius Antoninus Augustus, pulled his cloak over his head and died.

Commodus returned to Rome, to a reign of lust, extravagance, and bloodshed, culminating in his assassination twelve years later. The Danube war was allowed to languish, and as Marcus foresaw, the day would one day come when the limes would collapse, the barbarians would flood the western empire, and, as later poets said, the lights of the world would go out.

Yet, within the bosom of Rome, there lay another kind of courage, born not of Stoicism but of hope. Four years after Marcus's death, the aging Senator Apollonius was identified by a recreant slave as a closet Christian. For this service, both the slave's legs were broken, the state's usual penalty for an informer against a master. This, however, did not mitigate the charge. Was Apollonius yet another instance of a renegade member of Rome's noble families who had treasonously allied himself to that crucified Jew? The prefect Perennis would have an answer, please. Christians, replied the senator, were taught to pray for the emperor. Would the senator then swear by the genius of the emperor? The senator would not. Perennis, a true Roman, respected courage, however ludicrous the cause. He would therefore submit Apollonius to the judgment of his peers and schedule a public hearing by senators, counselors, and philosophers.

Before this august assembly, the senator made his confession. Yes, he believed in Christ. Did not the worthy philosophers before him believe in "the divine logos?" Indeed they did, and so, too, did he. But he believed that this logos had been made into a man, became flesh, and dwelt among us. No longer, therefore, could he worship the gods, mere "corpses," as his forefathers had. Neither would he make oath or burn incense to a supposedly divine emperor-god.

Furious, the assembly passed its sentence—death. Since Apollonius was a Roman citizen, it would be a merciful death by the sword. He went to that death with the same tranquil equanimity he had shown at his trial. Like Marcus, he died bravely. Unlike Marcus, he died in triumph, not in despair.

He also died alone. Persecution had not always been so selective. Seven years earlier, and some 450 miles to the northwest, the Christians of Lyon had likewise suffered Rome's loathing of this new faith. But they died neither swiftly nor in solitude, but slowly, in degradation, and by the dozens, while the mob howled its approval.

MCNEELY

*The slave Blandina is thrown by a bull in the arena at Lyon (Lugdunum), but the animal's attack fails to kill her. Having endured unspeakable torture for several days, she has refused to deny her faith and, surviving the attack of the bull, is eventually stabbed to death, the final victim of the persecution of the summer of A.D. 177.*

# CHAPTER 5

# The mass slaughter of Lyon's Christians

## The first great French Christian, Irenaeus faced two foes: one, false teaching; the other, the mob

Blandina gazed up into the summer sky as if searching for a familiar face. Thunder rolled in the distance, but the sky was bright and clear. Summers in Gaul's Lugdunum, a city that would later be known as Lyon, had always been pleasant. Standing in the sunshine in the center of the arena, she welcomed the soothing warmth after the long days and nights in the cold, damp prison cell that made her frail, bruised body ache with sickness and pain.

Thunder reverberated again, and Blandina lowered her gaze to the only other survivor, the badly beaten teenager Ponticus, who lay helplessly on his back, his eyes also fixed on the sky. She started to ask him if he thought a storm was coming, but her voice was drowned out by another thunderclap, closer and louder, and then the roar of ten thousand voices as the interrogator struck her and repeated a question she had heard many times before. The cacophonous crowd fell silent, waiting expectantly for her answer. Her mind turned to Bishop Ponthinus, to Attalus and Biblias, and the nearly fifty others who had gone before her.

The question came again, underscored by another painful blow, and Blandina answered strongly: "I am a Christian, and there is nothing vile done by us!"

The public torture in the year 177 of the brave Christian slave Blandina and scores of other Christians drew large and attentive audiences for many days to Lyon's amphitheater. Lyon was the capital of Gaul, and Gaul was considered the "giant of the empire," Rome's most cherished possession, populated by huge people, or so the Romans thought them.[1]

"*Gallia est omnis divisa in partes tres*," Julius Caesar had written famously in 53 B.C., providing translation practice for generations of students learning Latin: "All Gaul is divided into three parts." He continued: "One part of these, which it has been said that the Gauls occupy, takes its beginning at the river Rhone. . . ."[2]

Within the borders of Gaul, encompassing 535,000 square miles, lay all the lands of what would become France, Belgium, and Luxembourg, and large portions of the Netherlands, Germany, and Switzerland. It was a wild place of rushing rivers, strong winds and tides, thick forests, and impenetrable marshlands that served as borders for the several Gallic nations which were rich in agriculture, natural resources, and people.

In 43 B.C., Gallic War general Lucius Munatius Plancus, appointed governor of Gaul by Caesar, founded Lugdunum as the capital of all three Gauls on the hill of Fourvière (from *Forum Vetus*, or Old Forum), at the confluence of the rivers Rhone and Saone. Roman Lyon sat astride the major road connecting modern-day Cologne and Marseilles. Lyon became the western empire's cultural center and its imperial mint, because of its location on a major trade route and despite the river swamplands that gave it a reputation as an unhealthy place to live. At its peak, its population approached fifty thousand, and the city counted among its natives the future emperors Claudius (A.D. 41–54) and Caracalla (A.D. 212–217), and Claudius's ill-fated brother Germanicus who died in 15 B.C.

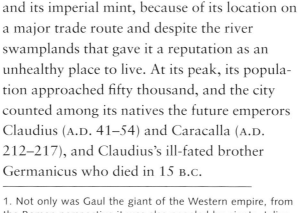

1. Not only was Gaul the giant of the Western empire, from the Roman perspective it was also peopled by giants. Julius Caesar reported that the Atuatuci of northern Gaul laughed at the sight of the smaller Romans setting up large siege engines at the walls of their principal city in 57 B.C. (They didn't laugh for long, however, for the city fell). A century and a half later, the historian Lucius Annaeus Florus described the Alpine Gauls as "superhuman in size." According to J. P. V. D. Balsdon (*Romans and Aliens*), the Gauls were on average two or three inches taller than the Romans.

2. The Romans had known of the area they called Gaul from the eighth century B.C. It was occupied by several Celtic groups, one of them, the largest, known as the Gauls, inhabited most of the area that would one day be France. Julius Caesar expanded Roman control over the whole area, including the lands occupied by the Belgae in the northeast and those occupied by the Aquitani in the south, near the Pyrenees.

South of the Fourvière and across the Saone sat the amphitheater dedicated to the emperor Augustus in A.D. 19 and expanded during the reign of Hadrian (A.D. 117–138). It could seat ten thousand spectators. It was here that the bloody gladiatorial games were held, and where, in the year 177, Gallic Christianity received a terrible baptism: immersion in the blood of innocent martyrs.

Lyon had not always been a city of prominence. Before the Roman conquest, the region's principal city was Vienne, twenty miles to the south. An intercity rivalry flourished across the decades, including a civil war between them during the final years of the first century A.D. Lyon would be sacked a century later, in 197, after backing the losing side in a civil war between two Roman generals. One result was the assumption of its economic functions by Vienne and two other cities.

*These marble statues of dying, wounded, and defeated Gauls were produced in Asia Minor after the Greeks stopped a Gallic invasion in 239 B.C. Whether these are Greek originals or Roman copies art historians debate. (1) The Wounded Gaul, the Louvre, Paris. (2) The Dying Gaul, Capitoline Museum, Rome (3) A Gaul Killing His Wife and Himself, National Roman Museum. (4) The Wounded Gaul, Museo Archaeologico, Naples.*

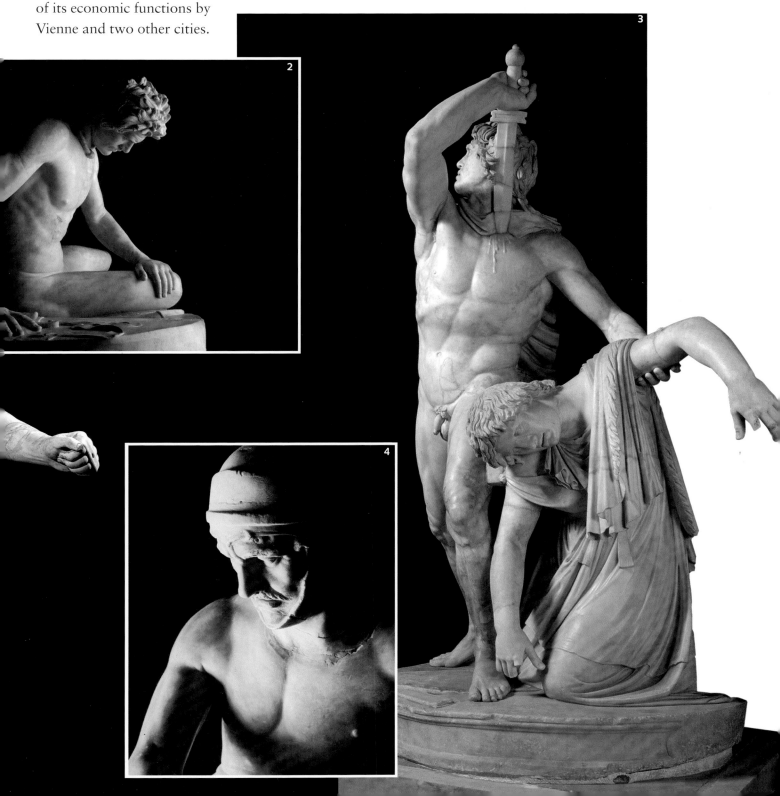

# Unlike today's, the old Druids served their gods with fire, blood and dagger

## The Gallic rituals of human sacrifice claimed both criminals and innocents

What passes for Druidism in the twenty-first century—a peaceful "spirituality" of environmentalism, crafts, and costume, blended in the woods by weekend worshipers—has almost nothing in common with the ancient cult whose name it takes.

Contemporary Druidic lore is so entangled in myth, legend, and fantasy that separating out the truth is almost impossible. Most probably, however, Druidism originated as early as the second century B.C. among the Celtic peoples of what is now Ireland. The Romans found the cult already well established in Gaul, and nearly all the written history of the ancient Druids comes from Roman sources, chief among them Julius Caesar. As conqueror, Caesar was unswervingly prejudiced in favor of his own culture—yet his chief informant on the details, Divitiacus, was apparently a Druid himself, and he remained unrefuted in the ancient accounts.

"In public, as in private life, they observe an ordinance of sacrifices," Caesar writes. "(They) use figures of immense size, whose limbs, woven out of twigs, they fill with living men and set on fire, and the men perish in a sheet of flame." The victims were often thieves or robbers, Caesar allows, "but when the supply of such fails, they resort to the execution even of the innocent."

The Greek author Diodorus Siculus, writing in about 8 B.C., describes other bloody Druidic sacrifices: "When they attempt divination upon important matters, they practice a strange and incredible custom, for they kill a man by a knife-stab in the region above the midriff, and after his fall, they foretell the future by the convulsions of his limbs and the pouring of his blood."

Whatever their barbarisms, Caesar also reports that the Druid priests in Gaul were of "definite account and dignity," serving as authorities in ritualistic and religious matters and even as judges. "In fact, it is they who decide almost all disputes, public and private; and if any crime has been committed, or murder done, or there is any dispute about succession or boundaries, they also decide it, determining rewards and penalties."

While Rome tolerated native religions, it did not, however, tolerate local rule, except under strict Roman oversight. Hence Druidic law, and with it

This is a bronze Celtic sacrificial knife of the early Roman period, beneath an engraving of Teutates, the Celtic god of war, fertility, and wealth, shown accepting human sacrifice. The bloodthirsty cult of the Celtic Druids bore little resemblance to the peaceful environmentalism associated with it in the modern age.

Druidism itself, was almost completely suppressed, and Druidic human sacrifice prohibited, though it persisted secretly for many years.

In the eighteenth and nineteenth centuries, a flood of romantic books and dramas revived interest in a fanciful and harmless Druidism that is further elaborated in modern-day gatherings, including those at the mysterious Stonehenge site in Britain, whose inhabitants were also Druidic. There can be no doubt, though, that some latter-day adherents—and those who adapt darker Druidic lore to role-playing games like "Dungeons and Dragons"—enjoy the delicious shudder that comes with whispering of those forbidden practices at Druidic gatherings long ago. ∎

Human sacrifice was a central part of the cult of Druidism. "When they attempt divination upon important matters they practice a strange and incredible custom, for they kill a man by a knife-stab in the region above the midriff, and after his fall they foretell the future by the convulsions of his limbs and the pouring of his blood, wrote Diodorus Siculus in 8 B.C., describing Druidic worship.

## Roman Gaul and Germany

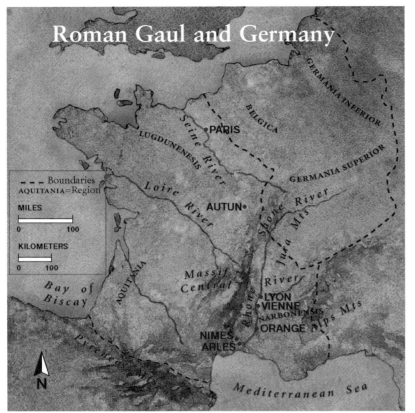

In many respects, Lyon was no different from the major trading centers of the late twentieth century, with its unending ethnic immigration and the myriad religions that accompany the movement of peoples. Gallic, Celtic, Greek, and Roman gods dominated the pantheons of Lyon and all of Gaul. Julius Caesar writes that Mercury was one of Gaul's most popular gods. The Near-Eastern deities Silenus and Isis, and Cybele, the "Great Mother" of the Phrygian gods, were also revered. Though officially prohibited, human sacrifices and cannibalism were still practiced, particularly among the Druids (see sidebar). But Druidism was on the decline, after a final outbreak of Druidic nationalism during a rebellion that resulted in what is known as the Year of the Four Emperors in A.D. 69, prior to the accession of Vespasian the following year. The most important cult in Lyon, however, involved worship of the Roman emperor.

Into this theological and philosophical mishmash came Christian traders and settlers from Asia, Phrygia, and other parts of the Roman world where "The Way," as the Christians originally called themselves, had taken root. The new Christian citizens of Lyon practiced their faith both in their private lives and in their businesses; they prospered and their influence grew. They also provoked fear and suspicion among the pagans, who viewed the followers of a crucified Jewish criminal as atheists at best. By the summer of 177, Christians were seen as the fount of every calamity, including war, plague, drought, and economic downturn.

Pagan writers of the time regarded the main body of Christians as the illiterate dregs of the population, the outcasts of Greco-Roman civilization. This characterization was far from true in Lyon, where Christians were to be found among the physicians and lawyers. As such, they spoke Latin and Greek, and in the ordinary fashion of the time, some of them owned slaves. Often these slaves did not subscribe to the new faith of their masters, and took every advantage to spread scurrilous tales about unspeakable acts they claimed to have witnessed at Christian gatherings. Such fabrications contributed to the gruesome persecutions that were shortly to befall Blandina and forty-seven other Christians.

As Lyon and its fledgling Christian community were growing, the Apostolic Age was ending. John, son of Zebedee and last of the original apostles, is generally believed to have died around the close of the first century at Ephesus. Early Christian accounts, the accuracy of some of them disputed, record that he appointed Polycarp as bishop of Smyrna on the Aegean coast, in what would become Turkey. Polycarp, it is said, in turn taught what he had learned from John and from others who had seen and talked with Jesus, to those who would lead the Church through the first century of the Post-Apostolic Age.

Perhaps Polycarp's most eager student was Irenaeus (pronounced *I-re-NAY-us*), a young man born some time between 115 and 140 to Christian parents in Antioch, where followers of Jesus had first been called Christians (Acts 11:26). In his later writings, Irenaeus described how his teacher Polycarp "related his life together with John, and with the others who had seen the Lord, and how he remembered their words, and what he heard about the Lord from them, about his miracles and teachings."

Sometime around the year 150, twenty-five years before the Lyon persecutions began and about five years before his own martyrdom, Polycarp appointed another of his pupils, Ponthinus, as the first bishop of Lyon and all of Gaul. Irenaeus was sent to accompany his older fellow student, probably because he was from Asia, home to many of the new citizens of Lyon. Irenaeus employed his knowledge of Greek, Latin, and Celtic to

The modern city of Lyon, France, with St. John's Cathedral in the foreground (top) is twenty miles north of the Rhone River bridge at Vienne (bottom), where lay the region's principal Celtic settlement before the Roman conquest. The ashes of the Christians of Lyon and Vienne slaughtered in A.D. 177 were eventually thrown into the river.

*A Roman sandstone relief shows Cybele, the "Great Mother" and goddess of mountains and wild nature. In addition to local Gauls, the population of ancient Lyon included immigrants from all over the Roman empire. They brought with them the worship of a variety of pagan gods, including Cybele seen here in the upper left corner as a priest makes her an offering.*

spread the gospel, even though he considered the latter the language of barbarians. And while the church of Lyon was multi-ethnic, the Greek Scriptures used in worship were not translated into the local languages.

Because Lyon was a Christian center of the Western empire, it attracted all manner of offspring practices, including the rapidly growing Gnosticism that had taken a firm hold in Christianity by the middle of the second century. The licentious version of Gnosticism became particularly active at Lyon and attracted women in search of escape from the superficially stringent cultural and sexual mores of Roman society.

Irenaeus therefore faced two problems. On the one hand, his flock was threatened with extermination by the mob hostility rising against them. On the other, they faced spiritual doom, as he saw it, if they fell into the hands of the Gnostics. To Irenaeus, the Gnostics were the more dangerous influence. They were mentally ill and void of morals, he declared, particularly in their sexual practices and in their habit of stealing Christian wives. He would later write that the disciples of the Gnostic luminary Valentinus embraced all forms of pleasure and lust, ate meat offered to idols, attended gladiatorial games, and seduced women.

But he directed his harshest criticism on the flashy Marcus, whose Gnostic sex clubs pulled in many Christians of Lyon with their elaborate and expensive ceremonies. Their practices in magic and mathematical tricks caused consider-

Roman Lyon sat astride the major road connecting modern-day Cologne with the port city of Marseilles. This location helped make Lyon the western empire's cultural center and home to an imperial mint. The ruins of the impressive Odeon are shown at right. It is one of two Roman theaters still preserved in the city.

able consternation among the non-Christian populace, who tended to lump in the Gnostics with the Christians. Such anxiety may have contributed to the great anti-Christian pogrom to come.

Marcus was a smooth operator who knew the right things to say to the right people. He attracted society women, the rich and elegant of the landed and political classes.[3] According to Irenaeus, Marcus would convince a woman that by sharing his learning, she would be given the gift of prophecy. More often, however, she would be bewitched and bewildered, filled with the pride that comes with the acquisition of special prophetic powers. It was obvious to Irenaeus that such women suffered from infatuation, that their property and their bodies were easy prey for Marcus. Thus Irenaeus wrote:

3. The Gnostic Marcus was not alone in his awareness of the phenomenon of female infatuation. Galen, physician to Marcus Aurelius, was tending to a woman patient when he noticed that a visitor's mentioning the name of a famous dancer caused his patient's color to change and her pulse to become erratic. Intrigued, Galen had an assistant call out the names of other dancers over the next three days, but to no effect. He concluded that the woman's ailment was psychological, not physical. "Irenaeus says that women were accustomed to hand over their property as well as their person to Mark," notes Robert M. Grant in his biography of Irenaeus. "Galen's services were less expensive."

Gaul's importance to the Romans can be judged by the sheer size and grandeur of public works that remain. The massive structure of the Pont du Gard Aqueduct (top) in Provence, France, built in 19 B.C. and still almost intact, dominates the valley of the River Gard. The Trophée des Alpes (left), at La Turbie, was built by the Emperor Augustus in 6 B.C. to commemorate Rome's victory over the Gauls. Truncated remains of the once-massive monument still tower over the village and are visible from many miles away. The first-century Roman Amphitheater at Arles (below) is today used to stage bullfights (see photo pages 158—159).

# Across France, splendid visions of Rome still shape daily life

**The empire may be long dead and gone, but ruins proclaim its former glory**

Preserving the essence of Roman government and culture is now largely a matter for the historians, but the glory of the fallen empire continues to influence daily life throughout Europe. This is particularly true in Italy, of course, but also in France and Germany. In England, Spain, Greece, and elsewhere, the triumphal arches, columns, and monuments of Rome stand as a backdrop to modern living. Tourists and residents sit casually amid still-sturdy remnants of Roman temples. They cheer modern-day spectacles within ancient arenas, maneuver twenty-first-century vehicles through archways erected two millennia ago, and visit and work in the shadows of aqueducts bearing continual witness to the empire's lost ascendancy. Though its political power withered long ago, millions of Europeans still live today with Rome all around them. ■

*Roman ruins abound throughout France in the former Roman province of Gaul. This mosaic (top) showing the treading of grapes, uncovered at St. Romain-en-Gal, dates from the third century. The impressive limestone columns of the Maison Carrée (above), a popular tourist spot in the heart of the city of Nîmes, are what remains of a Roman temple built by Agrippa around 20 B.C. The Porte d'Arroux in Autun (left) is a Roman gateway from the first century—still sturdy enough to permit the passage of traffic beneath its arches.*

Some of his disciples, too, addicting themselves to the same practices, have deceived many silly women and defiled them. They proclaim themselves as being "perfect" so that no one can be compared to them with respect to the immensity of their knowledge, not even were you to mention Paul or Peter or any of the other apostles. They assert that they themselves know more than all others, and that they alone have imbibed the greatness of the knowledge of that power which is unspeakable. They also maintain that they have attained to a height above all power, and that therefore they are free in every respect to act as they please, having no one to fear in anything.

The Gnostics did not, however, charm all of the Christians in Lyon. The orthodox faithful scorned them for eating food sacrificed to idols and for denying their faith in the face of opposition. Although Gnostics agreed with Christians and Jews that martyrdom atoned for sins, the ultimate act of sacrifice was seen as a means for personal enlightenment rather than as a victory over evil. In later years, Irenaeus noted with derision that very few Gnostics died with their martyred orthodox brothers and sisters. "The church does in every place send forward, throughout all time, a multitude of martyrs to the Father; while all others, not only have nothing of this kind to point to among themselves, but even maintain that such witness-bearing is not at all necessary, for that their system of doctrines is the true witness."

If weak or prideful persons always found a reason to turn away from God, and if traveling salvation-shows always found their way to town, what was the great concern over the arrival of another faddish sect from the East? For Irenaeus, Gnosticism was less a rival to traditional Christianity than it was a threat to the eternal salvation of his people: "Those who do not partake of him [Christ] are neither nourished into life from the mother's breasts, nor do they enjoy that most limpid fountain which issues from the body of Christ, but they dig for themselves broken cisterns out of earthly trenches, and drink putrid water out of the mire, fleeing from the faith of the Church lest they be convicted; and rejecting the Spirit, that they may not be instructed."

Irenaeus knew that the physical death of each member of his flock was as certain as Roman taxation; and that although heaven was not a certainty for anyone, Gnosticism did not provide the keys to the kingdom. To the Christian historian Eusebius, Gnosticism created division within the church, which he believed to be a greater threat than persecution. That was a bold contention, considering the events that would turn the summer of 177 into one of the darkest periods in the early history of Christianity.

No one can say with any certainty what finally set the pagans of Lyon so decisively against their longtime Christian neighbors. It may have been a combination of seemingly unrelated events, including a war and the need to find scapegoats for the ills of everyday life. A war, indeed, had broken out in the spring of 177, and angry eyes turned upon the Christians. Was it not obvious that all major disasters—wars, earthquakes,

*The cost of buying condemned criminals from the authorities, for use in the arena, was expensive—six gold aurei a head, or the equivalent to six months' wages for a legionary—but a lot less expensive than the cost of buying or hiring a gladiator. Six such Roman coins are shown, taken from among the thousands that survive to this day in collections all over the world.*

floods, and prolonged droughts—were caused by the displeasure of the gods at these Christian "atheists?"

Moreover, you could see they weren't really part of the community. Many did not partake in the revelry of Roman life, which included the frequent games and festivals with their accompanying gladiatorial contests and bloody public executions. Christians refused to make sacrifices to the popular gods and did not participate in emperor worship. And if rumors and innuendos could be believed, in their meetings they were worse than the Druids—after all, they engaged in sorcery, sexual orgies, human sacrifice and incest. Worse still, they refused to worship the Great Mother Cybele, who had been made an official god of Gaul in 160.

## Soon Christians were banned from the baths, markets, other public places, and then their own businesses. If caught in the streets, they were beaten or stoned.

Others no doubt saw in the Christians an opportunity to cut costs. It fell as a duty upon the wealthy to provide and fund the great festivals, to sponsor the games and the lavish entertainment that was involved. The cost was stupendous and bankrupted more than one family. But the highest cost of all was the purchase price of gladiators, and the provision of victims for public execution. Taking human life in the arena was not cheap.

To ease the burden, the emperor and the Senate had agreed to allow rich landowners and others to acquire condemned criminals from the imperial procurators for about six gold *aurei* coins a head. This was a substantial sum (roughly five or six months' wages for a soldier), but it was nevertheless a fraction of the cost of hiring or buying a gladiator on the open market. Now the Christians who refused to repudiate their faith automatically became criminals, and while most could not serve as gladiators, their public torture and prolonged execution was always a dependable crowd-pleaser. A roundup of Christians therefore represented a veritable bonanza for those who had to fund the big shows, and their torture and death a major attraction for those who would attend them. It would be a win-win situation for everyone, except, of course, for the ill-fated Christians destined to provide the entertainment.

The pogrom in Lyon and Vienne began slowly, with the occasional assault on a Christian citizen or merchant. It escalated into enforced isolation, robberies of Christian homes and businesses, then stonings, imprisonment, and torture. Details are given in the dramatic *Letter from the Churches of Vienne and Lyon* to the faithful in Asia and Phrygia, distributed widely among the Christian churches of the Roman world and included in Eusebius's *Ecclesiastical History*.[4]

4. The author of the remarkable description of the martyrdoms at Lyon is not known. The letter begins: "The servants of Christ residing at Vienne and Lyon in Gaul, to the brethren throughout Asia and Phyrgia who hold the same faith and hope of redemption, peace and grace and glory from God the Father and Jesus Christ our Lord." The story is so well told that some historians speculate that Irenaeus himself wrote it.

The protracted nightmare was so great that the writers of the letter warned from the start that recording all the events would be impossible.

In the beginning, the Christians endured the scorn of the townspeople silently, but that only further infuriated the mobs. Soon, Christians were banned from the baths, the markets, other public places, and then their own businesses. If caught in the streets, they were beaten or stoned. When Christians could no longer be found outside their homes, the mobs broke down their doors and dragged them into the streets, where they were beaten and bloodied. Apparently none of their personal property was ever confiscated, however, and for that reason some scholars believe the persecution had a more personal agenda, with the

*A youthful Irenaeus confronts a belligerent crowd at Lyon, striving to persuade them that the shameful things they have heard about the Christians are not true. His hearers seem far from persuaded. The men on either side of him are Christians on hand to defend him if the reception becomes violent.*

*The bullfight, still popular in the French region of Provence as well as in Spain and Portugal, is thought to be a vestige of Roman culture, which included frequent games and festivals with accompanying gladiatorial contests and bloody public executions. This bullfight takes place in the Roman Arena at Arles, Provence, France.*

targeting of specific individuals. If so, this would explain why Irenaeus was free to leave the city in the middle of the crisis.[5]

Another important consideration is that the persecution began when the governor was away and the soldiers and city magistrates were in charge of law and order. After many days of violence, the authorities ordered several dozen Christian leaders taken into custody, saying it was for their own protection. In reality, they were forced from their homes and taken to the forum, where they were questioned in front of the mob. After confessing their faith, they were thrown into the foul, dark prison to await the return of the governor.

Trials of the Christians began at some point after the governor's arrival. There was no record of distrust or animosity in the governor's attitude toward the Christians prior to the persecution. The question that must be asked, then, is why the governor would so quickly sanction a series of events whose goal was the death of the prisoners. The basic human and political drive for self-preservation was likely at work. A crowd was a powerful political force in the Roman

5. Historians can only speculate about why Irenaeus was not arrested in the roundup of Christians in Lyon. One theory is that he had by then been made bishop of Vienne, which was not within the jurisdiction of the governor at Lyon. He seems to have been free to travel to Rome in the midst of the persecution.

Empire, one that could threaten even the emperor himself, unless it was placated with sufficient quantities of bread and blood. For a mere governor, lacking the emperor's protection of several thousand soldiers, a basic policy of appeasement was a matter of survival.

When summoned, the prisoners were asked to give a declaration of faith, either voluntarily or after a round of torture. Their treatment was such that Vettius Epagathus, a Christian who had not been rounded up with the others, stepped forward to protest to the governor. According to the letter from the martyrs, Vettius "could not endure the unreasonable judgment against us, but was filled with indignation, and asked to be permitted to testify on behalf of his brethren, that there is among us nothing ungodly or impious." After those surrounding the judgment seat raised vehement objections, the governor rejected the request, and then asked if Vettius was a Christian himself. In a loud voice, Vettius proclaimed that he was. He was arrested immediately and given the unenviable role of advocate for the Christians.

The accused fell into two groups. The first witnesses to the faith eagerly confessed their belief; the rest were not so ready. Some appeared confused, weak, and unable to endure the physical and spiritual conflict. About ten recanted their faith, causing the brethren much consternation. Among those who had not been arrested

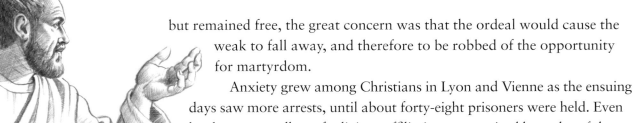

but remained free, the great concern was that the ordeal would cause the weak to fall away, and therefore to be robbed of the opportunity for martyrdom.

Anxiety grew among Christians in Lyon and Vienne as the ensuing days saw more arrests, until about forty-eight prisoners were held. Even the slaves, regardless of religious affiliation, were seized by order of the governor. Heathen slaves, "being ensnared by Satan, and fearing for themselves the tortures which they beheld the saints endure," accused the Christians of many things, including Thyestean banquets, meaning cannibalism (because they spoke of devouring the body and blood of their leader); Oedipal intercourse, meaning incest (because they spoke of "loving" their brothers and sisters in Christ); "and deeds which are not only unlawful for us to speak of or to think, but which we cannot believe were ever done by men."

The entire community was so incensed by the testimony of the slaves that the people were described as raging like wild beasts "so that even if any had before been moderate on account of friendship, they were now exceedingly furious and gnashed their teeth." As a result, all of those who confessed their faith were tortured "beyond description."

How long these ordeals lasted is not known. It is possible they took place over several days. During this time, "the wrath of the populace, and governor, and soldiers" was concentrated on four individuals. Sanctus was a deacon from Vienne, who may have been visiting Lyon when he was arrested, since Vienne was not in the governor's jurisdiction. Maturus was a recent convert. Attalus was from Pergamum, where he was a leader in the Christian community. And Blandina was a slave in a Christian household, her mistress also one of those facing martyrdom.

Sanctus suffered greatly at the hands of his torturers, but he was like a prisoner of war who gives only his name, rank, and identification number, even when the questions were reinforced with pain. What is your name? Where are you from? What do you do? Are you a free man? To every question, Sanctus replied in Latin: "*Christianus sum*" ("I am a Christian.") This pleased neither the governor nor the torturers, who increased the torment and expanded the methods by which it was inflicted. At the end of the day, when Sanctus would not add to his declaration, the torturers pressed red-hot brass plates against his genitals. Those witnessing the spectacle were amazed that he held firm to his confession, "refreshed and strengthened by the heavenly fountain of the water of life flowing from the bowels of Christ." Sanctus was returned to prison "one complete wound and bruise, drawn out of shape, and unlike a human form."

The Christians were not sure what to expect when it was Blandina's turn to face the torturers. She was not strong, and there are indications that she may have suffered from a deformity. She was described as possessing an appearance that was "mean and obscure and despicable." The Christians feared that her weak physical condition would cause her to succumb to her tormentors and deny her faith. She proved them wrong, astonishing her friends and foes by enduring broken bones and mangled flesh, and every form of torture that would have killed another individual.

Biblias, another Christian woman but otherwise unidentified, who had been arrested in the early days of the persecution and denied Christ upon initial interrogation, was brought before the governor at the judgment seat for additional torture, in the hope her weakened condition would allow her to add to her recantation details of wickedness performed by the other Christians. She refused to aid the spread of falsehoods and, "as if awakening from a deep sleep, and reminded by the present anguish of the eternal punishment in hell," took back her earlier confession as well. Against the charge that Christians committed

## Enraged, some in the crowd pummeled the old man with their fists or feet, fearing they would be thought guilty of wickedness and impiety if any possible abuse were omitted.

cannibalism, she demanded: "How could those eat children who do not think it lawful to taste the blood even of irrational animals?" (The church was presumably observing the Old Testament proscription against consuming the blood of animals, Gen 9:4).

One of the next to be dragged in by the soldiers and civil magistrates was the aged and sick bishop, Ponthinus. He was more than ninety years old and illness made his breathing labored.

"Who was the God of the Christians?" the governor asked the bishop.

"If you are worthy, then you will know," Ponthinus replied.

That was not the answer the crowd wanted to hear. In their rage, some advanced and pummeled the old man with their fists, their feet, and anything else they could immediately get their hands on. Those not close enough to strike him picked up whatever they could and threw it at him, "all of them thinking that they would be guilty of great wickedness and impiety if any possible abuse were omitted." When the savagery abated, Ponthinus was returned to his prison cell, which was about the size of a small closet. There, two days later, he died.

All the prisoners were taken back to their cells and subjected to more torture, including the "stretching of the feet to the fifth hole in the stocks." Many were suffocated. Others were hauled before the crowd for more abuse after several days. Sanctus was one of them. The mob remembered how he had been beaten and broken, how his "most tender parts" had been burned, and how he could not bear the touch of a human hand. A stunned silence must have come over the crowd as Sanctus was led into the amphitheater. Against all expectations, "his body arose and stood erect in the midst of the subsequent torments, and resumed its original appearance and the use of its limbs, so that, through the grace of Christ, these second sufferings became to him, not torture, but healing."

It was at this point that those who had recanted their faith in hopes of escaping further tortures were tossed into prison with the faithful, where they were

*The Basilica of Fourvière sits on a hill overlooking the center of modern Lyon.*

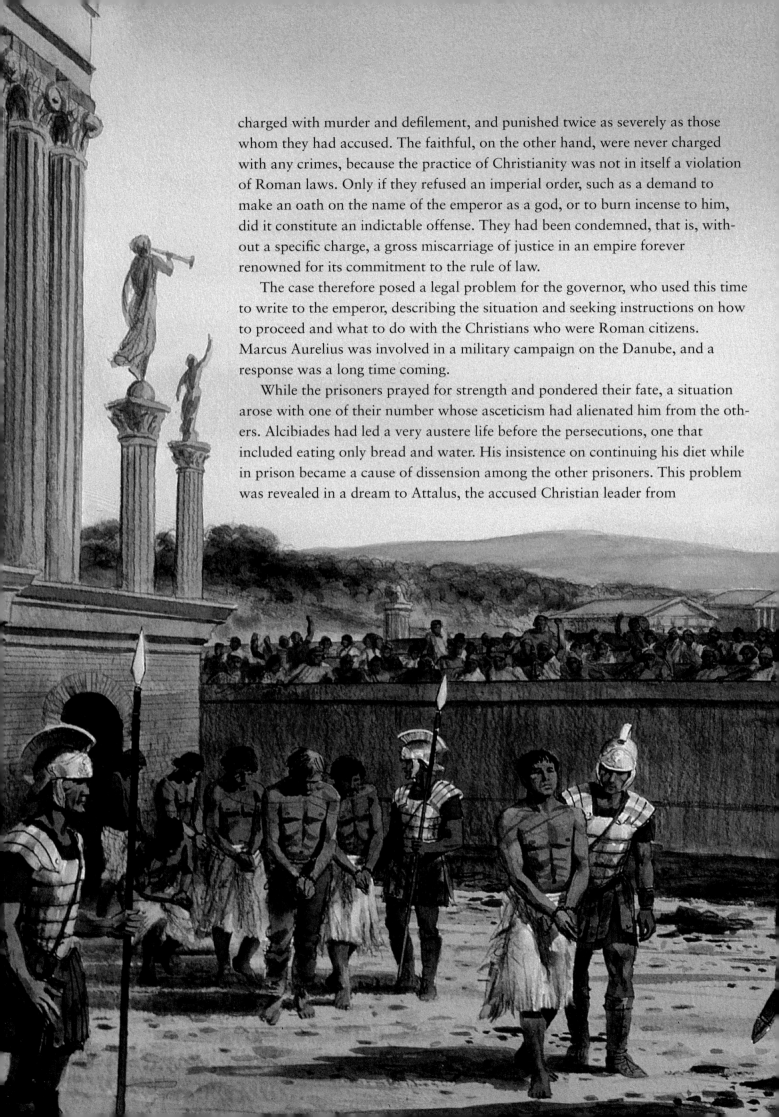

charged with murder and defilement, and punished twice as severely as those whom they had accused. The faithful, on the other hand, were never charged with any crimes, because the practice of Christianity was not in itself a violation of Roman laws. Only if they refused an imperial order, such as a demand to make an oath on the name of the emperor as a god, or to burn incense to him, did it constitute an indictable offense. They had been condemned, that is, without a specific charge, a gross miscarriage of justice in an empire forever renowned for its commitment to the rule of law.

The case therefore posed a legal problem for the governor, who used this time to write to the emperor, describing the situation and seeking instructions on how to proceed and what to do with the Christians who were Roman citizens. Marcus Aurelius was involved in a military campaign on the Danube, and a response was a long time coming.

While the prisoners prayed for strength and pondered their fate, a situation arose with one of their number whose asceticism had alienated him from the others. Alcibiades had led a very austere life before the persecutions, one that included eating only bread and water. His insistence on continuing his diet while in prison became a cause of dissension among the other prisoners. This problem was revealed in a dream to Attalus, the accused Christian leader from

Pergamum, who spoke about it with Alcibiades. From that moment on, he ate the same food that was prepared for all the prisoners.

The second round of tortures began on June 2, the day later set aside to commemorate the martyrdom of the Christians of Lyon. The prisoners were led out into the amphitheater, carrying themselves in a manner that made the faithful among the spectators believe their brethren were clothed in beautiful garments, "as those of a bride adorned with variegated golden fringes; and they were perfumed with the sweet savor of Christ." The others, those who had recanted their faith or who accused the Christians of indulging in unspeakable acts against God and nature, were dejected "and filled with every kind of disgrace, and they were reproached by the heathen as ignoble and weak, bearing the accusation of murders, and having lost the one honorable and glorious and life-giving Name."

Into this arena of suffering were led Maturus, Sanctus, Blandina, and Attalus, to do battle with the wild beasts, entertaining and fulfilling the blood lust of the pagan crowd. Maturus and Sanctus were subjected to another round of contests and tortures—running the gauntlet, battling the beasts, suffering all manner of physical abuse—which they endured as before.

The last of the tortures was the awful iron chair. This was a device into which

*The screaming crowd cries out for Attalus, a Roman citizen, as he enters the amphitheater behind a soldier carrying a sign which said, "This is Attalus the Christian." He went willingly, his friends said, because of his clear conscience and because his devotion to Christ removed his fear. Other Christians wait their turn.*

HIC ATTALUS
CHRISTIANUS

the victim was seated and placed amid flames. One does not need much imagination to picture what happened. The chair heated up to a red-hot level, cooking the victim alive. The goal was to force a victim to confess before dying amid the fumes of his roasting flesh. Sanctus, however, further enraged the crowd by repeating his earlier statement. What Maturus said is not recorded, but we are told that both men were sacrificed "after their life had continued for a long time through the great conflict."

Next up was the slave girl Blandina. She was suspended from a stake in a way that made it appear as though she were crucified, but according to the *Letter*, that only strengthened the will of the Christians, who "beheld with their outward eyes, in the form of their sister, him who was crucified for them." Then, wild animals were turned loose to eat her alive. They circled her as the crowd cheered them on. "Blandina looked upon them and prayed for strength to her Father in heaven, and when the animals turned away and would not touch her, she was removed from the stake and returned to her prison cell."

The people then cried out for Attalus, who entered the amphitheater willingly, because of his clear conscience, and because his devotion to Christ removed his fear of the fate that awaited him. A tablet, on which was written "This is Attalus

## Marcus Aurelius ordered that anyone who recanted the faith was to be set free, but all who kept confessing their Christianity were to be condemned to death.

the Christian," was carried in front of him as he was led around the amphitheater in front of the screaming mob. At some point the governor was informed that Attalus was a Roman citizen, and therefore could not be condemned to be eaten by the beasts. The governor ordered him returned to the prison until the response from the emperor was received.

The imprisoned Christians used the following days to their best advantage, caring for their wounds and tending to the spiritual strength of the wavering. Their influence and demeanor caused many of those who had recanted to reaffirm their faith. The time was also spent discussing their concerns about fellow Christians outside Gaul, particularly those involved in Montanism. The Christians of Lyon did not like dissension and conflict within the body of the Church. This attitude may have been the reason the prisoners wrote letters regarding their feelings about the Montanist controversy in Asia and Phrygia. The letters, urging peace in the churches along with the recounting of what was happening in Lyon, were given to Irenaeus to take to Bishop Eleutherus in Rome. According to Eusebius, the prisoners also recommended Irenaeus to the bishop as highly worthy of his position as priest. The persecutions had ended by the time Irenaeus returned to Gaul as the new bishop.

The emperor's response to the governor's query about the Romans among the prisoners finally arrived before August 1, the start of Gaul's great festival commemorating the dedication of the temple to Augustus in 12 B.C. Marcus Aurelius ordered the continuation of Trajan's policy of sixty years earlier: Anyone who recanted his faith was to be set free, but all who persisted in asserting they were Christians were to be executed. Roman citizens confessing the Christian faith were to be beheaded, a method of death said to be quick and possibly even painless.

The festival games began with the faithful brought before the governor and the judgment seat, "to make a show and a spectacle for the multitude." The governor asked each prisoner if he or she was a Christian. Those who recanted the faith "blasphemed The Way through their apostasy." Roman citizens who confessed were beheaded. Some of those who had earlier denied Christ now confessed him, and were added to the rest who had held firm in their faith from the beginning.

During the interrogation, Alexander, a Phrygian physician who had lived in Gaul for several years and who was known for his Christian belief, used hand gestures to encourage the others to confess their faith. The crowd noticed him instructing those who had recanted earlier and furiously blamed him for causing them to change their testimonies. The governor heard the commotion, called Alexander to stand before the judgment seat, and asked him, "Who are you?" "I am a Christian," Alexander replied, for which he, too, was sentenced to face the wild beasts.

The next day, Alexander and Attalus were returned to the arena, where they were tortured for a long time with every instrument available. Alexander would not speak, and was finally stabbed to death. Attalus, although a Roman citizen, was placed in the iron chair. As his flesh burned, he spoke in Latin to the crowd, saying, "Look! This which you do is devouring men; but we do not devour men; nor do any other wicked thing." He was asked for the name of God, and he answered before he died, "God has not a name as man has."

Finally, just two of the Christians remained. Blandina and the fifteen-year-old Ponticus were brought into the arena for what would be the final day of the games. They had been forced each day to watch the suffering and death of their friends, and had repeatedly been urged to recant and to swear by the idols. Because they would not yield, the crowd granted them no mercy. Each was taken through every round of torture and treated to the pain of every instrument, all the while being asked to swear by the idols. Blandina encouraged the boy to stay strong and to keep focused on God, and so he did until he died.

The last to die was Blandina, "having, as a noble mother, encouraged her children and sent them before her victorious to the King." After the whippings and beatings, the wild beasts, and the iron seat, and after her continued refusal to swear, a net was placed around her and she was thrown before a bull. When the bull tossed her about but failed to kill her, Blandina was stabbed to death. "And the heathen themselves confessed that never among them had a woman endured so many and such terrible tortures."

But the madness of the crowd did not stop with Blandina. The bodies of those who had died in prison were fed to the dogs, and a twenty-four-hour guard was

**IRENAEUS ON HERESY**

*Indeed, when I myself reveled in the teachings of Plato, and heard the Christians misrepresented and watched them stand fearless in the face of death and of everything that was considered dreadful, I realized the impossibility of their living in sinful pleasure.*

placed around the remains, the Romans knowing that bones and bodies of martyrs could be venerated later, and that the Christians believed in bodily resurrection. After six days, all of the remains were burned and the ashes were thrown in the river, thus ending the summer of terror for the Christians of Lyon and Vienne.

Irenaeus would live another twenty-five years. Scholars disagree as to whether or not he, too, died a martyr in 202. His remaining years, however, were spent studying Gnostic beliefs and writing the definitive works against them, the most famous of which was the *Adversus Haereses*, or the *Against Heresies*. He also intervened in the date-of-Easter controversy about 188, urging the bishop of Rome to be tolerant of different practices regarding the Lenten fast and the dates used to celebrate Easter (see page 280).

Although Irenaeus was a vociferous opponent of heresies, in particular those of Valentinus and Montanus, he was averse to dividing the body of the Church, as witnessed by his position in the debate regarding Easter, and also by his pleading in Rome on behalf of the imprisoned Christians of Lyon regarding the Montanist controversy. In *Adversus Haereses*, Irenaeus provided a warning for Christians of his time, and for future Christians who would face great controversies that would splinter the Church: "He shall also judge those who give rise to schisms . . . who look to their own special advantage rather than to the unity of the Church . . . men who prate for peace while they give rise to war."

Though it would never die, Gnosticism would fade, and the violence and brutality of the Roman amphitheater would one day be prohibited. What would not fade, however, was witness borne by the Christians at Lyon, and the valor of the young slave girl who perished with them—simple people with a simple faith, whose light would shine as a beacon for the Christian millions in the centuries that lay ahead.

# Montanus, the prophet, lured away thousands and saw himself as Father, Word, and Spirit

**Though the chosen date and place for the world's end didn't see it happen, his sect flourished, then fell, but such ecstatic spirituality was far from finished**

The Christian faith has never suffered from a lack of dissent and dispute, or of colorful and compelling individuals who insist they have gained unique insight into the most profound questions of human existence and theological truth. The apostles were not beyond questioning Jesus when the Way did not accord with their way. This attitude of independence was perhaps in part inherited from Jewish forebears, including Abraham, who famously questioned God about the upcoming destruction of Sodom. "You will sweep away the innocent with the guilty?" This spirit of independent thought is very much with us in the twenty-first century, belying the charge that people of faith are participants in a massive exercise of groupthink.

On some occasions, however, individual "revelations" run so contrary to accepted Christian doctrine that they threaten the coherence of Christ's message. Few have been more interesting and colorful than the Montanist movement, which appeared between the 150s and 170s. It sprang to life in the Asia Minor district of Phrygia and eventually spread to Rome, Lyon, Syria, and North Africa. Though it was largely extinguished within a few centuries, echoes of Montanism are heard to the present day.

Montanus was apparently a neophyte presbyter, increasingly given to visions and states of "ecstasy." In and of itself, this would not have set him apart from other Christians of his region. Montanus, however, claimed to be about much greater things. "I am the Father, the Word, and the Paraclete," he insisted. "I am the Lord God omnipotent" who has descended into man. In this case, into Montanus.

These were grand and startling assertions, and the focus of Montanus's message was on an equally epic scale: He claimed to know the time and place of the appearance of the New Jerusalem promised in the Book of Revelation.

*The religious ecstasy and visions at the heart of mid-second-century Montanism survive into modern times. This photo from 1942 shows delegates to the Twentieth Annual Convention of the International Church of the Four Square Gospel in Los Angeles. Some lie on the floor and sob in religious fervor, while others seek comfort from sister Aimee Semple McPherson, the founder of the church.*

According to Montanus and his two prophetesses, Priscilla and Maximilla, the Heavenly City would descend on the Phrygian village of Pepuza in the year 177. The Day of the Lord was indeed at hand. The believer's duty was to prepare the soul for this event.

These prophecies, while perhaps harrowing to modern ears, were powerful balm to many who heard them. For most people in second-century Phrygia, life was not distinguished by its luxury. Apart from the usual poverty and disease, survival itself was always tenuous. For Christians there was the added fear that a great persecution was on the way. Polycarp of Smyrna, the preeminent Christian leader in Asia Minor, had been executed in 155. If one so great as Polycarp could be killed, what Christian was safe?

The Montanist message put these earthly worries into perspective. Yes, Christians should expect persecution at the hands of the Romans, who, after all, were agents of the devil, Montanus said. Yet the devil would be getting his due soon enough, and for the martyrs,

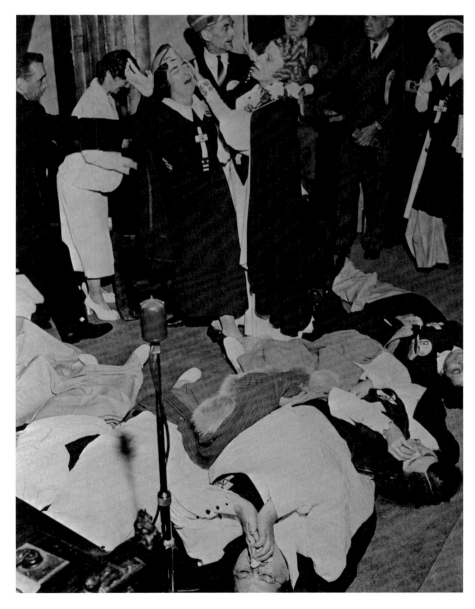

a life of eternal peace and heavenly bliss would follow.

Even so, Montanism should not be confused with "pie-in-the-sky" escapist eschatology. Quite the contrary. It set a hard path for adherents, establishing a host of new fasts, including dry fasts—food taken without water. It advocated a diet whose centerpiece was the radish. It counseled the abandonment of family and worldly possessions and forbade second marriages. It also called for a turning away from public life and military service, as well as a full and willing embrace of persecution. "Do not look forward to dying in your bed, in childbirth, or in lassitude of fever," Montanus counseled, "but in martyrdom, so that he who has suffered for you may be glorified." Such teachings were to face hard scrutiny, but initially, they attracted thousands to worship services whose drama and ecstatic vibrancy matched that of the doctrines espoused.

Women were central to Montanist worship, as one would expect of a movement with two prophetesses at its core, and that alone set these services apart. One can imagine the additional sense of awe, wonder, and perhaps daring, when at a climactic moment, seven white-clad virgins appeared before the assembly. Their faces were brilliantly painted, as if they were beings from a higher sphere. Their hands bore beautiful lamps, and their tongues bore divine prophecy. The congregation was often borne away to states of high excitement, many falling into fits of ecstasy, tears, and tongues. They had received the Truth directly from the Holy Spirit. How else could they respond?

Not everyone was ecstatic, of course. Soon enough, authorities both secular and ecclesiastical turned their scorn on the Montanists, for reasons obvious and, in some respects, entirely defensible.

The secular authorities viewed the Montanists, with their demands to shun military service, and indeed, anything having to do with the state, as dangerously subversive. So profound was their concern that they began viewing all Christians as being in league with these radicals—a clear case of overreaction, as historian Marta Sordi explains in *The Christians and the Roman Empire*: "In reality, of course, it was a tragic misunderstanding. Neither the Great Church nor the majority of Christians actually shared the anti-Roman, anti-state ideal of the followers of the New Prophecy," as Montanists sometimes described themselves. Nonetheless, Rome would

*Delegates raise their arms to receive the Holy Spirit at the opening on July 20, 1977, of what at the time was the largest meeting ever of the charismatic movement. The conference was held at Arrow Stadium, home of the Kansas City Chiefs football team.*

bar conversion to Christianity, as well as Judaism, in 201, largely as an attempt to suppress these intimations of independence.

Christian leaders were perhaps even more disturbed, for reasons both institutional and theological. "As time went on," writes historian W. H. C. Frend in *Martyrdom and Persecution in the Early Church*, "Montanism took on more and more the character of a revolt, the prophetic and eschatological religion of the native countryside against the Hellenized Christianity of the towns."

At the heart of the problem posed by Montanus's extravagant assertion of his personal indivisibility with the Holy Spirit lay some disconcerting implications. After all, if a man truly enjoyed such status, who could question his authority? Who was to stop him from revising Christianity in any way he pleased? Montanus may have provided religious cohesion and leadership to his followers, but to other Christians, he represented nothing less than spiritual anarchy.

*Recalling Jesus' prophecy that his followers would pick up serpents unharmed (Mark 16:18), serpent-handlers at the Pentecostal Church of God prove their faith at Harlan County, Kentucky, in 1946.*

Indeed, to his growing host of critics, Montanus represented something much worse. Aviricius Marcellus, a Phyrgian merchant and devout Christian, charged that Montanus, "in the unbounded lust of his soul for leadership, gave access to himself to the Adversary"—a charge of demonic possession that would be echoed by others, including two bishops, who attempted to exorcise the occupying demon. The fourth-century Christian historian Eusebius, with his typical literary flair, observed that Montanus spoke in an "ecstasy, in which he is without shame or fear. Beginning with purposed ignorance, he passes on to involuntary madness of soul."

Meanwhile, rumors and gossip were circulated to undermine the movement: Its leadership had expended church funds on rich living; a trustee of the church had floated into the sky during a period of ecstasy, only to suddenly drop to earth and die from his injuries. Bishop Claudius Apollinarius of Hierapolis took special interest in Montanism, initially attempting, it is believed, to persuade Montanus to return to the fold. When that failed, the bishop's denunciations became white-hot. Then in 193, Bishop Serapion of Antioch pronounced that "the lying organization called the New Prophecy is held in abomination by the whole brotherhood in the world." In 200, Bishop Zephyrinus of Rome added his voice to the condemnation.

While traces of Montanism could be found six centuries after its beginning, especially in Phrygia, these early attacks took their toll, and were greatly bolstered in 331, when the emperor Constantine ordered public prayer sites maintained by the Montanists expropriated. Just to make sure, in 550, the bishop of Ephesus ordered the bones of Montanus, Maximilla, and Priscilla exhumed and burnt. Montanus's date of death is not known, though detractors claimed that he and Maximilla, whose death supposedly occurred in 179, had hanged themselves. Evidence for that charge remains elusive.

Yet for all these efforts, the spirit of Montanism was never eradicated. Bold and independent voices calling for repentance, rejection of worldly security, and dedication to the faith, even in the face of death, have been heard throughout the Christian centuries. Theologian Richard J. Foster in his *Streams of Living Waters* hears an echo of the yearnings of Montanism in the Gregorian Liturgical Movement (seventh century to present), the Franciscans (thirteenth century to present), the Pentecostal Movement (begun in the twentieth century), the Charismatic Renewal (twentieth century), and the Modern Liturgical Renewal (twentieth century).

He hears the voice in individuals as varied as Joan of Arc, Hildegard of Bingen, and Oral Roberts.

What is this voice? It proclaims that the spirit of God animates each believer, no matter what his or her standing in society. It proclaims that the Good News is found not only in ancient texts and ecclesiastical pronouncements, but springs eternal in this moment and in all moments. It is a voice that sometimes reaches the level of obvious falsehood, but it has also, to some degree or another, echoed in every Christian soul. ■

# CHAPTER 6

# The feisty lawyer who spoke for Christianity

**Sharp, witty, logically lethal, Tertullian took the fight into the enemy's camp, but died as a church of one**

Because it has never been easy, and almost never safe, to be an outspoken defender of their faith, many Christians hunker down in quiet anonymity. They live unobtrusively, inconspicuously; they leave no mark. After all, as the "common man" reminds us in Robert Bolt's play *A Man For All Seasons* (about the martyrdom of Sir Thomas More): "I'm breathing. Are you breathing too? It's nice, isn't it? It isn't difficult to keep alive, friends . . . Just don't make trouble—or if you must make trouble, make the sort of trouble that's expected."

In the second century, Roman authorities regarded Christians as immensely troublesome. Not only were their rituals immoral, their repudiation of the gods caused fires, earthquakes, floods, all manner of natural calamities. How should Christians respond? Most considered it reasonable to "suffer in silence." After all, didn't their own leaders preach loving one's enemy, turning the other cheek, accepting those who were placed in authority over them?

On the Mediterranean's southern coast, near the modern city of Tunis, the ruins of Carthage can still be seen. There, about A.D. 160, a boy named Quintus Septimius Florens Tertullianus was born into a pagan family. Scholars differ about the exact date and circumstances of his conversion, but one thing was clear. Even after he became a Christian, turning the other cheek did not appeal to him, and yielding to mindless authority was out of the question.

Tradition has it that Tertullian was a lawyer; whether or not he acquired his combativeness in studying the law (he was also an expert in literature and philosophy), he was an implacable adversary. Against those who attacked Christian beliefs, against those who impugned the Christians' practices and slandered their names, Tertullian fought back boldly.

Not a military man (in fact a self-declared pacifist), Tertullian had only ideas and words for weapons, but he wielded them fiercely. In treatises, pamphlets, essays, and sermons (it was common then for laymen to be invited to preach in Carthage though not in some other Christian centers)—in polemics of all kinds—Tertullian took on all opponents. We know of more than thirty of his written works, but some scholars speculate that twice that number may have been lost. His writings span a period of two decades, from A.D. 195 until about 215.

Tertullian coined a splendid phrase, *militia Christi* ("Christian warfare"), and applied it to his own life. It is apt. By sixteen hundred years, he anticipated the counsel of the nineteenth-century Anglican hymnologist John Samuel Bewley Monsell, echoing Paul: "Fight the good fight with all thy might/ Christ is thy strength and Christ thy right."

The setting in which Tertullian waged his warfare was Carthage. *Kart Hadasht*, "the new town," was the name used by the Phoenicians when they founded it about eight hundred years before the birth of Christ. Carthage was a formidable power in the ancient world, with a population estimated at two hundred thousand, remarkable for that time. By the fifth century B.C., however, the Carthaginian Empire found itself challenged by the rising power of Rome. Carthage's greatest general, the elephant-employing Hannibal, nearly captured

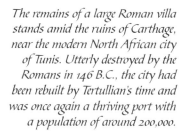

*The remains of a large Roman villa stands amid the ruins of Carthage, near the modern North African city of Tunis. Utterly destroyed by the Romans in 146 B.C., the city had been rebuilt by Tertullian's time and was once again a thriving port with a population of around 200,000.*

Rome in 216 B.C. In his treatise *On the Pallium*, Tertullian expresses nostalgia for the glory days, "the good old days when Carthage was Carthage."

Nostalgia was in order because, in the third Punic War (149–146 B.C.), Carthage was conquered and utterly destroyed by Rome. Before the war had even started, Cato the Elder had pronounced a curse—*Carthago delenda est*, "Carthage must be destroyed"—which he repeated in speech after speech until it became Rome's mission. When the Romans finally overcame Carthage, they salted its soil to ensure its barrenness. One might have thought that her glory was all in the past. But not so. In about 44 B.C., Julius Caesar decided to rebuild Carthage as a colony of Rome.

By the time of Tertullian's birth more than two centuries later, Carthage was second only to Rome in grandeur. "Little Rome," it was sometimes called. It rivaled Alexandria as the empire's second largest city. Immense in geography, Carthage extended inland for many miles, enjoying wealth and, thanks to a busy port, a highly prosperous trade. Sunken Roman vessels are still occasionally discovered in the waters around Carthage.

Due to Roman engineering, Carthage had dams, reservoirs, and aqueducts that allowed fields to be irrigated and agriculture to flourish. Water from as far away as thirty-five miles arrived in the city by an ingenious system of aqueducts at a volume estimated at eighty gallons per second. The Roman Emperor Antoninus Pius (138–161) had built elaborate public baths, and as the scholar Paul Petit has noted, the *Pax Romana* throughout the region—peace, order, and good Roman government—was preserved by the Thirteenth Urban Cohort and a small mounted force, while the fleet from Alexandria discharged the task of surveillance.

Carthage was also a center of learning, so much so that the Roman writer Lucius Apuleius, who would satirize the vices of the age in *The Golden Ass*,

Roman North Africa

abandoned Athens to study in Carthage and then remained there to teach philosophy and rhetoric.

The Romans worshiped many gods and goddesses, as Tertullian mocked: "new gods and old, barbarian, Greek, Roman, foreign, captive, adoptive, private, public, male, female, rustic, urban, military, and naval." Schoolteachers were required to teach the genealogies of these little deities, but predominant was the cult of Saturn, whose adherents believed that all things, large and small and good and evil, were willed by a god who could be appeased only by sacrifice. Initially, this meant human sacrifice, usually involving children under four years of age. By Tertullian's day, human sacrifice had been prohibited, the children being replaced by animals.

Carthage was also an important center of rabbinical training, and its schools had graduated several notable rabbis who taught in local synagogues. When Tertullian was a teenager, the city government decreed that there would be an elaborate annual festival. Houses would be garlanded, lavish banquets staged, and sacrifices offered to the emperor. Devout Jews considered this idolatrous and generally declined to participate.

Just how Christians got to Carthage, and from where, scholars continue to debate. Some contend that Carthaginian traders or merchants, whose commerce took them to Jerusalem, heard the first apostles speak in tongues on the day of Pentecost. The book of Acts (2:6–11) says the apostles were heard by many, including pilgrims "from the parts of Libya." Or perhaps the Christian community began with homegrown converts from among Carthaginian Jews. By the time of Tertullian's birth, Christian cults (as the authorities considered them) were common throughout North Africa.

**TERTULLIAN ON PERSECUTION**

*With our hands thus stretched out and up to God, rend us with your iron claws, hang us up on crosses, wrap us in flames, take our heads from us with the sword, let loose the wild beasts on us—the very attitude of a Christian praying is one of preparation for all punishment.*

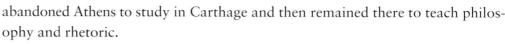

## Christians posed real security problems for the authorities. They seemed to speak in revolutionary terms, of a future when God would rule, having broken the world's kings.

Christians were easily identifiable. They kept one day in seven free from business; they worshiped in their own house churches; they had their own burial grounds, some of which archaeologists have unearthed and identified. They believed in one God, who had taken upon himself the lineaments of a man, had been crucified by the Romans and buried, rose from the dead, ascended into Heaven, and was accessible through prayer. A starker contrast with the beliefs of pagan religions is difficult to imagine.

Second-century Christians posed real security problems for the authorities. The Christians seemed to speak in revolutionary terms, pitting Caesar against God. They taught of a coming millennium, based upon old dreams of Jewish prophets and psalmists. They envisaged a future when God would rule, having first broken the kings of the world like a potter's vessel. In his *Annals*, the Roman historian Tacitus dismissed such beliefs as "pernicious superstitions," but they could just as easily be considered treasonous. Archibald Robertson, in *The Origins of Christianity*, points out that among early Christians there was the expectation of an imminent end time, "of which the communal feast in which church members joined weekly was a sort of foretaste and pledge."

The emperor Marcus Aurelius died in Rome on March 17, A.D. 180, and his son Commodus took the throne. Times of transition are always times of uncertainty, and perhaps it was uncertainty that motivated the North African proconsul, Vigellus Saturninus, to mount a crackdown on the Christians.

In his *Apology*, published in about 197, shortly after his conversion, Tertullian mocks the authorities for blaming their difficulties on Christians and persecuting them: "If the river Tiber reaches the walls, if the river Nile does not rise to the fields, if the sky does not move or the earth does, if there is a famine, if there is plague, the cry is at once: 'The Christians to the lion!'" Then, with that acerbic touch so characteristic of him, Tertullian adds: "What, all of them to one lion?"

Whatever his reasons, Saturninus demanded that Christians take a loyalty oath that, until then, had been required only sporadically. The person charged had the usual two options: burning a pinch of incense or swearing an oath to the emperor's "genius" on the one hand, or death on the other. Then, on a date known precisely (July 17 in the year 180), from a town called Scillia (whose name and exact location—perhaps in the province of Numidia—remain matters of conjecture), Saturninus provoked a showdown between twelve peasant Christians and the might of Rome.

These twelve, five of them women, would come to be known as the "Scillitan martyrs." Tertullian claimed they were the first Christian martyrs in Africa.

*This is an artist's impression of Carthage's naval harbor. Built in the days of the city's epic struggle with Rome, the harbor was later transformed by the Romans into a monument to their gods and their military power.*

# Rome builds on North Africa's wealth

## Severus's monuments still stand

As they are throughout the Mediterranean world, the ruins of Roman towns and cities are abundant along the coast of North Africa, which produced not only a wealth of goods for export but also many distinguished Roman senators, lawyers, and literary figures. Christianity arrived early in the province of Africa, and the church there soon developed an advanced episcopal structure. In the wealthy commercial center of Leptis Magna, one of a group of three cities within the district of Tripolitania (modern Tripoli), Roman construction projects multiplied following a visit by the emperor Septimius Severus, who had been born there himself. Among Roman structures built at Severus's behest were a forum, a basilica, and a colonnade leading from a modernized harbor to a massive piazza. In Djemila, Algeria, called Cuicul in Roman times, the Severan period saw creation of a new forum and basilica. Dougga (ancient Thugga) was the prosperous home of a mixed population of Punics and native Libyans, and even after annexation to the Roman province of Africa its citizens continued to run their own government into the early third century, while benefiting from construction of such Roman standards as a temple, forum, and Senate house. ∎

The ancient colonnade of the Roman forum area at Cyrene, Libya (opposite page, top), built in 27–18 B.C., was damaged in an earthquake in A.D. 365 that destroyed much of the city. Overlooking the Roman amphitheater of Leptis Magna, Libya (opposite, bottom) is a statue of Ceres, probably installed when the theater, with its view of the Mediterranean Sea, was constructed in A.D. 1–2. In the former Numidian capital of Dougga (top left), now all but deserted, a Tunisian sits amid impressive Roman ruins. A colorful and wonderfully intact mosaic (above) lines the fish ponds in a Roman villa's garden at Utica, Tunisia. At Djemila, Algeria (below), founded in the first century, the sprawling ruins of this first-century military garrison constitute one of the best preserved Roman sites in North Africa. The ancient marketplace at Leptis Magna, Libya (left), boasted a series of marble slabs containing standard Roman volume measures that can still be seen, installed so shoppers could verify the honesty of vendors.

(They would hardly be the last. Far more Christians were to be murdered in Africa during the waning years of the twentieth century and the early years of the twenty-first than in Tertullian's long lifetime.)

Very little is known about the Scillitan twelve as individuals, or about what brought them to Saturninus's attention, but it is certain that the cult of the emperor was anathema to committed Christians. The twelve were put on trial in the Judgment Hall at Carthage. Apparently, none was tortured; instead, the proconsul Saturninus interrogated them.

The ensuing dialogue is restrained, earnest, almost Socratic in tone. Although the historian Henry Chadwick writes that some Christians appeared almost to "court martyrdom" when questioned, by being "contumacious, dissident, and disrespectful to the governor," the Scillitan twelve were models of courtroom decorum and resolute courtesy. The terse brevity and Latin composition of the transcript of those proceedings have led some to suggest that its author may have been none other than Saturninus himself.[1] In any event, the drama and pathos of the encounter remain gripping eighteen hundred years later in this more contemporary rendering of J. A. Robinson's translation:

> **Saturninus, the proconsul**: You can win the indulgence of our lord the emperor, if you return to a sound mind.
>
> **Speratus [acting as spokesman]**: We have never done ill, we have not lent ourselves to wrong, we have never spoken ill, but when ill-treated we have given thanks, because we pay heed to our emperor.
>
> **Saturninus**: We too are religious, and our religion is simple, and we swear by the genius of our lord the emperor, and pray for his welfare, as you ought also to do.
>
> **Speratus**: If you will peaceably give me your attention, I shall tell you the mystery of simplicity.
>
> **Saturninus**: I will give you no such attention, if you begin by speaking evil of our sacred rites, but rather I command you now: Swear by the genius of our lord the emperor!
>
> **Speratus**: The empire of this world I know nothing about, but rather I serve that God, whom no man has seen nor with these eyes *could* see. I have committed no theft. If I have bought anything I pay the tax, because I do know my Lord, the King of Kings and Emperor of all nations.
>
> **Saturninus**: Then stop being of this persuasion.
>
> **Speratus**: It would be bad advice for me to murder someone, or to tell lies.
>
> **Saturninus**: Get yourself out of this foolishness.

---

1. The *Acts of the Scillitan Martyrs* is the earliest dated document from the Latin Church and the first to mention a Latin Bible. "Most scholars have felt that this document, like the court protocol in the *Acts of Cyprian* [covered in the next volume of this series] is the closest of all the extant 'Acts' to the primitive court records," writes historian Herbert Musurillo.

**Cittinus [another prisoner]:** We have nothing to fear, except our Lord God who is in Heaven.

**Donata [a female prisoner]:** We honor Caesar as Caesar, but we fear God.

**Vestia:** I am a Christian.

**Secunda:** What I am, that I wish to be.

**Saturninus [to Speratus]:** Do you persist in being a Christian?

**Speratus:** I am a Christian.

[With him all the rest agreed.]

**Saturninus:** Do you want time to reconsider?

**Speratus:** In a matter as straightforward as this, there is nothing to reconsider.

**Saturninus:** What are those things in your shirt?

**Speratus:** Books and epistles by Paul, a just man.

**Saturninus:** Listen, you people! Take another thirty days and think this over.

**Speratus:** I am a Christian.

[And again, they all agreed with him.]

**Saturninus [reading out the decree from a tablet]:** Speratus, Nartzalus, Cittinus, Donata, Vestia, Secunda, and the rest having confessed that they live according to the Christian rite, after opportunity was offered them to return to the custom of the Romans, have obstinately persisted. It is determined that they be put to the sword.

**Speratus:** We give thanks to God.

**Nartzalus:** Today we are martyrs in Heaven, thanks be to God.

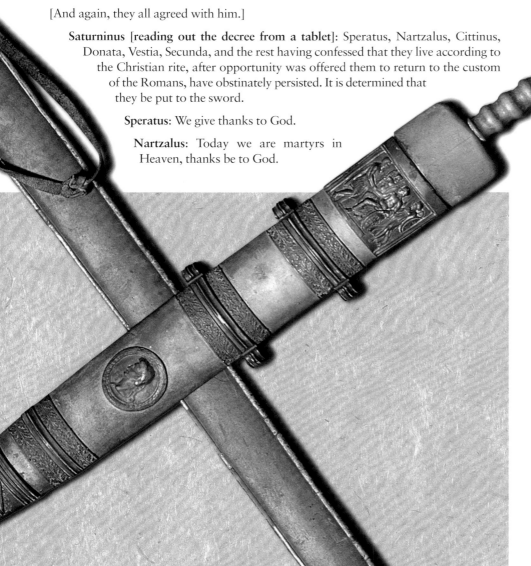

*The Scillitan martyrs were not sent to the arena to be stoned, crucified, or thrown to the beasts. They were "put to the sword"—perhaps with weapons similar to these—though such a death was usually reserved for Roman citizens.*

The twelve were then beheaded,[2] all, according to most accounts, on the same day.

Such courage as the Scillitan martyrs demonstrated has a tendency to humble observers, then and now; it provokes admiration even from those who do not share the martyrs' convictions. After all, these men and women had no greater strength to face persecution than anyone alive in the twenty-first century. They knew what awaited them; indeed, they sometimes discussed among themselves whether the executioner's sword would hurt and if death would be instantaneous. Yet their faith overcame their fear. Henri Daniel-Rops describes them: "Encouraging one another, exchanging the kiss of peace, even more united in the moment of sacrifice than in their everyday lives, where it was only human that discords and dissensions should have existed, they went steadfastly to execution, bearing in their hearts that peace which Christ had promised them."

The effect of such martyrdoms on the Christian community of North Africa was mixed. Some Christians became more circumspect or went underground, but for many others a "martyr's crown" became the desired culmination of a life of spiritual dedication. "May you gain your crown" became a common North African salutation, and anniversaries of the deaths of the martyrs began to be celebrated, giving rise to the earliest church calendars.

Clearly, the example of Christian martyrs had a profound and lasting impact upon Tertullian. Though he was not yet a Christian when the Scillitan martyrs

---

2. Why were the Scillitan martyrs beheaded? Beheading was a nobler form of execution, reserved for condemned Roman citizens. Christians were more often stoned, crucified, or thrown to the beasts. Could it be that the proconsul Saturninus was moved by their courage and serenity and therefore mitigated the harshness of the penalty?

were beheaded, their example was the cause of his conversion. Later he contended that their deaths had accelerated the vigorous spread of Christianity throughout North Africa. His best known and most quoted maxim is usually mistranslated into English as: "The blood of the martyrs is the seed of the church." What he actually wrote was: *Semen est sanguis Christianorum*, "The blood of the Christians is [i.e., serves as] seed."

Who was this Carthaginian rebel, this lawyer-convert, this pacifist who scorned a military career like his father's to enlist in the *militia Christi*? Who was this man of privilege who abandoned the powerful to stand with the oppressed?

We do not know even what Tertullian looked like. He was probably born into a well-to-do family, and his father may have served in the proconsul's guard. Almost certainly he studied law in Rome, and he wrote two early legal treatises. He frequently employed legal terminology and often argued as though he were in court. For example, he once wrote as if he were himself cross-examining someone who purported to be a Christian astrologer: But if you could truly foretell the future, Tertullian asks, would you not have foreseen your own conversion? And if you had foreseen your conversion, would you not also know that Christians scorn astrology?

Tertullian's writings show the breadth of his reading; he quotes from Herodotus, Pliny, Juvenal, and Plato, all philosophical and literary luminaries of the ancient world. This was important because the early Christian church had few advocates who were "intellectuals." To the Corinthians, Paul had written: "Remember, brethren, the circumstances of your own calling; not many of you are wise, in the world's fashion, not many powerful, not many well born" (1 Cor. 1:26). But if Christians were to prevail in what was becoming, at least in part, a war of ideas, they would have to equip themselves for a vigorous defense of their faith. As Gerald Lewis Bray points out in *Holiness and the Will of God*: "The Apostolic Age and those who remembered it had passed from the scene, and with them had gone the last living link with the historical revelation." Was not Christ himself the embodiment of truth? Had he not promised: "You shall know the truth, and the truth shall make you free"? Tertullian would defend his newly acquired faith with the skill of a lawyer and the subtlety of a philosopher.

As a young man, Tertullian had been attracted to the theater and the games, spectacles of violence and eroticism serving much the same audience as movies and professional sports today. After his conversion, he expressed remorse about how much time he had wasted. His description (*De Spectaculis*) of a pious Christian meditating on the eternal verities while watching with one eye the bloodletting in the arena suggests that the lure of the games was never entirely lost on him. To his fellow Christians who attended, Tertullian quoted Psalm 1:1: "Blessed is the man who enters not the assembly of the ungodly." What assembly, he asked rhetorically, could be more ungodly than those in the

**TERTULLIAN ON ABORTION**

*We may not destroy even the fetus in the womb. To hinder a birth is merely a speedier man-killing; nor does it matter whether you take away a life that is born, or destroy one that is coming to the birth.*

amphitheater screaming for the blood of Christians? Moreover, he went on, spectators who are ostensibly Christians often acclaim one gladiator as "the greatest," forgetting that only God is great.

Ridicule and sarcasm were among Tertullian's favorite techniques. He did not suffer fools gladly; in fact, he seldom suffered them at all. In his *Apology*, he mentions the widespread concern about the dwindling revenues of the pagan temples, for which the Christians were being blamed. "We cannot cope with men and gods begging together," he writes. And in any event, Christians compensate for the lost revenue because, unlike just about everybody else, they don't cheat on their tax returns. Defending the early Christian practice of communal property, he quips: "We Christians have everything in common—except our wives."

An idea of what it was like to joust verbally with Tertullian may be gleaned

# Tertullian's advice to his wife

## Don't wed again because God couldn't make another such perfect marriage

If drawing up instructions for the disposal of mere property after a man's death is important, the great Christian theologian Tertullian (c. 160–220) tells his wife in a remarkable letter, then preparing a spiritual will, dealing with those "things divine and heavenly" accumulated during a lifetime, is far more urgent.

What Tertullian wrote for his wife was just that, his advice for her spiritual conduct if he should die before she did. In the letter, preserved now for nearly two millennia, he tells her this: When I'm gone, don't get married again. Don't even think about it.

Few writings have been more misunderstood than Tertullian's "Letter to His Wife," observes Eric Osborn in *Tertullian: First Theologian of the West*. After all, in a text that runs to nearly a dozen pages in modern typescript, Tertullian's spiritual counsel depicts marriage as the worst state anyone could enter, short of plunging into the flames of Hell. What a benediction for a man to leave for his own widow!

It's not that he wants to "prescribe an end to marrying," says Osborn. Indeed, Tertullian agrees with the apostle Paul that "to marry is better than to burn," meaning that taking a wife or husband is better than being consumed to distraction by lust. Marriage, after all, channels the otherwise unruly fires of passion. But in that sense marriage is good, Tertullian says, only because "burning" is worse. "A thing is not 'good' merely because it is not 'evil.'"

Tertullian is also unconvinced by the practical argument that marriage provides "a husband to the female sex as a source of authority and of comfort or to render it safe from evil rumors . . . (and from) the fleeting desires of beauty and youth." It would be far better, he argues, as did Paul, to keep oneself completely free of all that.

What's more, says Tertullian, the notion that a woman should marry for economic reasons, "to roost on another's wealth, to extort splendor from another's store," is a grave error. God, not a husband, is to provide for all one's needs. Christ promised that God would care for us just as he "clothes with such grace the lilies of the field and feeds the fowls of the heavens." And God, Tertullian admonishes, "knows what is needful for each of his servants—not indeed ponderous necklaces, not burdensome garments, not Gallic mules nor German bearers, which all add luster to the glory of nuptials, but 'sufficiency' which is suitable to moderation and modesty."

Tertullian likewise dismisses the argument that "anxiety for posterity" compels marriage. He seems particularly well acquainted with the pitfalls of parenthood when he writes of "the bitter, bitter pleasure of children." (He may have had teenagers in mind.)

When a woman's husband dies, "the marriage, likewise, by the will of God, deceases." So "why should you restore what God has put an end to? . . . Let us love the opportunity of continence as soon as it offers itself, let us resolve to accept it, that what we have not had strength to follow in matrimony we may follow in widowhood."

But after all that, after excoriating marriage as a horror of barely controlled lust and shameful dependency and extolling widowhood as a divine blessing, he

*Tertullian's "Letter To His Wife" contains nearly a dozen pages of advice on dealing with "things divine and heavenly"—should he die before her. Despite depicting marriage in a less than flattering light, he writes lovingly of his own: "Whence are we to find words enough fully to tell the happiness of that marriage which the church cements . . . which angels carry back the news of to Heaven?"*

suddenly, in the final paragraph of his letter to his wife, stands his argument on its ear. Clearly describing his own marriage, Tertullian is as woozily romantic as a new bridegroom on his wedding night. His real concern finally shows through. A second marriage could never work for either of them, because it could never begin to recapture the joys of the first.

"Whence are we to find words enough fully to tell the happiness of that marriage which the church cements . . . which angels carry back the news of to Heaven? . . . What kind of yoke is that of two believers, partakers of one hope, one desire, one discipline, one and the same service? Both are brethren, both fellow servants, no difference of spirit or of flesh; nay, they are truly 'two in one flesh.' Where the flesh is one, one is the spirit too. Together they pray . . . together perform their fasts; mutually teaching, mutually exhorting, mutually sustaining.

"Equally are they both found in the church of God; equally at the banquet of God; equally in straits, in persecutions, in refreshments. Neither hides anything from the other; neither shuns the other; neither is troublesome to the other. . . . There is no stealthy signing, no trembling greeting. . . . Between the two echo psalms and hymns; and they mutually challenge each other as to which shall better chant to their Lord. Such things, when Christ sees and hears, he joys. To these he sends his own peace. Where two are, there is he himself. Where he is, there the evil one is not."

Tertullian's warning to his wife, it turns out, is that a marriage for the wrong reasons, a marriage for the sake of comfort or for society or for marriage itself, is an invitation to disaster, putting the unfortunate couple a single step away from Hell. On the other hand, a marriage under Christ—a spiritual union such as he and his wife apparently enjoyed—is cause for rejoicing in Heaven. And it's not likely to be offered twice to anyone. ■

from his goring of Praxeas, an influential Christian writer who expressed doubts about both the triune nature of God and the kind of spirit-filled "charismatic" worship favored by the Montanists (see p. 166). In one memorable sentence, Tertullian made Praxeas infamous over the centuries: "He has accomplished two bits of the devil's business: he put to flight the Paraclete [the Holy Spirit] and crucified the Father."

Some authors have speculated that Tertullian was eventually ordained a presbyter. On two occasions, he classes himself with the laity, as though calling attention to an anomaly. But his ordination is unlikely. However, he was certainly the first example of a Christian satirist, a sort of second-century forerunner of the twentieth century's Hilaire Belloc or Malcolm Muggeridge.

Tertullian's polemics are vigorous defenses of Christian orthodoxy. His subjects were wide-ranging: on prayer, on fasting, on suffering, on repentance, on baptism, on marriage, on women, on the Incarnation, and his most influential work, *The Apology*. He defends both the historicity and rationality of

## Tertullian focuses on Christ and his death on the cross, beyond words or reason: 'It is credible because it is foolish. It is certain because it is impossible.'

Christianity against all objections. He contrasts the piety and sobriety of Christians with pagan prejudices,[3] pointing out that Christians pray to God at their meetings and are led in worship by wise elders who are chosen for honesty, not wealth. Christians spend their money not on riotous living, he writes, but in support of the orphan, the widow, and the stranger, and "the only shame or regret [a Christian] feels is at not having been a Christian earlier."

In his earlier works (roughly 195 to 205), Tertullian focuses on Christ and the cross. God's saving love for man, he contends, was demonstrated beyond words, beyond theories, beyond reason itself, by the sacrificial death of Jesus. "It is credible because it is foolish," he writes. "He was buried and rose again. It is certain because it is impossible." He meant, that is, that nobody inventing a religion would have invented one so outlandish.

In *The Sword and the Cross*, Robert M. Grant credits Tertullian with two major contributions to Christian history. First, he pioneered the idea of the "gathered" church: a small community of believers, beset by enemies, facing persecution and death, faithful only to the truth revealed in Jesus Christ, a remnant to be eventually vindicated by God. "We are a society," Tertullian wrote, "with a common religious feeling, a unity of discipline, and a common bond of hope."

---

3. Tertullian saw nothing wrong with Christians behaving as pagans do, so long as there was no religious significance to what they were doing. Men might wear the toga, for instance, or rings could be exchanged during marital vows. However, he warned Christians to be careful of what words they used in conversation because of the way paganism had infused conversational language. He mentions a Christian, for example, who used the term, "By Jupiter!" It was a common exclamation, he said, but it was one Christians should avoid.

Whatever his delight in philosophy, Christianity had now carried Tertullian beyond it, a point he succinctly summed up in his most-repeated observation: "What has Athens to do with Jerusalem? What has the Church to do with the Academy?" It meant that Jerusalem did not need Athens because in Christ it had surpassed and moved beyond mere human philosophy. Grant says that this remark "succinctly summarizes his attitude toward pagan culture. We have the truth; they do not; we do not need them. He literally created the African ecclesiastical mentality." At the same time, he drew a sharp distinction between Caesar's kingdom and God's. "What is more foreign to us than the state?" he dangerously asked.

Such challenging, not to say subversive, views kept Tertullian embroiled in controversy, not only with civil, but also with ecclesiastical authority. Most bishops considered that the survival of the Christians required keeping a low profile, that something less than hostility to civil authority was the wise course. But Tertullian scorned this clerical prudence. When bishops waffled, he jeered them. A bishop who shies away from controversy, he once wrote, is like a soldier who runs away from battle.

How did it happen, then, that an apologist whose earliest polemics were in defense of orthodoxy should, during his late middle age, fall in with the Montanist sect that the Christians had condemned? And why then did he turn on the Montanists, abandon them, and, in effect, establish his own church? Why die old, tired, solitary, estranged?

Eric Osborn in his biography, *Tertullian: First Theologian of the West*, suspects that he was not able to cope with the spectacle of sin being committed by baptized Christians within the fold of the faith. "The fulfillment of all things in Christ and the effectiveness of baptism required the absence of deadly sins from Christian lives," he writes. "He was driven to despair by the abundance of Christian sin. . . . This estrangement was no passing problem; in every age there have been as many repelled by a 'sordid' church as by the folly of faith."

Bray observes: "Tertullian's writings became controversial at the very moment when his works were more widely circulated and more generally read than ever before. The objection made was not that they taught false doctrine . . . but that they portrayed the Church as an exclusive body of saints which rejected any kind of compromise with the world."

Others would perhaps find that the best explanation lies in the nature of Christianity itself. Over the ages Christians would find themselves torn in an unending struggle between the pursuit of further Truth and the acceptance of established doctrine, between zeal and survival, between individual charisma and collective authority, and finally between martyrdom and the accommodation of authority. Tertullian witnessed one such struggle most starkly in the year 203, when he became acquainted with the fate of a young woman known to history as St. Perpetua of Carthage. Tertullian's tract, *To the Martyrs*, was prompted by her story, which follows this chapter.

Tertullian lived on for several decades after Perpetua's martyrdom. His

**TERTULLIAN ON FREEDOM**

*The prison does the same service for the Christian which the desert did for the prophet. Though the body is shut in, though the flesh is confined, all things are open to the spirit. The leg does not feel the chain when the mind is in the heavens.*

declining years were marked by controversy and schism. The asceticism and the explicit appeal to martyrdom of the Montanists irresistibly attracted him, and several of his works are in their defense, written with the same vigor with which he had once defended Christians against pagans. Tertullian's vision was always of a beleaguered and persecuted community of ascetics and martyrs, engaged in warfare:

> Even to Christians the prison is unpleasant—yet, we were called to the service in the army of the living God. No soldier goes out to war encumbered with luxuries, nor does he march to the line of battle from the sleeping chamber, but from light and cramped tents where every kind of austerity, discomfort, and inconvenience is experienced. In like manner, O blessed, consider whatever is hard in your present situation as an exercise of your powers of mind and body. You are about to enter a noble contest in which the living God acts the part of a superintendent, and the Holy Spirit is your trainer; a contest whose crown is eternity, whose prize is angelic nature, citizenship in Heaven and glory forever and ever.

However, true to form, Tertullian eventually quarreled with the Montanists, going off with a handful of his own closest followers, who became known as *Tertullianistae*. (In the fourth century, they would be reintegrated into the Christian community.) Finally, Tertullian quarreled even with the Tertullianistae, finishing up, in effect, as the sole member of a church of one.

And though condemned, his writings were preserved and have been read by Christians in every generation ever since, a tribute to his originality and genius.

Born to rebel, never to compromise, Tertullian might be dismissed as a fanatic, one who saw Christians and the world as locked in conflict, forever incompatible; a man almost nostalgic for the days when the Scillitan Martyrs and Perpetua had spilled their blood to demonstrate that incompatibility. But ironically, Tertullian himself did not die in the arena but in bed, of old age, in about 240. By then the North African church had ninety bishops, and beneath them a hierarchy of

*The Zaghouan-Carthage Aqueduct stretches over the countryside of northern Tunisia. Its massive ruins parallel a modern highway across a rolling green plain near Tunis. Carthage had dams, reservoirs, and aqueducts that allowed fields to be irrigated and agriculture to flourish.*

presbyters, deacons, and thousands of lay adherents. It was a growing and powerful institution. But Tertullian died alone, having cast himself out of the community he had labored most of his life to establish and defend.

Meanwhile, fifteen hundred miles to the east along the Mediterranean coast, in the city of Alexandria, another voice had been raised that would carry farther and more clearly than even Tertullian's, and that story too had begun with a martyrdom.

# *Will it be loyalty to God or to her child? A young mother, Perpetua, had to decide*

**Despite the pleas of her father and the judge who tried her, her answer provides an example that informs Christian history**

In the year 201, the emperor Septimius Severus published a decree forbidding Christians and Jews from seeking converts. It marked the start of a new campaign of persecution against the growing North African Christian community. Yet when a young Carthaginian mother, Vibia Perpetua, was arrested and charged, it was not for proselytizing, but simply for being a Christian. Because of this charge, she would not only suffer death, but she would also keep a detailed diary of her thoughts and dreams as she awaited it, conferring upon the Christians for centuries to come the moving account of a faith that persevered against the pleas of an aggrieved father and the needs of an infant child.

The diary tells little of Perpetua's life before her arrest in the year 203. "She came of a good family; she was well brought up and a respectable married woman," is the only background provided by its anonymous third-century editor. Because of her diary, however, we know a great deal more: we know that her immediate family included her parents and two living brothers (another brother had apparently died in childhood). We know that her father was a man of property with slaves and influence in high places. Perpetua's use of language suggests that she was well-educated.

We also know that when she was arrested, she was nursing her firstborn son. Since we hear nothing of her husband (he is never referred to in the diary and makes no appearance at her trial), some have speculated that he deserted Perpetua when she became a Christian. She is generally thought to have been about twenty-two years old.

How would such a privileged young woman of Carthage have become a convert to Christianity? In her incisive and moving 1997 study *Perpetua's Passion: The Death and Memory of a Young Roman Woman*, author Joyce Salisbury estimates the number of Christians in Carthage at about two thousand. They met regularly in believers' homes, and newcomers tended to be invited guests of family or friends. So it is likely that Perpetua first attended as the guest of someone she knew, perhaps Felicitas, her maidservant, one of four other Christians arrested with her.

Perpetua must have been intrigued by what she heard and saw. Christians cared for one another. (Tertullian, the renowned Christian apologist who would be profoundly influenced by her example, refers to the scope of Christian charity as cause for bewilderment in Carthage.) Christians taught about an afterlife, and they claimed to have the Divine Spirit in their midst. Perpetua soon became acquainted with the sacred texts in use in her congregation: the Gospels of Matthew, Mark, Luke, and John, the Epistles of Paul, the Pentateuch, the Book of Revelation, and certain apocryphal books then in wide circulation, like *Enoch*, the *Apocalypse of Peter*, the *Gospel of Thomas*, and the *Shepherd of Hermas*.

At some point, Perpetua must have moved beyond curiosity to affirmation, because she became a catechumen, as did one of her brothers. A catechumen participated in some aspects of Christian worship, but did not receive the bread and wine of the Eucharist until baptism, after a preparation period of up to three years. However, Perpetua, although only a catechumen, soon exerted a leadership role within the congregation, a role she carried on in prison, and eventually in the arena.

Why the authorities chose to arrest her and her companions is not known. The diary's ancient editor says only: "A number of young catechumens were arrested, Revocatus, Felicitas, Saturninus, and Secundulus, and with them Vibia Perpetua." Sometimes congregations were betrayed by an informer. Sometimes family members who had "lost" a child to what they considered a dangerous cult demanded action from the authorities. Sometimes arrest and prosecution were random. At least one member of Perpetua's congregation, Saturus, was not initially arrested with the others; he gave himself up voluntarily, joining the others in prison and resolved to share in their martyrdom. Certainly women were shown no preference; proportionate to their numbers, more women than men were then being martyred.

The prosecutor in Perpetua's case was the acting procurator, Hilarianus. Tertullian reports that there had been much anti-Christian agitation at that time; perhaps Hilarianus was trying to appease the mob by making an example of Perpetua and her little band. At first, she was placed under house arrest only, but for Perpetua, this was particularly difficult, as the diary explains:

> While we were still under arrest, my father, out of love for me was trying to persuade me and shake my resolution. "Father," said I, "do you see this vase here . . . ?"
> "Yes I do," said he.
> And I told him: "Could it be called by any other name than what it is?"
> And he said: "No."
> "Well, so too I cannot be called anything other than what I am, a Christian."
> At this my father was so angered by the word "Christian" that he moved towards me as though he would pluck my eyes out. But he left it at that and departed, vanquished along with his diabolical arguments.

*Perpetua's father brought her baby and pleaded with her to perform the ritual sacrifice. "Have pity on your father's old age; have pity on your infant son," he urged. "Offer the sacrifice for the welfare of the emperors."*

*The inexperienced gladiator's first thrust struck Perpetua just below the collarbone, injuring but not killing her. She took his trembling hand and guided it to her own throat.*

Instead of renouncing her faith, Perpetua chose the first days of her house arrest to be baptized and received into full communion. At her baptism, she experienced a vision, foreseeing that her future would be short and end in martyrdom. Then she was taken away.

The prison was close to the governor's residence, on the Byrsa hill in the center of Carthage. The dungeon where Perpetua and the others were held was underground, fetid, and crowded: "I was terrified," she writes, "as I had never been in such a dark hole. What a difficult time it was! With the crowd, the heat was stifling; then there was the extortion of the soldiers; and to crown it all, I was tortured with worry for my baby there."

Perpetua was nursing ("I nursed my baby, who was faint from hunger"), and she continued to do so as long as that was possible, before giving the baby over to her own mother. Later during her imprisonment, she had a nervous breakdown, upon which her captors reunited her with her baby. "At once I recovered my health, relieved as I was of my worry and anxiety over the child. My prison had suddenly become a palace, so that I wanted to be there rather than anywhere else."

One morning, the five prisoners were led under guard from the jail to the forum. Perpetua noted that "a huge crowd" had gathered to witness the proceedings. When it came her turn to be questioned, her father appeared, carrying the baby. "Perform the sacrifice—have pity on your baby," her father called out. Even Hilarianus was moved: "Have pity on your father's old age; have pity on your infant son," he urged. "Offer the sacrifice for the welfare of the emperors."

"I will not," Perpetua replied. Hilarianus then asked the inescapable question: "Are you a Christian?" "Yes, I am a Christian," Perpetua replied. Hilarianus quickly passed sentence. Perpetua writes: "We were condemned to the beasts, and we returned to prison in high spirits."

Now when she sought to get her baby back, her father refused. She had broken her ties to both family and country. Harrowing as that moment must have been, her faith found grace even then: "As God willed, the baby had no further desire for the breast, nor did I suffer any inflammation; and so I was relieved of any anxiety for my child and of any discomfort in my breasts."

The bulk of Perpetua's prison diary is devoted to her visions and dreams. To today's mind, these may seem odd, even bizarre, but to a second-century Christian, steeped in the tradition of ecstatic prophecy, dreams were highly meaningful.[4] One of her dreams involved ascending a ladder made of swords, spears, and spikes; at the top, she found a "tall gray-haired man sitting in shepherd's garb . . . milking sheep," who said to her, "I am glad you have come, my child." In another dream, she was taken from prison to the arena, where she was stripped, rubbed with oil, and, discovering that she had become a man, was made to fight an Egyptian warrior, whose face she crushed in the dust. In yet another dream, she is joined by Saturus, the Christian who had volunteered to join the other martyrs. The two were transported by four angels to Heaven, where she heard the endless refrain, "Holy, holy, holy." The martyrs kissed the face of their Lord, and Perpetua said: "Thanks be to God, for I am now even happier than I was in the flesh."

Whatever their psychological significance, Perpetua's dreams convinced her

---

4. In his treatise *On the Soul*, Tertullian devoted several chapters to the significance of dreams. They originated, he argued, either from God or the devil. Dreams that originated from God were prophetic and trustworthy; dreams originating from the devil could be either true or false, but they were never to be trusted. In *The Shepherd of Hermas*, a popular second-century text which some, like Tertullian, advocated as worthy of inclusion in the then-assembling New Testament, Hermas is led into wisdom by five dreams. Since Perpetua was familiar with *The Shepherd of Hermas*, she may have thought that, by recording her dreams, she was following this example.

*The ruins of the amphitheater in Carthage. On March 7, A.D. 203, Pepetua was led through the tunnels beneath the arena to meet her fate in front of a crowd of thirty thousand jeering spectators. At the center of the ruin stands a chapel dedicated to Perpetua and Felicitas.*

that what was happening to the Christians was God's plan. By the time she was led from prison to the arena, singing and radiant, she was convinced that she was to become a bride of Christ's, going not to a painful and squalid death, but to a wedding feast where she would see her beloved face-to-face, and dwell with him forever.

Perpetua's diary ends with her prison dreams. As she put it: "So much for what I did up until the eve of the contest. About what happened at the contest itself, let him write of it who can."

The anonymous diary editor adds one bittersweet prison story. Felicitas, the serving-girl who was arrested with Perpetua, was eight months pregnant. "She became greatly distressed that her martyrdom would be postponed because of her pregnancy, for it is against the law for women with child to be put to death." So Perpetua and the others prayed with her, and God answered their prayers; two days before the execution date, Felicitas went into premature labor and was delivered of a baby girl, who was then turned over "to one of the sisters [who] brought her up as her own daughter."

Any important Roman city had an amphitheater. Carthage's amphitheater, located on the city's northwest edge, was particularly impressive. Its arena measured roughly the size of an American football field, and the steeply raked stands encircling the arena accommodated thirty thousand spectators. Today visitors can still walk the subterranean tunnels through which wild beasts and martyrs were herded to their deaths.

On March 7 in the year 203, the birthday of the emperor's youngest son, Geta Caesar, Perpetua was led through the dank underground tunnels, singing a psalm. Then she and Felicitas were stripped and propelled naked into the arena before a jeering crowd. Two of the Christian men had already faced a leopard and a wild boar and had been injured, although not mortally. But for the women the authorities had chosen a mad cow. This was meant to add insult, in that the women were to be humiliated by being killed by an animal of their own sex.

Suddenly there was silence. "The crowd was horrified when they saw that one was a delicate young girl and the other was a woman fresh from childbirth with the milk still dripping from her breasts. And so they were brought back again and dressed in unbelted tunics."

The mad cow attacked, tossing Perpetua and knocking Felicitas to the ground. Perpetua went to Felicitas and helped her to her feet. But the cow seemed to lose interest in the proceedings, and with nothing much happening, the two women were led out of the arena, a temporary reprieve. This gave Perpetua an opportunity to tell the other Christians who were awaiting their fate: "You must all stand fast in the faith and love one another, and do not be weakened by what we have gone through."

Then a platform was erected in the center of the arena, and all of the Christians were led in, in a group. When they had mounted the scaffold, a gladiator plunged his sword into the neck of each, one by one.

The last to die was Perpetua. She bared her throat willingly, but her gladiator was inexperienced; his first thrust of the sword tore into her flesh just below the collarbone, at which she shrieked in pain. Perpetua "then took the trembling hand of the young gladiator and guided it to her own throat."

Joyce Salisbury writes: "For centuries the faithful of Carthage remembered the martyrdom of Perpetua. The recollection was strengthened by the presence of her remains in the basilica. . . . Her deeds were annually recalled by the public reading of her diary, and constantly made relevant . . . by churchmen commenting on the text."

The date of Perpetua's canonization is unknown; like that of other very early martyrs, her sainthood was long recognized by the faithful before it was formally acknowledged. Perpetua and Felicitas appear as martyrs in both the Philocalian calendar of Rome and the Syriac calendar by the fourth century. They are mentioned in the first eucharistic prayer of the Roman rite. Perpetua's feast day is March 7.

History would record one final irony. There is a column to Septimius Severus in Rome. There are churches dedicated to St. Perpetua all over the world. ■

*Part of an ancient inscription from the Basilica Majorum, built to hold the remains of Perpetua, bears the names of those martyred in the Carthage arena in March, A.D. 203.*

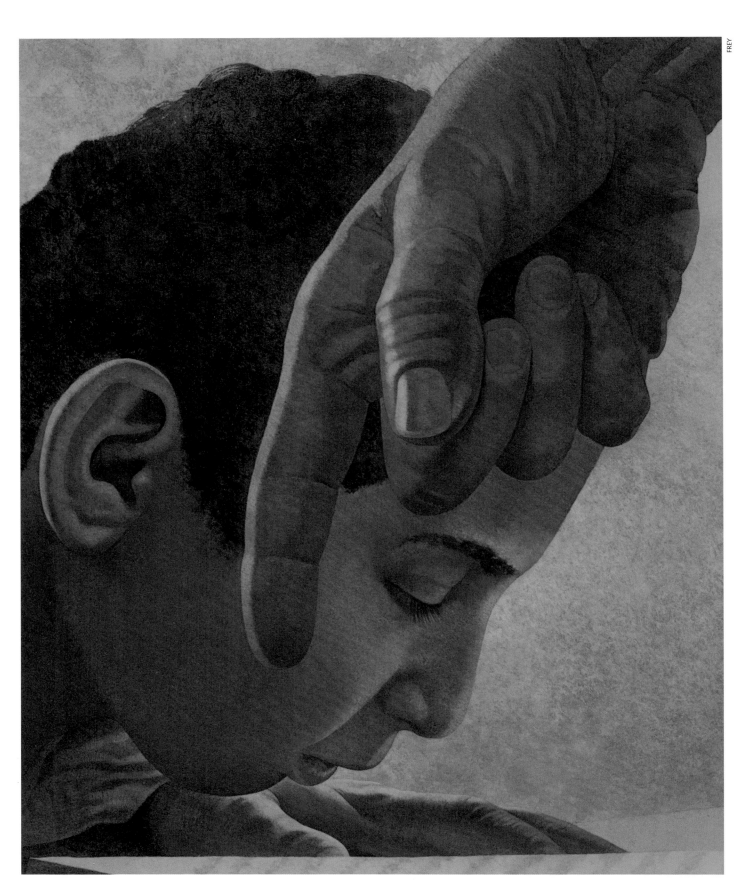

*Origen was a good student. Quick at his studies, he memorized the lines of Scripture his father, Leonides, gave him every day, and raised penetrating questions about their meaning. But Leonides was not just a father and teacher to Origen. He was also his hero.*

# CHAPTER 7

# A Christian giant arises in Egypt

## His father martyred, the boy Origen, saved by his mother, becomes an evangelical powerhouse and a teacher whose students one by one perish

Young Origen of Alexandria could not remember a time when he had never heard of Jesus Christ. He was a product, that is, of a Christian family, a growing phenomenon in the second-century Roman Empire as couples were converted and raised their children in the new faith. It was also a phenomenon that many authorities would have liked to suppress and much of the populace would have liked to destroy. Christians were "atheists," after all. They offended the gods and brought needless ruin on the world. Such was the popular view. As Origen had known since infancy, being a Christian was a very dangerous business.

Still, he and his six younger brothers felt a powerful security in the figure of their father, Leonides (pronounced *Le-ON-i-dees*), a loyal Roman and a prominent resident of the empire's second most important city. In the past, few Christians had been arrested in Alexandria, though it was certainly happening elsewhere in the empire. Moreover, no official felt strong enough to take down Leonides, despite the fact that he made no secret of his faith and spoke boldly of it in public. His sons not only loved him, they lived in awe of him. He was their father and their hero.

He was tough, too, especially in his insistence that they use the minds God had given them to learn the faith they must live by. Origen (his name in English is pronounced like the word "origin") was a particularly good student. Quick at his studies, he not only memorized the lines of Scripture his father gave him every day, he raised penetrating questions about their meaning. Don't go prying into things too great for you, his father had admonished him. He was just a boy; he must be content with the simplest understanding of these passages.

Leonides was, of course, pleased. As his young son lay sleeping the father would quietly kiss his chest, dwelling place of the Holy Spirit.[1] The flame of faith was burning bright and hungry in this lad. He was an unfolding treasure. What would he become when he grew up?

But Leonides did not live to see his son grow up. There came one day the dreaded knock on the door, or so at least one may suppose. A new governor named Laetus (pronounced as *LAY-tus*) had been appointed for Alexandria, a new regime was in office, and a crackdown on Christians was under way. A warrant had been issued for the arrest of Leonides. He was taken away, says the Christian historian Eusebius. The penalty was high. Not only would he face death, his property would be seized, his family made homeless and destitute, and his wife left solely responsible for raising the seven children. All this he could escape by simply denying Christ, swearing the oath or burning the incense.

His eldest son inscribed an urgent letter to him. "Be sure that you don't change your mind because of us," he wrote—don't relent, but die as a martyr in the faith all the family holds dear. Origen need not have worried. Leonides knew what he had to do. How long the trial lasted, history does not record. There is no record of proceedings. But when the day came that the judge pronounced the death sentence, the teenaged Origen resolved to join his father and perish with him.

---

1. In the Coptic (i.e., Egyptian) tradition and in that of other churches, the kiss is a gesture of veneration. Just as Leonides kissed the breast of his sleeping little boy because the heart was discerned as the dwelling place of the Holy Spirit, a Coptic priest kisses the altar of the church and also the book containing the Gospels, indicating that through them the Holy Spirit acts and speaks.

Frantically he searched for his clothes, but they were nowhere to be found. Die as a martyr, he was prepared to do. Run through the streets of Alexandria naked, he was not. St. Leonides died that day beneath a Roman executioner's sword. The year was A.D. 202. Origen was sixteen. He lived because his mother had hidden his clothes—lived to become the man many regard as the greatest Christian writer, theologian, and evangelist of the postbiblical period. All Christendom for the next two thousand years would become the beneficiary of his mother's action.

Origen was also an Egyptian and an Alexandrian, and that meant something. Alexandria was a fascinating, powerful, and volatile city. Rome was the capital

*Leonides did not live to see his son grow up. A warrant had been issued for his arrest. The penalty for his faith would be high. Not only would he face death, his property would be seized and his family made homeless and destitute.*

of the empire, but Alexandria was wealthier and more cosmopolitan; the center of learning and the site of renowned landmarks. The port's lighthouse rose four hundred feet into the air and was accounted one of the seven wonders of the ancient world. There was a zoo, a museum, and an astonishing library comprising almost a million books, by far the greatest collection in antiquity.

Geography favored this queen of cities. Situated near the westernmost of the four mouths of the Nile River, it linked the worlds of Europe, Africa, and the

*One of the Seven Wonders of the Ancient World, the Pharos, or Lighthouse, of Alexandria was forty stories high (about 380 feet) and the tallest building on Earth. It was said the light from its mirror could be seen more than thirty-five miles offshore, reflecting sunlight during the day and fire at night. Built on an island at the entrance to the harbor, the lighthouse survived almost intact until severely damaged by earthquakes in A.D. 1303 and 1323. In 1480 Egypt's Mamluk rulers built a fort (right) on the spot where it had stood, using the fallen stone and marble. In the ancient world the image of the Pharos was so recognizable it was often used on coins (as happens with famous monuments today). This example (above), an Egyptian bronze coin from the reign of Emperor Antoninus Pius (A.D. 138–161), shows the god Isis holding out a sail towards a depiction of the famous lighthouse.*

Far East, and through it the grain of Egypt, breadbasket of the empire, poured across the Mediterranean to Italy and Rome. Alexandria was a crossroads for populations as well. In addition to the native Egyptians who spoke Coptic,[2] the city was inhabited by Greeks and Jews. These bore a habitual grudge against each other, frequently resulting in massive bloodshed. The rest of the empire thought of Alexandrians as clever, boastful, sarcastic, and, finally, defiant of authority—a product of their imaginative ingenuity that was destined one day to cost them their language and national identity. A Roman admirer of the city wrote that if he were assigned the task of defending Alexandrians and proving that they were neither irresponsible nor treacherous, he would find the task

2. The word Copt and the word Egypt both derive from the Greek word *aigyptos*, which has provided the name for the country in most modern languages. Thus the "Coptic Church" is simply another way of saying the Egyptian church. The Coptic language, which descended from the language of the Pharaohs, was spoken in Egypt until the tenth century A.D., when it was supplanted by Arabic. It survives today, however, as the liturgical language of the Coptic Church.

hopeless. "I could make a long speech, but it would be a wasted effort," he said.

Within this ferment, many religions mixed. Judaism was flavored with Platonism, and Greek gods were grafted onto Egyptian deities. Jews had long maintained a strong and scholarly presence in Alexandria, and one of lasting historic significance, for it was here that the Greek version of the Old Testament, the Septuagint, was created (see Chapter 3, *The Veil Is Torn*, p. 72). The indigenous Egyptian religion tended toward animal worship, and each town might have its own animal, bird, or fish as a deity, leading to rivalries that could turn bloody.[3] Romans thought this Egyptian proclivity ridiculous. However, they learned that Egyptians took it very seriously when a Roman soldier accidentally killed a cat and was lynched by a mob.

The historian Eusebius describes Alexandria as a "large . . . company of believers, men and women alike . . . with an extremely severe rule of life." Such "asceticism" as it is called, from the Greek word used to describe athletic training, went back to Paul's observation that "I pommel my body and subdue it" (1 Cor. 9:27). It involved strict fasts, indifference to material possessions, a celibate life, contempt for the body and physical comfort, and removal of oneself from the security of even a home. This stern regimen would characterize Egyptian Christianity for centuries to come. But it probably originates in one of the two conflicting versions of Gnosticism (see sidebar, p. 218), both of which took deep root in Egypt and Alexandria during the first and early second centuries.

By then, Alexandria had surpassed both Rome and Athens as the empire's liveliest center of intellectual inquiry. The church at Alexandria shared this robust mood. It was the most theologically active and the wealthiest Christian body in the empire. Five strong figures had dominated early Christian history in Alexandria. Origen was to become the sixth.

The first of those figures was that ubiquitous personage of the New Testament, John Mark. He is identified by Paul as the cousin of Barnabas (Col. 4:10), who quit the Paul-Barnabas mission into Galatia, costing him Paul's confidence (Acts 15:37–41). He later accompanied Barnabas on a mission to Cyprus (Acts 15:39), and still later, having reconciled with Paul, turned up in Rome (Col. 4:10; 2 Tim. 4:11; Philem. 24). Mark is also associated with Peter (1 Pet. 5:13), whose memoirs Mark wrote, says the first-century Christian historian Papias. These became the Second Gospel of the New Testament.

---

3. The first-century Greek historian Plutarch records that in his time, citizens of an Egyptian town whose religion sanctified dogs had eaten a kind of snouted fish called an oxyrhynchus, which was the deity of a neighboring village. Those citizens responded in indignation by sacrificing and eating a dog. A bloody battle ensued that was not settled until the Roman army intervened.

Tradition, though not the Bible, also identifies Mark as the son of the Mary in whose house at Jerusalem the Last Supper took place, and where some seven weeks later the Holy Spirit descended on the apostles at Pentecost. Finally, it is reasonable to conclude that the young man who escaped naked after Jesus' arrest in the garden of Gethsemane is the same John Mark (Mark 14:51), since none of the other three Gospels mentions the incident. Eusebius adds to the story: From Rome, Mark traveled to Alexandria, he writes, and became the first bishop of the Egyptian or Coptic Church.

In the Coptic tradition, Mark had been born into a Jewish family in Libya, where Berber attacks on his village forced his parents to flee. They resettled in Cana of Galilee. Thereafter, Coptic accounts vary. In one version, Peter became a family friend, and, after the death of Mark's father, took a hand in raising the boy. Peter refers to Mark in his first epistle as his son, using the Greek term indicating a familial rather than a merely spiritual relationship. By the time of the Resurrection, Mark's widowed mother had moved to Jerusalem, where he, now a teenager, became part of the Christian community. The ancient tradition calls him "stumpy-fingered," which may have meant that his hands were deformed or mutilated, but the mysterious disability did not prevent him from being Peter's scribe.

The Copts record a miracle on Mark's first arrival in Alexandria, around A.D. 45. The story goes that on disembarking from his ship, he went looking for a cobbler to repair a broken sandal strap. He found a workman named Anianus,

*The ancient tradition calls Mark 'stumpy-fingered,' which may mean his hands were deformed, but the mysterious disability did not prevent him from being Peter's scribe.*

who tackled the stubborn leather with too much zeal and drove the awl into his own left hand. As Anianus howled with pain, Mark made clay of spittle and dust, prayed, and anointed the wound, healing it instantly. Anianus, already a Christian, took Mark to his home. Another very early believer from Alexandria was the mysterious Apollos, who later moved to Ephesus and Corinth, and assisted Paul. However, there is no known connection between Apollos and Mark (see *The Veil Is Torn*, p. 144).

Coptic Christians believe that Mark served as Alexandria's bishop until the year 62, when his labor for the Gospel began to attract hostile attention. Appointing Anianus as bishop, along with twelve priests and seven deacons, he fled the city—not an act of cowardice, say the Copts, since Jesus himself had said, "When they persecute you in one town, flee to the next" (Matt. 10:23). A few years later, Mark slipped back into Alexandria, and was greeted joyfully by his spiritual children. But this time he could not evade the Christians' opponents. He was captured, tied to the tail of a horse, and dragged over the cobbled streets of Alexandria until his body was torn to pieces. The year, say the Copts, was A.D. 68.[4]

However historically substantial these Coptic traditions of Mark's ministry in Alexandria, one thing seems very substantial indeed: the next sixty to one hundred years of Christian history in the empire's second city are a blank. Eusebius, who composed the first comprehensive history of the church in the early fourth century, lists the names of the bishops who succeeded Mark—Anianus, Abilius, Cerdon, and so forth—but it is not until the tenth bishop, Julian, that he supplies more than a bare name, and by then, more than a hundred years have passed.

"If Christianity was taken to Egypt by the middle of the first century," writes C. Wilfred Griggs in his authoritative *Early Egyptian Christianity*, "an inexplicable silence in Christian sources concerning the leaders of the movement and the development of the church over the next 125 to 150 years is probably unique in the history of Christianity."

Oddly, it was not until the twentieth century that any real clue to the missing years of early Egyptian Christianity came to light. At Nag Hammadi, sixty miles downstream from modern Luxor on the Nile, a collection of thirteen papyrus codices was found in a jar buried in a pagan cemetery, eleven of them complete with their leather

**St. SARGIUS CHURCH**
The Oldest Church in Egypt

WHERE THE HOLY FAMILY LIVED FOR SOME TIME DURING THEIR STAY IN EGYPT

*An Epiphany service (above) at the Coptic Cathedral of St. Mark in Cairo, named for the first bishop of the Coptic or Egyptian church. Martyred in A.D. 68, in the Coptic tradition Mark played a central role in establishing the Christian community in Egypt, which still survives in Cairo's Church of St. Sargius (below), built, says the plaque (left), on the spot where the Holy Family—Joseph, Mary and the infant Christ—rested at the end of their journey from Bethlehem.*

4. The remains of Mark's body, or what the Copts believed are his remains, were stolen by the Italians in the ninth century and removed to Rome. In 1968, the relics were returned to the Coptic Church on orders from Pope Paul VI.

The influence of the Greek philosopher Plato (above) was so important in the early Christian era that both Basilides and Clement of Alexandria used elements of Platonism to enhance their own teachings.

bindings. Written in Coptic and dated from the third to fifth centuries, they constituted a library of Gnostic texts, evidence of early Egyptian preoccupation with Gnosticism. Significantly, another discovery, made a half-century earlier at the Faiyum Oasis, 250 miles north of Nag Hammadi, included a fragment of John's Gospel dated to the beginning of the second century, equally tangible evidence of very early Christian activity in Egypt (see p. 31).

So what happened? Were the Christians and Gnostics in keen dispute during these missing years? There is no evidence of it. One theory is that the story of Mark's evangelism in Alexandria is a myth, and that Christianity came to the city later from an unknown source. But Alexandria was the second city of the empire, and it would not have been long neglected by Christian missionaries. Then there is the further evidence of the gospel fragment. So the mystery remains.

By the year 130, the fog suddenly lifts. The second great figure of Alexandrian Christianity appears in the person of a man who was later denounced as not Christian at all. His name was Basilides (Bas-i-LIE-dees). He began as a conventional Christian, but in his quest to enhance Christianity with elements drawn from Judaism, paganism, and Platonism, he developed in Alexandria a full-flowered Gnosticism. It was an immense project, his influence

# Devout believer or ancient con man?

**Despite a criminal past, Peregrinus became a Christian hero, then bilked the brethren—Was he a total phony? The historians still can't decide**

His unflattering nickname was "Proteus," after a mythological sea god given to assuming various shapes, just as Proteus kept changing his religion. But his real name, Peregrinus, means "wanderer." Down through the centuries, those who have examined the life of Peregrinus Proteus have asked several questions: Was he sincere but misguided? Or was he a self-promoting sham, a second-century forerunner of the twentieth-century religious con man, warming the hearts of the faithful while emptying their pockets? And whatever he was, why did he suicidally set fire to himself after the Olympic games?

The case for Peregrinus as a fraud is laid out by the skeptical satirist Lucian of Samosata in a detailed account of Peregrinus's life. Lucian wrote fiction, but Peregrinus was not one of his invented characters, since he's mentioned by other contemporary writers, including Tatian, Athenagoras, Tertullian, Maximus Tyrias, and Eusebius.

Born to a wealthy family at Parium on the Hellespont, the straits known to later history as the Dardanelles at the northeast corner of the Aegean, he first ran afoul of authority by committing adultery. He then "corrupted a handsome boy," and managed to escape the consequences by paying off the boy's impoverished parents. Those misdeeds might have been passed off as youthful indiscretions, but Lucian also reports that Peregrinus's criminal activity rapidly expanded. He strangled his father to death "and bought his way out of justice by deeding his property to the city."

No longer welcome at home, he began roaming from one country to another. When he discovered the community of Christians in Palestine, he quickly joined, learning everything he could about their beliefs. "In a trice he made them all look like children," Lucian writes, "for he was prophet, cult-leader, and head of the synagogue. . . . He interpreted and explained some of their books, and even composed many."

After being seized and imprisoned for his participation in the new faith, he received "every form of attention" from the Christians whom he had dazzled. "From the very break of day, aged widows and orphan children could be seen waiting near the prison," Lucian writes. "Elaborate meals were brought in for him, and sacred books were read aloud. . . . Indeed, people came even from the cities in was enormous, and since it had no self-correcting boundaries, it rapidly grew into the bizarre.

Just how bizarre was explained in the Christians' response to Basilides. Irenaeus, the bishop of Lyon, in his *Against Heresies* written in 180, reports that Basilides taught that there is an ultimate God who existed before all things, and that he begot Thought, Logos, Prudence, and other powers. From these powers proceeded yet further powers, and by successive steps, there emerged 365 levels of "heavens" between this earth and the original or ultimate God. According to Basilides, this Earth is ruled by the God of the Jews, Yahweh, whom he saw as a minor and corrupt deity. When conflict arose among the spiritual powers of this earth, Yahweh appealed to the "unoriginate" God for help, and in response he sent his "first emanation." This was Thought, who was to be born as Christ on earth. Since it is impossible for such a lofty entity to suffer, at the time of the Crucifixion, Jesus switched places with Simon of Cyrene. . . . On and on it goes, Basilides' disciples adding their own further details, as did Valentinus, Heracleon, and other Gnostic teachers during the second century.

Alexandrians reveled in all this. Always creative and imaginative, they delighted in finding hidden mysteries behind ancient texts, in exploring ever-deepening

Asia, sent by the Christians at their common expense, to succor and defend and encourage the hero. They show incredible speed whenever any such public action is taken; for in no time, they lavish their all."

Adds the skeptical Lucian: "The poor [Christian] wretches, their first lawgiver persuaded them that they are all brothers of one another, after they have transgressed once. . . . So if any charlatan and trickster, able to profit by occasions, comes among them, he quickly acquires sudden wealth by imposing upon simple folk."

Having impressed the Syrian governor with his philosophies, Peregrinus was freed and began again "to roam about, possessing an ample source of funds from the Christians, through whose ministrations he lived in unalloyed prosperity."

Eventually, however, he slipped up. He was seen sneaking food that the Christians forbade, and he was ejected from their company. After trying unsuccessfully to recover his property from the city where his father was slain, he dabbled in Yoga and Brahmanism, taking up residence in Rome as a Cynic philosopher until he was expelled for publicly mocking the emperor. So off he went to Greece, where he "libeled a man outstanding in literary attainments and position" and barely escaped a mob bent on stoning him to death.

"At last, he was disregarded by all, and no longer so admired," Lucian writes, "for all his stuff was stale, and he could not turn out any further novelty." Still craving acclaim, he announced that after the end of the Olympic games in 165, he would burn himself to death in public. He seemed confident that the crowd would "cling to him and not give him over to the fire, but retain him in life—against his will, naturally."

So he arranged for a pit full of wood to be set ablaze outside the city of Olympia. However, instead of begging him to save himself, the crowd began chanting, "Carry out your purpose!" After exclaiming, "Spirits of my mother and my father, receive me with favor," he jumped into the flames, which consumed him.

"I could not control my laughter," says Lucian, at the thought of Peregrinus invoking the spirit of the father whom he had murdered. In the end, Lucian sums him up as a "poor wretch" who "never fixed his gaze on the verities, but always did and said everything with a view to glory and the praise of the multitude." By some accounts, Peregrinus had a cult following for a brief time after his death, and a statue was erected in his memory.

His story reveals important details about Christianity in the mid-second century. There were food laws (which he broke); worship still took place in a synagogue (which he for a time led); and there was extensive communication between communities separated by hundreds of miles (which sent emissaries to feed and comfort him in prison).

The classical scholar A. M. Harmon in his translation of *Lucian* observes that many critics see Peregrinus not as a fake, but as "an earnest seeker after truth." However, Harmon writes, such events as his attempting to get back the inheritance he renounced after murdering his father "make it impossible to see in him an 'earnest and steadfast man'." ∎

levels of illumination through arduous stages of initiation, and finally, in joining the predestined few who had finally arrived at the doorstep of secret wisdom. The more preposterous it sounded, and the more complex the "truths," the more likely its validity, they said, because it involved realities that ordinary, unenlightened people could never deduce for themselves.

As for the human body and how the individual should regard it, Gnosticism took two diametrically different paths. Some schools taught that the body was a "cage of mud," in which an evil god (often the Jewish Yahweh) had imprisoned pure souls. The body must therefore be despised, they said, and extreme disciplines followed from this. Others, like the Gnostic and avowed Christian Carpocrates (pronounced *Car-po-CRA-tees*), considered the body irrelevant, and taught that therefore one could do with it whatever one pleased. All constraints could be ignored. The excesses that followed from this can be imagined.

### 'You're our next bishop,' someone declared. Demetrius's first reaction was to turn and run. Placed in fetters, he had to be 'forcibly' persuaded to assume the office.

To the Christians at Alexandria, it rapidly became clear that unless some means could be found to distinguish Christianity from Gnosticism, the former would disintegrate into a chaos of theological gibberish and moral squalor. The man who first realized this, and did something about it, became the third great figure of Alexandrian history, and the one about whom the least is known. His name was Pantaenus (*Pan-TEE-nus*), and the method he chose to correct the problem was to establish a school in about 190, known as the Catechetical School of Alexandria. In it, he began training Christian teachers, evangelists, and other leaders, carefully distinguishing what Christians believed from what Gnostics believed. Pantaenus was a Jew, probably from Sicily because he was known as "the Sicilian Bee," a nickname conferred on him by one of his students who saw him as collecting nectar from "all the flowers of the prophetic and apostolic meadow." Schooled in Hebrew, he studied Greek philosophy in Sicily and became a Stoic, employing elements of Pythagorean Platonism before converting to Christianity. He brought with him to Alexandria a global wealth of knowledge, and was the first head of the school, an institution without equal in the ancient Christian world, probably the first Christian seminary.

Little else is known about Pantaenus, except for one curious story. His work at the Catechetical School was interrupted one day by unexpected visitors. A delegation from India had become so impressed with reports of his teaching that they asked him to come with them to engage and challenge the Hindu teachers of their land. The bishop of Alexandria agreed that Pantaenus should go, and the amazing accuracy with which other Alexandrian Christians, one of them Origen, later described the culture of India, lends great credibility to the story. The information doubtless came from Pantaenus's reports back to Alexandria, or from students he sent from India to the Catechetical School.

The fourth figure in Egyptian Christianity is the bishop credited with sending Pantaenus to India. This was Bishop Demetrius of Alexandria, who presided over the city's Christians from 190 to 233, a forty-three-year regime, during which he curbed the doctrinal and moral chaos wrought by Gnosticism and established Alexandrian Christianity as a major influence in Christian development for the next four centuries.

His own background was far from academic. In the Coptic tradition, he was an illiterate, married farmer, a Christian who became a bishop as the result of an odd occurrence. His predecessor, Bishop Julian, lay dying, and suddenly had a vision that the man who should be the next bishop would visit him the next day bearing a gift of fresh grapes. And on the following day, Demetrius, doubtless a faithful member of Julian's flock, came to his bedside bearing clusters of grapes from his vineyard. The scene that followed can be reconstructed. Those attending the stricken man would have stared wide-eyed as the farmer bearing his grapes entered the room. There would have been a moment of unbelief. This? Muddy boots? Rustic, weathered face? This, the next bishop of Alexandria? A man who could neither read nor write was to become bishop of what was probably the most literate Christian community in all the empire?

Still, the vision was the vision. "You're our next bishop," someone would have declared. Apparently, Demetrius's first reaction was to turn and run. He was seized by the others, says Eusebius. The farmer was plainly panic-stricken. Placed in fetters, he had to be "forcibly" persuaded to assume the office, but he became a tough administrator with a farmer's sense of practical reality. When he died, the Gnostic influence in Alexandria had been significantly diminished.

Pantaenus's successor as principal of the Catechetical School was the fifth of the five luminaries who preceded Origen. Given a proud Roman name, Titus Flavius Clemens (known as Clement) was born a pagan at Athens and became a convert to Christianity as a young man. He traveled widely in search of education, gaining instruction in the faith from teachers throughout the Mediterranean world, and enrolled as a pupil in Pantaenus's school. When Pantaenus departed for India, around A.D. 190, Clement succeeded him as principal.

He arrived at Alexandria just as

*This first-century Pompeiian mosaic, now held by the Museo Archaeologico in Naples, depicts the school of Plato, known as the Academy. The teacher is shown surrounded by his students. Origen would have conducted his school at Alexandria in much the same way.*

Clement instructs his students in the Catechetical School at Alexandria. He set out to forge a middle path between Gnostic speculation and the Christian anti-intellectuals. He wanted to show educated pagans that it was possible to become a Christian without sacrificing intelligence, and to show that even Plato and the Greek philosophers had grasped some elements of Christian truth.

Pantaenus had begun seriously addressing the Gnostic problem. The Christians were divided, some deeply into Gnosticism, others so bitterly appalled at the proliferation of bizarre competing theories masquerading as advanced knowledge that they had become hostile to any intellectual endeavor at all. Clement plunged into the fray. With the generous and optimistic spirit that made his writings appealing as well as persuasive, he set out to forge a middle path between Gnostic speculation and the Christian anti-intellectuals. He wanted to show educated pagans that it was possible to become a Christian without sacrificing their intelligence, and to show wary believers that even Plato and the Greek philosophers had grasped some elements of Christian truth (thanks, Clement believed, to their study of the Hebrew Scriptures).

Philosophy was to the Greeks what the Law was to the Jews, he said. It was a schoolmaster preparing them to receive the coming of Christ. "One indeed is the way of Truth," he writes, "but into it, as into an ever-flowing river, streams from everywhere are confluent." And while philosophy might inform faith, it was Scripture that ultimately ruled. But in reading Scripture, Clement proposed a twofold guide to prevent Gnostic excesses. First, that Christians never take literally any

## Clement's treatise opposing the Gnostic libertines was so graphic that the editors of an 1885 translation of his work put the offending passages in Latin, for 'scholars only.'

passages that seem to be fundamentally contrary to the nature of God (he thereby refuted the Gnostics who saw the God of the Old Testament as unreasonable and cruel). Second, they should consider each passage in the light of the Bible as a whole (a check on the Gnostics whose overactive imaginations could spin strange fantasies from a single verse).

Clement's works abound in quotations from classical philosophy, designed to put the cultivated reader at ease while leading him past the objections that classical thought presented to Christianity. For example, Platonists asked, if God is by definition unchanging, how could he leave Heaven and become human? Clement answered that what was unchanging was God's love for humankind. That love is manifested through his providence, which would necessarily adapt to changing human needs, and Jesus was a crowning example of God's never-changing love, expressed in God's breakthrough into the natural world, an act of rescue.

Clement also worked to resolve another conflict, that between the Gnostic

---

5. Clement's attack on the sexual escapades of the Carpocratian Gnostics, considered by nineteenth-century translators too crude for all but the scholarly, would scandalize few twenty-first-century readers. In order to procreate the race, says Clement, God "has implanted in the male a strong and energetic sexual desire. Law cannot make this disappear, nor can social mores or anything else." However, sexual intercourse "while natural," is not "necessary," in that the individual can survive without it. There are therefore times when the "highly sexed young male" must restrain himself. But to give free rein to these instincts as do the Carpocratians who indulge in wife swapping and other disgusting practices, is to behave "like pigs and goats." And to suggest that "in some combination of immoderation and dirty language lies human freedom" is nonsense. As Scripture says, "Everyone who sins is a slave" (2 Pet. 2:19). As to the Gnostics of the other extreme, the ascetics, "who yearn to be free from marital agreement and participation in decent food," they too are in error.

**CLEMENT ON POSSESSIONS**

*Not a single thing we possess is properly our own. We are truly owners of one possession alone—godliness. When death overtakes us, death will not rob us of this. But from all else, it will eject us.*

libertines and the extreme ascetics.[5] His treatise opposing the former was deemed so graphic in its descriptions that the editors of an 1885 English translation of Clement's *Miscellanies* rendered the passages relating to Carpocrates in Latin so that "scholars only" might peruse it. Yet Clement was also skeptical of a trend among Christians to pursue excessive and demonstrative physical rigors.

The middle way was best, he taught. The rich man need not reduce himself to poverty, but should give generously to the poor and handle his wealth with detachment. Virginity was good, but marriage was better. Clement, in fact, wrote more positively of marital love than did any other Christian of his time. Death by martyrdom, he taught, was no more valuable than a daily martyrdom of the will in which the tumult of selfish desires is stilled and the heart turned toward God. The person is blessed who progresses on this path, immersed in the study of Scripture, ever growing in knowledge of God and tranquil self-control, and actively caring for others.

However, the phenomenon of martyrdom posed further problems for Clement, because Gnosticism made death for the faith unnecessary under any conditions. To the Gnostics, Jesus was often little more than a phantom, so why bother to suffer physically for something so unsubstantial? Second, if the whole of Christianity had to do with "secret" knowledge, how could you bear public "witness" to it (for "witness" is what the Greek word for "martyr" meant)? Finally, if a mystical inner transformation was the most important thing, why balk at doing something as trifling as to offer a pinch of incense to the emperor? After all, Basilides had taught,

## To the Gnostics, Jesus was little more than a phantom, so why suffer physically for something so unsubstantial? And why balk at offering a pinch of incense to the emperor?

or so his critics said, that such capitulation was no crime, and that faith could be denied conveniently and "lightheartedly."

While such a doctrine was poison to a people at the doorstep of suffering, a parallel danger lay on the opposite side. Panicked Christians, like the youthful Origen, might rush into martyrdom, courting it as a way to swiftly resolve the intolerable tension. Some believed that such a headlong action would erase any sins committed in this life and usher the martyr directly into paradise—an easier step, all told, than a life of patient, daily self-discipline. Once again, Clement pointed to the middle path. He opposed "impious and cowardly" Gnostics who mocked true martyrs as foolish, and he upheld martyrdom as an honor for those forced to endure it, a path of cleansing and glory. But those who purposely "rush to their death" are "not martyrs" at all, he said. They "give themselves up to a futile death like Indian fakirs in a senseless fire."

Clement's work was brilliant and effective, but it had a hidden flaw, one which did not become apparent for generations. In all his emphasis on using philosophy to inform Christianity, he failed to question the underlying premise that

# Why the Bible condones slavery— all the ancient world depended on it

**But when the campaign to abolish it finally began, it was the Christians who would lead it—often against fierce opposition from other Christians**

Though it was Christians who during the next twenty centuries would lead the world in a battle to stamp out slavery—often against the determined opposition of other Christians—that battle began, during an era of almost universal acceptance of the practice, which had long been pervasive throughout the Greco-Roman world. As far as is known, Jesus had never preached against slavery; in fact, Paul described Christians as "slaves of God" (Rom. 6:22).

Until the fourth century, the only other mention of slavery by Christians was in the form of appeals to slave masters for compassion and to slaves themselves for obedience. "Slaves, obey your earthly masters with respect, fear, and with sincerity of heart, just as you would obey Christ," Paul wrote in Ephesians 6:9. "Masters, treat your slaves in the same way. And do not threaten them, since you know that he who is both their master and yours is in heaven, and there is no favoritism with him."

Slavery was everywhere accepted in the Mediterranean world, as it was in all major civilizations of the time from Mesopotamia to China. Both the Roman and Greek economies were actually based on slavery, in that slaves comprised the primary workforce in the countryside and the cities. Two cultural traditions made slave labor vital in the Roman Empire. First, it was not acceptable for freemen to take orders from anyone except their fathers or military

*A sculpture of a young black slave, from Aphrodisias, Turkey. With manual labor beneath the dignity of Roman citizens, slavery was omnipresent in the Roman world.*

leaders. Second, it was beneath the dignity of Roman citizens to actually perform manual labor.

By the time of Claudius (A.D. 41–54), historian Edward Gibbon estimates, slaves equaled freemen in number. Later historians put the proportion at perhaps one-third slave in most urban centers. A typical Christian congregation included both slave owners and slaves.

Moral concerns had seldom surfaced. Plato, for example, included a slave class in his ideal republic. Aristotle held that "from the hour of their birth, some are marked out for subjection, others for rule." He presented the view that prevailed among Greeks and Romans: Slavery was good for everyone. Masters gained workers, and slaves benefited from the guidance of their superiors. Only the small sect of the Essenes at Qumran and the Egyptian-Jewish community called the Therapeutae are known to have rejected slavery in principle.[1]

Slavery as practiced in the first-century Roman Empire differed significantly from that in later centuries. Race, for example, played almost no role. Slaves came from all races. Education of slaves was encouraged, and some were better educated than their owners. Many slaves held highly sensitive and responsible positions. They could own property (including other slaves). Their religious practices and responsibilities were the same as those of the freeborn. No laws prohibited public assembly of slaves. Most significant: Urban and domestic slaves could usually expect to be freed by age thirty.

Nor were legal and social status precisely linked. For example, a slave named Erastus was the treasurer of the provincial capital of Corinth, and was probably the most socially distinguished member of that city's Christian congregation. On the other hand, the relationships of masters and slaves were often ambivalent. Slaves or ex-slaves were generally treated as social inferiors, regardless of wealth.

However, many slaves led wretched lives. Those who had been sentenced to slavery by the court as convicted criminals had no hope of manumission, that is, release. Such convicts were usually worked to death

---

1. No Greco-Roman author had ever attacked slavery in principle, not even the philosopher Epictetus, who was raised in slavery. Among Jews, Hebrew law demanded that slaves be treated considerately, and according to Leviticus, Jews were required to treat Jewish slaves better than Gentile slaves (Lev. 25:44–46). Court-ordered slavery for debt payment was usually limited to six years.

in mines or rowing galleys, or forced to fight to the death as gladiators. In rural areas, many slaves performed arduous manual labor. In urban settings some were forced into prostitution, even as children.

On the other hand, domestic slaves often had only light duties, and many slaves worked in what were essentially civil service positions. Indeed, they pursued a wide variety of occupations. Slave ranks included doctors, teachers, writers, grammarians, accountants, agents, bailiffs, overseers, secretaries, singers, actors, and sea captains.

Romans followed practices already established by the Greeks to make the system work smoothly. Beyond receiving room and board, slaves were allowed to earn and save money, and to make contracts. They were given holidays. Often a time limit was placed on their servitude. After A.D. 200, they were allowed to marry, although it remained more usual for a monogamous couple to live in concubinage. For many, slavery provided not only economic security, but also an avenue to eventual prosperity. Most contemplated the prospect of eventual manumission as a reward for faithful work.

Besides being enslaved as a court-imposed punishment following criminal conviction, a variety of circumstances led to people becoming slaves.

Some were sentenced to slavery for debt. (Athens was unique among cities in outlawing enslavement for debt.) Some were born into slavery; some had been taken prisoner in war or captured by pirates. Stealing other human beings had been practiced in the Mediterranean basin for centuries. Often in these societies, people simply abandoned unwanted babies, leaving them to die of exposure. If found alive, these infants were usually raised as slaves.

Many people sold themselves into slavery: to pay debts; to obtain a special job; to climb socially (since Roman citizenship might be bestowed upon release); and most often, to live a more secure and less strenuous life than the freeborn poor could expect. Domestic slaves acquired the social status of the master's household. Slaves who saved enough money were often able to buy back their freedom. Some earned release by performing a particular service. Many were willed freedom at their master's death.

The frequency of manumission actually became a problem in the Roman Empire. Caesar Augustus introduced laws to limit the numbers who could be freed. After the first century, following the end of the great wars of conquest that had brought in a steady stream of captive soldiers, the children of slaves served as the primary source.

Meanwhile, even without explicit teachings in opposition to slavery, Christianity began to erode the system's foundations. Second-century Christians like Justin Martyr deplored the buying and selling of children. Others railed against the trade in gladiators. The spur for this growing Christian opposition to slavery lay in Christian insistence on the equality of all people in Christ. Christian salvation—faith's greatest gift—was equally available to slave and free, and was more important than earthly circumstances. Christians did not share the Roman contempt for work. They regarded converted slaves as brothers and sisters.

"For we were all baptized by one Spirit in the body—whether Jews or Greeks, slave or free," Paul wrote in 1 Corinthians 12:13. "There is neither Jew nor Greek, slave nor free, male nor female, for you are all one in Christ Jesus." In Romans 8:38, he declared that there should be no worldly impediment between believer and God. Thus, from that beginning, Christianity would come to play a decisive historical role in the elimination of slavery. ■

A relief of two actors performing a scene in which a slave is rebuked by his master. It is from the façade of a theater at Sabrata, Libya. Even Plato included a slave class in his ideal republic, reflecting the widespread belief in the ancient world that slavery was good for everyone: Masters gained workers, and slaves benefited from the guidance of their superiors. Only the small sect of the Essenes at Qumran and the Egyptian-Jewish community called the Therapeutae are known to have rejected slavery in principle.

knowledge—*gnosis*—was the real key to enlightenment. He challenged the content of Gnosticism, but tried to recover the word "Gnostic" for Christian use. He believed that some people were "true Gnostics," selected by God to receive advanced revelation and to teach it to others. In his *Miscellanies*, he scattered these revelations in a deliberately jumbled way, so that the illumined could perceive them and the less advanced, who might be harmed by what they could not handle, could not. In a recently discovered letter, Clement writes that Mark did, indeed, compose a secret Gospel which was given only to the inner circle of advanced believers. Thus elements of Gnosticism tarnished his monumental work.[6]

Consistent with his beliefs, when the persecution that claimed Origen's father broke out, Clement fled to Cappadocia in Asia Minor. There he spent his last years with a student, Alexander, and died around 217. The circumstances of his death are not known.

Leonides had been killed, Clement had fled, and the city's Christian community was in disarray. Young Origen struggled to feed his family. But to do so, he must first complete his education. God, as he no doubt saw it, helped him. A wealthy woman, otherwise unidentified, generously provided him with room and board while he finished his studies. He rapidly progressed from student to teacher and was able to contribute to the support of his mother and brothers.

But his father's martyrdom still weighed heavily on him. Should he somehow have persisted in joining his father in death? Was he really as committed to

**CLEMENT ON LOVE OF ENEMIES**

*Loving one's enemies does not mean loving wickedness, ungodliness, adultery or theft. Rather, it means loving the thief, the ungodly, and the adulterer.*

## *Origen soon realized his self-mutilation was an act of folly. He wrote that those who practice it are reviled by people both inside and outside the Christian faith.*

Christ as his father had been? Or was he in reality just a coward? Finally, he resolved on an act which, he decided, would make his own commitment unmistakable. In the ancient pagan religion of Egypt, there had been a means by which young men proved their loyalty to their gods. Why not emulate it as a Christian? Did not the Scripture say that some men "made themselves eunuchs for the kingdom of heaven's sake?" (Matt. 19:12). Suppose he in fact had this done? Would this not once and for all give the lie to all the gossip that Christians were sexually promiscuous? The expedient finally seemed obvious to him. He had himself castrated.

He determined to keep it a secret. But, says the historian Eusebius, this proved impossible. "However much he might wish it, he could not possibly conceal such a thing." When the incident came to the attention of Bishop Demetrius,

---

6. The name of Clement of Alexandria was included in an early Christian calendar of martyrs. But as time passed, Clement slipped from favor. Future generations found much of his work inspiring, but some of it as speculative and as strange as the Gnostic writings he sought to refute. The ninth-century Patriarch of Constantinople, Photius, drew attention to objectionable passages in Clement's writing, and in the sixteenth century Pope Clement VIII had Clement of Alexandria's name removed from the church calendar.

**CLEMENT ON SELF-KNOWLEDGE**

*To know oneself has always been the greatest of all lessons. For, if anyone knows himself, he will know God; and in knowing God, he will become like Him.*

he was "amazed at Origen's headstrong act." He perceived it as evidencing "great courage and devotion, but also reckless immaturity." He nevertheless told the young man to put it in his past, a mistake to be repented and forgotten.

Origen himself realized it had been an act of folly. As an old man, crippled by torture and near death, he wrote a commentary on Matthew's Gospel. When he came to the twelfth verse of the nineteenth chapter, he wrote that those who practice self-mutilation "subject themselves to reviling" from people both inside and outside the faith. They may be motivated by "an imagined fear of God and an intemperate love of sobriety," but they only bring on themselves "troubles and bodily amputation and whatever else the one who gives himself over to such deeds may suffer." He concluded: "True purity does not consist in doing violence to the body, but in mortifying the senses for the kingdom of God."[7]

The Christian community in Alexandria, meanwhile, seemed to be disintegrating. After Clement's departure, there was no one of adequate age and experience to run the Catechetical School. Yet Origen, himself a former student of the school under Clement, was winning an ever-widening reputation as both a teacher of secular philosophy and a Christian evangelist. He was only eighteen, but he had all the other qualifications. Was not a school with an underaged prin-

## The Alexandrian mob hated Origen, on one occasion tried to stone him, and threatened his home so frequently that soldiers had to be stationed around it to prevent riots.

cipal better than no school at all? Bishop Demetrius thought so, and invited Origen to take on the job.

It would be no sinecure. Laetus's persecution had only begun, and one of its chief aims was to put a stop to Alexandria's religious ventures, in particular Christianity. To become a Christian was therefore a perilous step to take, and to register in the Catechetical School was to invite immediate arrest. To actually operate the Catechetical School would seem an act of almost deliberate defiance. Origen certainly knew all this, but he accepted the post anyway. Here perhaps was a far better way of following in his father's footsteps.

But would the students come? Come they did, one by one, all the dangers notwithstanding—young men like Plutarch and his brother, Heraclas, who would one day become bishop of Alexandria, Severus, Hero, and Serenus; and young women like Herias and Potamiaena (pronounced as *Po-ta-mee-AY-na*—see sidebar)—names that would be recorded for perpetuity in Eusebius's history, as all but Heraclas went to their deaths over the next three years, each steadfastly refusing to deny belief in Jesus Christ. Origen himself accompanied each to

---

7. Voluntary castration was never countenanced by the Christians, and a century later, the Nicene Council made it clear that anyone who had been voluntarily castrated could not be a priest. If a man was mutilated against his will, that was not to be charged against him. But to seek the act was to try to escape a common temptation artificially, rather than by growing in self-control. The act was therefore a sign of weakness, an evasion of the daily struggle for holiness that works a far greater transformation in the soul.

prison, visited them all there, and accompanied them to the arena itself to bestow on them the final kiss of peace.

Some came to the school as students, some just to hear him teach and preach, their numbers all the while growing. The abiding mystery of those three years is why the authorities never arrested Origen himself. The Alexandrian mob detested him, on one occasion tried to stone him, and threatened his home so frequently that soldiers had to be stationed around it to prevent riots. Someone high in the Roman administration, probably a Christian, must have been protecting him. It was God who protects him, the Christians would have said.

If so, Origen kept God busy. One day the mob grabbed him, dragged him to the steps of the Temple of Serapis, cut his hair in a pagan rite, dressed him up as a pagan priest, and ordered him to perform the office of priest by distributing palm branches to the worshipers. Origen complied, put the palms in the people's hands, blessed them, and shouted: "Come and receive the palms, not of idols,

# She wouldn't yield to her master's advances

**So a plucky Christian slave is sent to her death, jeering her executioners, later her admiring Roman guard becomes Christian and he too is killed**

The most celebrated of Origen's students to suffer martyrdom at Alexandria was a comely and very determined female slave named Potamiaena, who, according to the fourth-century historian Eusebius, was turned in as a Christian by her master because she kept refusing his advances. Just to make sure she was persuaded to submit, her owner bribed the judge, who ordered her tortured into compliance and then returned to him.

But Potamiaena did not comply, reports the historian Palladius, so she was subjected to more tortures, "dreadful and terrible to speak of." Her mother, Marcella, was charged along with her. Finally the judge threatened to turn Potamiaena over to the gladiators "for bodily abuse" if she did not comply. Palladius describes her response: "After a little consideration, being asked for her decision, she made a reply which was regarded as impious."

She and her mother were then ordered executed forthwith. However, as she was led to her death, a strange thing happened. As the mob crowded in upon her, jeering and insulting her, the Roman officer escorting her drove them back, expressing his sympathy for her and no doubt his admiration for her astonishing courage. She thanked him for his kind words. His name was Basilides.[1] She would speak on his behalf to her Lord, she promised, as soon as this ordeal was over.

It wasn't over yet. The historian Eusebius describes how they dripped burning pitch on various parts of her body, from the soles of her feet to the crown of her head, then finally lit the fire that consumed her.

"Not long after this," writes Eusebius, "being asked by his fellow soldiers to swear for a certain reason, Basilides declared that it was not lawful for him to swear at all, for he was a Christian, and he confessed this openly. At first they thought that he was jesting, but when he continued to affirm it, he was led to a judge, and, acknowledging his conviction, was imprisoned."

Amazed, the Christians visited him in jail. What had caused this? they asked. Three days after her martyrdom, said Basilides, Potamiaena had come to him by night. She had placed a crown on his head "and said that she had besought the Lord for him and had obtained what she asked." Soon, she said, she would come and take him with her.

The Christians baptized him. "The next day," concludes Eusebius, "after giving glorious testimony to the Lord, he was beheaded." ∎

---

1. There are two men named Basilides in early Coptic history, one described in the accompanying chapter and rejected as a Gnostic, the other, this soldier, revered as a martyr.

HARLIN

*As the Christian martyrs are led through the streets of Alexandria on the way to their deaths, Origen boldly salutes them with a kiss, infuriating the accompanying mob to the point of rushing upon him.*

but of Jesus Christ." Amazingly, they let him go.

His school in those years was not really a preparation for a Christian life, says one historian, but a preparation for martyrdom. Yet Origen did not preach martyrdom. "If you want to receive baptism," he would say to his converts, "you must first learn about God's Word, cut away the roots of your vices, correct your barbarous wild lives, and practice meekness and humility. Then you will be fit to receive the grace of the Holy Spirit."

His own life mirrored his preaching. When he accepted the principalship of the school, he vowed to live in poverty, sold all the manuscripts that in earlier years he had carefully copied from the great philosophical works, and adopted what Eusebius calls an "extremely severe rule of life." He spent his days in strenuous labor and most of his nights in Scripture study. He alternated other forms of discipline, sometimes going without

*The Roman theater in Alexandria, Egypt is shown at right. A center of culture and social life in early Christian times, the area around the site contains some of the finest remains of buildings, streets and baths from the third century. Statues, sunken ships, gold coins and jewelry are among the treasures (above) that archaeologists have recovered from the ancient submerged city of Heracleion, off the coast at Alexandria.*

food, sometimes going without sleep, and always making his bed on the floor. He accepted as a stipend four *obols* a day, considerably less than a day's pay for a common laborer. He was said to "cultivate" poverty, going without shoes or warm clothing and eating only the minimum necessary to sustain life. His health soon suffered, and his behavior distressed his friends, who begged him to share their resources. He refused, and he became known to Christians as "Adamantius," the man of steel.

In 207, five years after it had begun, the persecution of Christians in Alexandria was suddenly stopped on imperial authority. Immediately, registration in the school soared. Heraclas, brother of the martyr Plutarch, became the assistant principal, teaching preliminary Christian doctrine. Origen's reputation and writings spread among Christian communities all over the empire. In 212, he was invited to Rome to give a lecture. Three years later, a soldier brought letters to Bishop Demetrius and the Roman prefect of Egypt. They came from the Roman governor of Arabia who sought Origen's advice on "a matter of doctrine."

What doctrine that was has never been discovered. In any event, Origen was dispatched forthwith, stopping along the way to preach in the church in

Caesarea at the invitation of Alexander, bishop of Jerusalem, and Theoctistus, Caesarea's bishop. He returned in 216 to find chaos both in the Christian community and around it. Bishop Demetrius was furious with him. Did he not know that a layman must never preach before clergymen, especially before bishops? But he had been invited by the bishops to preach, Origen said. Those bishops, responded Demetrius, had committed a major ecclesiastical offense, and Demetrius would certainly let them know.

But none of this meant anything to the citizens of Alexandria. They had far more to think about. One of the worst slaughters in the city's history had just occurred, and the instigator was the emperor himself. He was Caracalla, and his name would live in the city's annals as synonymous with monstrous depravity. He had planned a state visit to the city that year and his reputation had preceded him, a reputation for fratricide for he was known to have murdered his own brother, Geta, by treachery. The youth of Alexandria rather specialized in lampoonery, particularly of officialdom. "The witticisms that really irritate," said the historian Herodian, "are those that expose the truth of one's shortcomings." Caracalla had a great many shortcomings that could be exposed. He was a brother-killer, yet also a mother-lover, a pint-sized buffoon with the crazed idea that he was following in the footsteps of Alexander the Great—all fodder for great satire.

Of this frivolity, Caracalla had been fully informed. Approaching the city, he ordered a large public gathering for a gigantic spectacle, a mass slaughter of cattle as an offering to the dead. The citizens swarmed into the street to welcome him, showering him with flowers and accompanying him with music. He visited the tomb of Alexander the Great and set up his headquarters in the Temple of Serapis. From there, he announced plans for a special unit of his army to be recruited entirely from the young men of Alexandria, who should, he said, seat themselves in the front rows for the great festival.

As Caracalla addressed his new recruits, units of his German guard stole quietly behind the crowd, surrounding it. Others hurriedly dug pits on the outskirts of the assembly. At a signal, the heavily armed troops broke into the crowd, murdering all the young men, none of whom was armed. Their bodies were dragged from the field and dumped into the pits. Days of further carnage followed; hundreds of citizens were murdered in their homes; the city was looted as though conquered by a foreign army.

All the schools were closed, including Origen's. He escaped and made his way back to Palestine, with one thought no doubt pressing on his mind. The earthly fate of the Christians was entirely in the hands of the empire. Many of his pupils had been put to death under an imperial edict issued by Caracalla's father, Severus. So, too, had his own father, Leonides. Now the youth of Alexandria had been butchered through imperial whim. If conditions were to change, then the empire must change. And the center of the empire's power was not Alexandria.

# Gnosticism: If it began with Simon Magus, it enjoyed a far more respectable future

**Christian lore tells strange tales of the fate of Peter's old foe, but ideas like his of 'secret knowledge' would endure for centuries to come**

The story of Peter the Apostle's angry confrontation with Simon Magus, the Samaritan religious huckster, told in the Acts of the Apostles (8:18–24), leaves open the question of whether Simon repented. If subsequent records are right, he didn't. Or if he did, it didn't last. The third-century Christian writer Hippolytus records that Simon later turned up in Rome, traveling with a prostitute named Helen and claiming that he himself was God the Father while his companion was Sophia or

"Wisdom." Thus began a problem that would dog the Christians for the next two centuries and more. The problem was called Gnosticism.

As Simon's story went, shortly after he himself had created Wisdom at the beginning of time, she lost control of her fertility and gave birth to seven foolish angels who sought to claim supreme divinity for themselves. So they created the world and imprisoned their goddess mother here on

Earth in a series of females through history—Helen of Troy, for example. God, appearing human, had now come down to earth in the guise of Simon to rescue his bride, finding her in a brothel in Tyre. While on earth, he was offering to liberate from this evil world anyone willing to accept his secret and divine "knowledge," the Greek word for which is *gnosis*.

Such was the earliest manifestation in Christian history of the Gnostics, "the people in the know," a most resilient idea that would persistently reappear. In Rome, according to the apocryphal *Acts of Peter*, Simon encountered Peter and Paul, and also tried to impress the Emperor Nero by flying through the air, only to be dashed to the ground by the apostles' prayers. Another pious legend has him returning from Rome to Samaria where he promised he would die and rise on the third day. Accordingly, he had himself buried, but he stayed buried. Even so, he was later worshiped as the Messiah by a Samaritan sect. Other mystic teachers soon followed him. They included his fellow Samaritan, Menander, who taught in Antioch, as well as Menander's successor Saturninus, and Cerdo who had followed Simon to Rome.

Elsewhere, however, Gnosticism had far more respectable credentials; it is generally considered to have originated in Greek philosophy. Platonism in particular is believed to have shaped the views of Basilides in Alexandria and Valentinus who taught there before coming to Rome in A.D. 140. If these teachers were not inspired by Simon's personal example—none of them claimed to be themselves the Supreme God—they certainly emerged from the same cultural stew of eccentric Judaistic spiritualism, Greek philosophy, and Persian mysticism.

Most Gnostics claimed to be Christians—as they saw it, the true Christians— but also the inheritors of Greek and Eastern dualism, which sees good and evil as equally eternal and powerful and conducting an endless war on earth. To the Christians and Jews before them, God was the only eternal entity. He made the universe, with evil resulting as a corruption of good. The Gnostics could not accept the suggestion that the eternal God could pollute himself by taking on human flesh and enduring real agony in crucifixion. Nor could they accept that a good and all-powerful God could have created a world so evil.

In the mid-second century, the Christian gospel was still largely an oral

*Antiquities dealers originally sold several of the manuscripts from the Nag Hammadi library to a Swiss research institute. They were returned when the Egyptian government nationalized the collection. This photograph was taken in 1949, before restoration work at the Coptic Museum in Cairo.*

tradition, with an assortment of writings of widely varying reliability. So the Gnostics easily reinterpreted the tradition. The true God was entirely unknowable, they said, and the visible universe was the creation of a foolish or evil demigod, the Jewish Yahweh. The world and most of the people in it were completely unredeemable. However, through the intercession of the true God, some had been granted a divine "spark," or "spirit," or "pearl." Jesus Christ, a manifestation of God who merely appeared to be human, came to redeem those chosen ones—"as one who makes himself free and awakes from the drunkenness wherein he lived, and returns to himself," says the Gnostic *Gospel of Truth*.

What was needed for salvation was knowledge of one's divine identity, which was destined to escape material existence. The Gnostics offered to provide this knowledge—for a price, of course, because the Gnostics sold their secrets dearly. In practice, that knowledge was little more than myth, mysticism, astrology, and magic spells, differing from one Gnostic sect to another.

By the second century, with its intellectual centers in Antioch and Alexandria, Gnosticism had spread wherever there were Christian congregations: Rome, Carthage, southern Gaul, and Asia Minor. The apostles' immediate successors had been too busy teaching and caring for their communities to translate the good news into the categories of Greek philosophy. So since the Gnostics seemed the first theologians, they were welcomed into wealthy Christian homes in Alexandria. In Rome, Valentinus was almost elected a bishop.

Gnosticism's attraction for the effete and sophisticated Greco-Roman world was double-edged. Intellectually, it detached the revelation of Jesus Christ from its Jewish roots and gave a more flattering—for the chosen—explanation for the world's evil. Morally, in simply condemning the world and all human flesh, it

The Jabal al-Tarif cliffs at Nag Hammadi, 370 miles south of Cairo on the River Nile. In 1945 an Egyptian farmer found a large clay jar at the base of the cliffs. It contained more than a dozen early Christian manuscripts—including the only complete copy of the Gospel of Thomas. It was likely buried during a purge of heretical books ordered by the Orthodox patriarch of Alexandria in the late fourth century.

encouraged some to engage in extreme austerities—since nature was corrupt, sex and procreation were evil, they taught. Or more commonly, since the enlightened considered their minds to be "pearls to which no mud could stick," they were free to engage in anarchic sexuality—which they did with gusto.

The Gnostics began appealing to a succession of teachers, back, so they said, to the apostles Philip, Thomas, and Matthias. To these, they claimed, Jesus entrusted secret knowledge. Rejecting most of the Hebrew and many apostolic writings, they produced their own Scriptures. The Cainite sect—"descendants" of Abel's brother

Cain—produced *The Gospel of Judas*. The Alexandrian *Acts of Peter* describes Peter refusing to heal his paralyzed daughter to preserve her chastity. Other works included *Pistis Sophia* (Faith and Reason), *The Song of the Pearl*, *The Acts of Thomas*, *The Gospel of Mary Magdalene*, *The Wisdom of Jesus*, and *The Apocryphon of John*. Much fragmentary material was preserved by the Mandeans of the lower Tigris and Euphrates, the last continuously practicing Gnostic sect, whose existence was not discovered by the western world until the nineteenth century.

The Gnostic challenge forced Christians to respond vigorously. Already, in the late first century, Ignatius of Antioch had thundered against the Gnostic Docetists who taught that Jesus was purely divine and that his humanity was merely an appearance. A generation later, it was clear that Christianity's fundamental beliefs—that God's creation was essentially good, that sin was destructive, that God's salvation is rooted in the Jews, that God had entered human history as a real, not a sham, human being, and that the Christians were the continuing "body of Christ" on earth—all this would have to be defended as a package against the Gnostics.

The defenders, however, soon appeared. The Christian historian Hegesippus, among others, traveled from Rome to Palestine, documenting the succession of bishops back to the apostles to indicate there had been a person-to-person link from the apostles to the present. Clement of Alexandria, boring in on the

## It seems that wherever the Gospel spreads, some will reinterpret the message of salvation as purely intellectual, reject the body as unredeemable, and often wallow in mud.

Gnostics' contradictory attitudes toward sex, demanded they must concede the essential goodness of the created order. Polycarp, Justin and Irenaeus argued the continuity of the Jewish and Christian revelations, and condemned the Gnostics for their lack of charity—"trying with words devoid of meaning to gain hearers devoid of faith," as Irenaeus described them. "They set forth, indeed, the name of Christ Jesus as a sort of lure," he wrote, "but in various ways they introduce the impieties of Simon [Magus], and thus they destroy multitudes, wickedly disseminating their own doctrines by the use of a good name, and through means of its sweetness and beauty, extending to their hearers the bitter and malignant poison of the serpent, the great author of apostasy."

Valentinus's activity in Rome represented the high-water mark of the Gnostic threat, both because of the depth of his scholarship and the sophistication of his teaching. He was no smarmy poseur, but a speculative theological reformer who wanted to revise and incorporate Gnosticism into the emerging Christian orthodoxy. An inheritor of the teachings of Alexandria's Basilides, he moved to Rome in or about 143 and was a candidate to be its bishop. Though defeated, he nevertheless served as an aide to Bishop Anicetus ten years later. Valentinus's disciple

Ptolemy was able to present a view of Christianity which, says historian W. H. C. Frend, was particularly appealing to women because it gave them a central role in the acquisition of *gnosis*. Gnosticism had come a long way from Simon Magus and his prostitute partner. Not far enough, however. For when the Christians became fully conscious of the Gnostic threat, it ceased to be one.

By the mid-third century, the Gnostic challenge was on the wane, and by the fourth it had been supplanted by other controversies even more lethal in their divisiveness. But Gnosticism never did quite die. The Manicheans of the fourth-century North Africa, the Bogomils of the ninth-century Balkans, the French, German, and Italian Cathari in the twelfth century, the French Albigensians of the thirteenth century, and the Theosophist movement of nineteenth-century England and America are only a few of the recurring Gnostic revivals. And Gnostic influences can be seen in the alchemy of late-Medieval and early-Modern Europe. It seems that wherever the Gospel spreads, some will reinterpret the message of salvation as purely intellectual, reject the body as unredeemable, and often wallow in mud they believe will not stick to their "pearl."

Indeed, as late as the twentieth century, interest in Gnosticism revived with the discovery of a cache of thirteen Gnostic books near the southern Egyptian village of Nag Hammadi. These included the *Gospel of Thomas*, a collection of Jesus' sayings (including the strange assertion that "heaven and earth came into being" for the sake of the apostle James); *The Book of Thomas the Contender*, a dialogue between Jesus and Thomas just before Jesus' Ascension; a *Revelation of Adam* that has Adam telling Seth how Noah was saved from the Flood; and Valentinus's own *Gospel According to Philip*.

Spurred by these discoveries, Princeton scholar Elaine Pagels brought out a controversial reassessment of the early church in 1979. Based on and entitled *The Gnostic Gospels*, it won both the National Book Critics Circle Award and the National Book Award, and was praised for recovering an alternative form of Christianity, flourishing before the early church moved toward becoming an orthodox body with rules, rites and clergy. Simon Magus and Helen would, no doubt, have heartily concurred. ■

# CHAPTER 8

# The Christians pervade the imperial household

## In the midst of murder, mayhem, betrayal, and lies, the empress calls in Origen to advise her son; the tide seems to have turned, but it has not

The fate of the Christians—their fate in this life, anyway—depended upon the policies, moods, caprices, and ultimately the religious convictions of the reigning emperor. Origen had grim cause to know this firsthand. But it meant that safeguarding the Christians would involve persuading and perhaps converting the emperor himself, and in the blood-soaked era of Caracalla, this would have seemed so remote a possibility as to be preposterous.

However, before Origen died, he would see Christianity deeply infused in the imperial household, pivotally influencing the policies of one emperor and perhaps actually converting another, with Origen himself playing what was probably a key role in those developments.

Strangest of all, while the Christians stood for (and themselves usually evidenced) the mutual trust, sincerity and personal sacrifice that Jesus had enjoined upon them, the imperial household where Origen's influence was invited and felt was one of internecine feud, constant conspiracy, palace purges, assassination, betrayal, lies, and deception, all within a family in which brother murdered brother, sister murdered sister, and two emperors on separate occasions died in the arms of their mothers, each of whom helped bring about her son's downfall and perished along with him. Finally, it was the only era in the history of imperial Rome when the empire was run almost entirely by women, one of whom was the declared ally of Christianity and surrounded herself with Christian advisers.

Things had not gone well after the death of Marcus Aurelius in A.D. 180, about five years before Origen was born. Indeed, the conduct of the imperial court had descended sharply. Marcus's austere Stoicism was supplanted by the eventually insane delusions of his son, heir, and successor, Commodus, a devotee of the arena who fought a reputed seven hundred public battles, many against wild animals. From the start, Commodus's hold on office was insecure. A street

## Commodus then slipped into insanity, donning a lion's skin instead of a toga, proclaiming himself the son of Jupiter, and appearing in public carrying a Hercules-style club.

assassin, sword in hand, was narrowly thwarted soon after Commodus donned the purple toga. Next came a plot by the prefect of Rome that was stifled by the execution of the man himself, along with all his kinfolk and household servants. As plot followed foiled plot, so many people were executed, says the historian Cassius Dio, that recounting them all would be tedious.

Commodus, meanwhile, slipped into insanity, commanding senators to cheer him as "first of all men" in his frequent arena appearances, donning a lion's skin instead of a toga, proclaiming himself Hercules, son of Jupiter, and appearing in public carrying a Hercules-style club. He announced plans to designate himself the divine founder of Rome and rename the city *Colonia Commodiana* while retitling the months of the year after his own dozen names.

In the midst of this unpropitious household, however, a Christian made her appearance. Commodus's mistress, a freedman named Marcia, commandeered from the estate of one of his aides, acquired a strong influence over him, even before his father died. She was one of several Christians in his immediate circle, according to records left in the late 170s by the court physician Galen. While not a Christian, Galen was an open sympathizer who wrote admiringly of the Christians' discipline, their habitual honesty, and their fearlessness in the face of death. If only Christianity were rational, he wrote. At one point, Marcia was strong enough politically to intervene for Christians condemned to work in the Sardinian mines. Many were released, including a future bishop of Rome, Callistus.

However, neither she nor anyone else could fully control the mad emperor, and she gradually fell from his favor. When he announced to a few close friends his plans to publicly execute a number of senators in the arena, Marcia and others decided he had to be stopped, meaning assassinated. They almost botched the job. She gave him poison that he threw up, remaining very much alive, whereupon Narcissus, an athlete and his companion in arena appearances, strangled him in his bathtub. It was the eve of New Year's Day, 193. The Praetorian Guard, who were partying, were not there to defend him.

Acting swiftly, Marcia and her co-conspirators hastened to the home of Senator Pertinax, a respected bureaucrat under Commodus's father. Convincing him that he owed it to his now-dead benefactor Marcus to salvage the empire by accepting its crown, they escorted him to the barracks of the Praetorian Guard and declared that Commodus had died of a stroke, and that Pertinax, who could restore the high probity of Marcus's era, was the obvious successor. The Praetorians agreed, but reluctantly, and the following day, the grateful Senate ratified Pertinax, meanwhile hearing the motion that the would-be senator-killer Commodus should be stripped of his titles, that all monuments to him should be thrown down, that his body should be dragged by a hook into the stripping room of the gladiators and buried in disgrace. All in favor? Carried. And carried out it was.

But the Praetorians were not altogether in favor, especially when they discovered, much to their discomfort, that Pertinax actually intended to restore the disciplines and the severe honesty of Marcus's era. Their perks threatened, three hundred of them rose in revolt, and unrestrained by their officers, they marched on the palace. Pertinax, knowing their intent, walked out to meet them, declared his innocence, and cowed them into submission. However, one of their number, more brazen than the rest, strode forward and ran him through as the others cheered and joined in. Then, with Pertinax's head held high above them on a pike pole, they marched triumphantly back to the barracks.

He had reigned for eighty-six days. The imperial crown was theirs to confer, the Praetorians now knew, so they would auction it to the highest bidder. Edward Gibbon in his *Decline and Fall of the Roman Empire* calls this an "infamous offer, the most insolent excess of military license," which "diffused a universal grief, shame, and indignation throughout the city."

This shame was not quite universal, however. To a certain Didius Julianus, a veteran senator, vain, old, and wealthy, the auction came as a golden opportunity to achieve a rank otherwise beyond his wildest dreams. He won the bidding, offering a staggering 6,250 drachmas to each member of the Praetorian Guard.[1] The gates of the camp were instantly thrown open to the purchaser; he was declared emperor, and he received an oath of allegiance from the soldiers.

But when word of this connivance reached the frontline legions, three of their commanders, those in Britain, Syria, and Illyria, laid plans to march immediately on Rome, each aspiring to become at once Pertinax's avenger, Julianus's assassin,

In this late-first-century bust Commodus is depicted as Hercules, wearing a lion skin and carrying a club. No product of the artist's imagination, the emperor actually enjoyed appearing in public wearing this garb.

---

1. When vain old Didius Julianus bought the imperial crown at auction by bestowing upon each member of the Praetorian Guard a lump-sum gift of 6,250 drachmas, he was probably offering them the equivalent of ten or more years' pay. While the record of pay scales in the army is far from complete, the *Cambridge Ancient History* notes that Caracalla, whose reign began nineteen years after Commodus's assassination, raised the soldier's annual pay from five-hundred to 750 denarii. Since a denarius was the approximate equivalent of a drachma, the offer would be staggering.

and therefore his successor. None, however, could match the qualifications of the commander in the old province of Illyria, opposite Italy along the east coast of the Adriatic. He was the best strategist and had the sharpest mind, the best troops, and the shortest distance to travel to Rome. More than any of these, he had a very cunning and ambitious wife, as ruthless as he was, every bit as ambitious, and also stunningly beautiful.

The man was Septimius Severus, a North African by birth who rose rapidly in the army and under Commodus was given a command in Syria. There he was introduced to a little girl, Julia Domna, aged nine, who was the daughter of Julius Bassianus, high priest of the crossroad center Emesa, now called Homs, about halfway between Antioch and Damascus. Whoever marries this child, the astrologers predicted, she will make into a king. Severus was devoted to astrology, and both the girl and the fable fascinated him. He was either widowed or divorced from a first wife about whom almost nothing is known.

A great deal, however, was to become known about Julia Domna. Severus eventually married her. She would become the wife of one emperor, the mother of two, and the grandaunt of two more. Her younger sister, Julia Maesa, would be grandmother to two (see accompanying genealogy diagram). More powerful than either of those Julias would be a third, Julia Mammaea, daughter of Maesa and niece of Domna, who would rule the empire through her son for thirteen critical years, aiding, abetting, and perhaps even joining the Christians, though the last is doubtful.

But the founder of this female dynasty was Julia Domna, who presented her husband with two sons, one while he was proconsul in Gaul, the second when he was filling the same function in Sicily. However, her role in her husband's career was, first to last, far more than that of a wife. She became, in effect, his prime minister, and after his death she served in the same capacity for their elder son, popularly known as Caracalla.

*In the confusion following the death of Commodus, Septimius Severus, the Roman commander in Illyria across the Adriatic from Italy, moved quickly to secure the throne—founding a dynasty which would number five emperors, with his wife's family central to all five.*

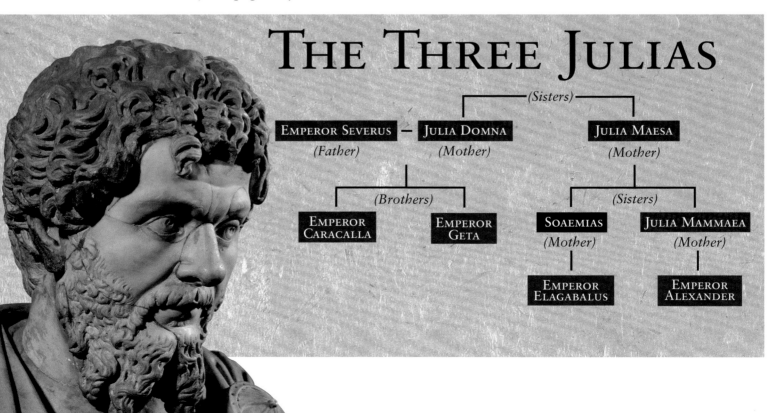

# THE THREE JULIAS

*(Sisters)*

**EMPEROR SEVERUS** — **JULIA DOMNA**     **JULIA MAESA**
*(Father)*          *(Mother)*            *(Mother)*

*(Brothers)*                    *(Sisters)*

**EMPEROR CARACALLA**   **EMPEROR GETA**     **SOAEMIAS**         **JULIA MAMMAEA**
                                             *(Mother)*           *(Mother)*

**EMPEROR ELAGABALUS**   **EMPEROR ALEXANDER**

An extraordinary woman, Julia Domna was learned in philosophy and she surrounded herself with rhetoricians, lawyers, astrologers, physicians, philosophers, and historians. Gibbon lists her attributes: "The attractions of beauty," he writes, "were united to a lively imagination, a firmness of mind, and strength of judgment, seldom bestowed on her sex." With soldiers, her popularity rivaled her husband's. She was declared "Mother of the Camp," "Mother of the Senate," "Mother of the Nation," "Mother of All the People." At one point, in Syria, there was a popular movement to have her declared a goddess.

*The ancient colonnade and arch of the Decumanus in Palmyra, Syria. The monumental arch was erected under the orders of Septimius Severus (A.D. 193–211) and was the symbol of Palmyra's prosperity. Julia Domna (inset) was Severus's popular Syrian-born wife and a power behind the throne.*

Spurred by his wife, Severus moved as soon as the news of the Pertinax murder reached his headquarters. His battle-hardened troops, many of them recruited from the wild Pannonians who lived along the south shore of the Danube, were on the march for Rome in short order. The Adriatic fleet went over to his side when he reached the coast, and his legions were soon at Ravenna, about 250 miles from the capital. There, both Julianus and the Praetorians were in a state of panic. The city-softened imperial guard had no stomach for a fight with, of all troops, the Pannonians. Gibbon portrays their terror:

> They trembled at the name of the Pannonian legions, commanded by an experienced general and accustomed to vanquishing the barbarians on the frozen Danube. They quitted, with a sigh, the pleasures of the baths and theaters, to put on arms whose use they had almost forgotten, and beneath the weight of which they were oppressed.
>
> The unpracticed elephants, whose uncouth appearance, it was hoped, would strike terror into the army of the north, threw their unskilled riders; and the awkward evolutions of the marines, drawn from the fleet of Misenum (the naval base near Naples), were an object of ridicule to the populace; whilst the Senate enjoyed, with secret pleasure, the distress and weakness of the usurper.

Julianus, meanwhile, had taken another precaution. Commodus's mistress, the Christian Marcia, and her co-conspirators, were duly murdered. But neither the Praetorians nor Julianus's makeshift fortifications around the city were of any use. The Praetorians conducted Julianus into a private apartment in the palace. There they beheaded him as a common criminal and surrendered the city without a fight. Julianus had purchased, with an immense treasure, an anxious and precarious reign of only sixty-six days, twenty days less than Pertinax. Always conscious that their own fate depended vitally on who was emperor and what were his religious views, the Christians must have seen all this violence as horrifying and looked anxiously for clues as to the attitude of the figure who now entered upon the scene.

But Severus at first gave no clues. He directed the Praetorians to assemble unarmed in a large field on the city's outskirts. A contingent of his Pannonians surrounded them with leveled spears, and the Praetorians waited in horror for the charge. It never came. Severus denounced them for treachery and cowardice. But he did not massacre or even disband them. In effect, he fired them and ordered them out of Rome. If any came within a hundred miles of the city they would be executed, he warned. Later, he reconstituted them as an elite frontline unit whose ranks the members of other legions could aspire to join.

Forty-one senators were executed as supporters of the rival claimant generals from Britain and Syria, both of whose armies Severus shortly defeated. For the next eighteen years, peace returned to the imperial household, Severus commanding the armies first in the East and then in the North, while Julia Domna ran the government, mostly from her native Syria, doing whatever it took.

What it occasionally took, according to some historians, was her own amorous activity. If this was true, Severus, always smitten by her charms, made no recorded objection to it. Sometimes they worked together on military strategy. "It may be argued," writes the historian Anthony R. Birley in his biography of Severus, *The African Emperor*, "that Severus and his wife had a keener realization of the importance of the eastern frontiers, and a shrewder perception of how they should be controlled, than any previous Roman ruler."

While all went well in the affairs of state under Severus, however, all did not go well with the Christians. In 202, the ninth year of his reign, Severus launched the five-year persecution against Christians that claimed the life of Origen's father, Leonides, and later those of Origen's pupils in Alexandria. The motive for this apparently sudden crackdown is not

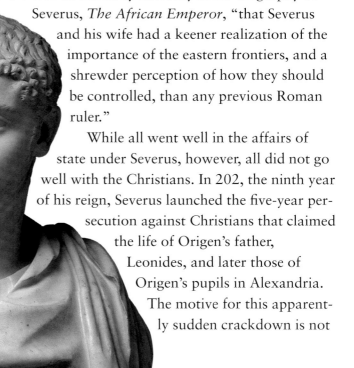

*Swaggering and brutish, the Emperor Caracalla (left), whom Gibbon called, "the common enemy of mankind," traveled the empire wreaking all manner of havoc, until he was stabbed to death by a soldier in Syria. (Right) Caracalla's brother, the soft and ineffectual Geta, was murdered by Caracalla's soldiers when he challenged his brother for a share of the empire. As their father had predicted, the stronger destroyed the weaker.*

easily explained. Severus for years had retained the services of a therapist named Torpacion or Proculus, a lifelong Christian. Moreover, Tertullian, notwithstanding Perpetua's and other martyrdoms, wrote that it was Severus who protected Christians of high rank against the fury of the mobs. In any event, the persecution was canceled in 207 as abruptly and mysteriously as it had begun.

In 211, sixty-five years old, weary, and in ill health, Severus crossed the English Channel to direct the war against the Caledonians in the north of Britain. He took his two sons—Caracalla, aged twenty-three, and Geta, twenty-one—along with him. He had held high hopes for these boys, but neither gave him any reassurance. Caracalla was swaggering and brutish, Geta soft, ineffectual, and given to the arts. From their infancy they had harbored an irrepressible hatred for one another, dividing the court into two factions. Severus carefully favored neither, bestowing the rank of Augustus on each, so that legally Rome had three emperors. But Severus was under no illusions. The stronger of the two will destroy the weaker, he said, and then will be himself destroyed by his own vices.

All this occurred precisely as Severus had foreseen. When he died that year at York, both sons hastened south to Rome and split the empire in two, as their father had unwisely recommended. The conflict between them grew worse. While Caracalla lavished money on the army, which became his unswerving supporter, their mother, Julia Domna, sought with fervor to make peace between them. Ostensibly bowing to her wish, Caracalla met his brother in her presence to settle their differences. Instead, his soldiers rushed into the room. Geta fled to his mother's arms, where they stabbed him to death, his blood spurting over her robe. Trying to ward off the blows, she was herself wounded in the hand. Caracalla darted from the room, screaming that his brother had tried to murder him. The story was doubted, but accepted by the Senate. The army was on Caracalla's side and the senators knew it.

On returning to the palace he found his mother weeping, with several noblewomen, for her dead son. Enraged, he threatened them all with instant execution. One of them, Fadilla, last surviving daughter of Marcus Aurelius, he did put to death; then he began the systematic execution of every ally of his brother, a purge that claimed the lives of thousands, say the Roman histories. Mother and son were reconciled, however. Julia Domna resumed her role as prime minister, while her son gradually sank into seeming imbecility.

He left Rome a year later, never to return, and became, says Gibbon, "the common enemy of mankind," traveling the empire, "every province by turns the scene of rapine and cruelty," typified by his slaughter of the young men in Alexandria recounted in the preceding chapter. Finally,

*A painted wood panel showing Julia Domna and Septimius Severus, with a young Caracalla below. The face of their other son, the murdered Geta, has been erased (bottom left). Caracalla had his younger brother's name and image removed from all inscriptions and portraits.*

he was stabbed to death by a soldier in Syria. The assassin was promptly executed, and in the resulting void of leadership a lawyer serving as a commander of the Praetorians in Syria had himself declared emperor. His name was Macrinus; he would remain in office and alive for the next year.

The new emperor first ordered Julia Domna, by now aging and exhausted, to retire to Emesa, her birthplace. She refused, then quietly starved herself to death at Antioch, or so most accounts record. But her younger sister, Julia Maesa, a woman of equal beauty and ambition but without intellectual pretension who had used her court connections to accumulate considerable wealth, saw that her hour had now come. She had two daughters, both widows. The elder, Soaemias, had a son, Bassianus, who would go down in history as the emperor with the virtually unpronounceable name of Elagabalus (pronounced as *E-la-GAB-a-lus)*, from the name of the sun god for whom his great grandfather had been high priest at Emesa. The younger and by far the brighter daughter was Julia Mammaea, who likewise had a son, Alexander (see family chart, p. 226).

Julia Maesa returned to her native Emesa, where her power and influence were greatest. The proper heir, she resolved, was not this upstart lawyer but her grandson, Elagabalus. But he had no blood relationship with Severus at all, some said. Wrong, said Julia Maesa. He was actually the illegitimate son of his mother's cousin, Caracalla; there had been an indiscretion. The army in Syria leaned toward her grandson. Whatever his relation with the mighty Severus, he was from the same family. His grandaunt, Julia Domna, had been their heroine, the "Mother of the Camp." Her sister, his grandmother, was wealthy and most generous. Moreover, they didn't like the Praetorians and they didn't like lawyers. So "Hail the Emperor Elagabalus!"

The showdown occurred in Syria. The Praetorians at first distinguished themselves on behalf of the Emperor Macrinus, driving Elagabalus's force into a rout. But no one was going to rout Julia Maesa. Jumping from a chariot with her daughter, Soaemias, she chided the retreating soldiers for cowardice.

Elagabalus, in the only distinguished act of his life, led the troops to turn and stand against the Praetorians, then to counterattack savagely. The Praetorians fled. Macrinus was caught running away and was executed.

The year was 218, and Emperor Elagabalus then began a four-year, catastrophic reign. His grandmother instructed the young emperor to leave immediately for the capital, and thus made two dismaying discoveries: first that he had a mind of his own, and second that it wasn't a very good one. He dallied in Syria, and when he finally arrived, he scandalized the Roman populace by wearing silk, jewels and the finery of the Eastern nobility, his head adorned with a high tiara, his eyebrows blackened, his cheeks painted pink, all much to the horror of his grandmother.

In the ensuing four years, one such outrage followed another.

*A coin bearing the likeness of Julia Maesa, younger sister of Julia Domna and grandmother of two emperors— the eccentric Elagabalus and his cousin Alexander.*

*Only the intervention of Julia Maesa and her daughter Soaemias prevented a rout of Elagabalus's forces. As the women rallied the troops, the retreating Elagabalus turned and led them in a counterattack, and the Praetorians fled.*

*The ill-fated, Elagabalus (left), and his mother, the Syrian princess Soaemias (right), were the grandson and daughter of Julia Maesa. After a disastrous four-year reign Julia plotted to have them replaced. They were murdered together, and their bodies were dragged through the streets of Rome.*

Described by some historians as "a passive homosexual," he took four successive wives, all promoted by his grandmother, and each failed to produce children. When he announced plans to marry one of Rome's forbidden vestal virgins, this created another crisis. He lavished upon his male paramours the loftiest titles in the civil service—a dancer became prefect of the city, a charioteer prefect of the watch, a barber prefect of provisions. "Corrupted by his youth, his country, and his fortune," writes Gibbon, "he abandoned himself to the grossest pleasures with ungoverned fury, and soon found disgust and satiety in the midst of his enjoyments."

Very soon, it became evident to his grandmother that salvaging the family fate and fortune depended upon ending the reign of Emperor Elagabalus. She had, she knew, one card left to play: the other grandson, Alexander. At thirteen, he was four years younger than his cousin, and as different as her younger daughter was from her elder. For Julia Mammaea was rectitude itself. She lacked the glamorous beauty of her mother, aunt, and elder sister, but she was far from homely, and she was skilled in philosophy, religion, and history. Morals aside, she realized that unless an end was put to her imperial nephew, a coup by the army was inevitable, and in it the whole family would assuredly perish. Finally, she hated Elagabalus—the way he lived, the way he thought, and the peril into which he put them all. Together with her mother, therefore, she plotted his death, which would entail the death, as well, of her own sister.

Three things were necessary. First, the army must be won over. Well-placed "donatives" to the right officers, plus a claim to a blood relationship with the revered Severus, would accomplish this. The dead Caracalla was again the chosen agent. There had been two indiscretions, it seemed, with Alexander the consequence of the second. Next, and most difficult, Elagabalus must be convinced to "adopt" his cousin as his heir—for Elagabalus a suicidal move, but he must be

 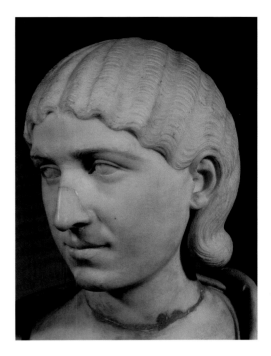

persuaded to make it. Finally, the reigning emperor must not only be assassinated but also disgraced, so that a clear distinction could be drawn between the two cousins. Such was the plan, and both women set about carrying it out.

Winning the army was not difficult. The soldiers were embarrassed by this effeminate incumbent. The Praetorians had in fact opposed him and naturally gravitated to a rival. Alexander's increasing presence in their camp and in public gained him a widening popularity. His grandmother undertook to solve the adoption problem. The emperor, she knew, had an infatuation with the sun worship of his ancestors which he was striving to make the state religion of Rome. She now championed this cause. Elagabalus could not adequately fulfill the role of the sun god's high priest in Rome, she said, when he was burdened with other state affairs. Why not let his young cousin shoulder some of the more routine responsibilities?

The emperor at first refused, then conceded, then began to suspect his aunt and grandmother of plotting against him. He tried to reverse the adoption, but the Senate would not agree. He next sought to subvert his cousin to his own lifestyle. When that failed, he twice attempted to murder Alexander, but was thwarted by the Praetorians. Elagabalus's own assassination soon followed. There are three accounts of it, the most probable and sanguinary that of the historian Cassius Dio. The assassins found the trembling emperor hiding in a palace closet and dragged him out. He fled into the arms of his mother, Soaemias. Both were then slain and beheaded. Their bodies were stripped and dragged through the streets. Elagabalus's body was thrown into the Tiber; the fate of his mother's body is not known. The date was March 11, 222. Two days later, his cousin, Alexander Severus, age fourteen, was declared emperor of Rome.

Alexander's accession brought radical change both to the imperial household and to the whole conduct of the administration. Behind the change lay the complex

figure of the emperor's mother, Julia Mammaea. She was a woman of two dominant qualities. An unswerving honesty in public affairs governed her conduct up to, but not including, her personal financial interest. Second, she had inherited from her mother an insatiable avarice, says the historian Herodian, which eventually worked her own ruin and her son's. Her mother, Julia Maesa, Herodian notes, went into a secluded retirement, died two years later and was buried "with imperial honors and deification."

Some doubt that she was deified—it would have alienated the Christians whom Julia Mammaea strongly supported. Historians generally agree that Julia Mammaea was not Christian herself. Like many heads of state nineteen centuries later, she was a religious syncretist. All religions had good in them, she would have said, and the state should welcome them all but favor none in particular. Rome, of course, had always embraced this view, provided that Rome's own imperial gods, including the divine emperors, were given their proper due. Rome drew the line at

Christianity because the Christians refused to make this last concession.

But Julia Mammaea did not draw that line. Like her aunt, Julia Domna, she studied the great religions and philosophies, thinking, no doubt, that to accept them within the fold of the state required, at a minimum, understanding them. She raised her son in the same rigorous virtuosity she demanded from her whole household, successfully shielding him against the depravities of his cousin. But of all the empire's myriad religions, Christianity in particular fascinated her.

Christians were numerous in her household, says the fourth-century Christian historian Eusebius, and when it became the imperial household, Christians moved into high positions within the state. Long before her son's accession, she had wanted to know more about their faith. Who, she once asked, would be a good instructor, both for herself and her son? There was a brilliant man at Alexandria, she was told, a man of widening influence among the Christians. His name was Origen. She sent for him.

Thus, Origen came into the presence of Julia Mammaea, then resident in Antioch, having been escorted there, he said, by the Praetorian Guard. The probable date was 218, four years before her son became emperor.

Origen by now had found himself leading a double life. In his beloved Alexandria, he was a man shunned by authority, deeply suspect to his bishop, on the verge of outright expulsion from the church for which his father had been martyred. Everywhere else in the Christian world, he was a man held in awe, his advice often sought to resolve conflicts between Christians, his books increasingly copied and read, his lectures in churches and public halls vastly attended.

Origen's troubles with Bishop Demetrius had begun on his first trip to Palestine, when the bishops there, Theoctistus and Alexander, had heard him preach in their churches. On learning of this, Demetrius was shocked. He wrote to the two bishops: "It has never been heard of, and it never happens now, that laymen preach homilies in the presence of bishops." The two bishops replied that "where there are men capable of doing good to the brethren, they are invited by the holy bishops to address the people." Demetrius rejected their case, and from

**ORIGEN ON CREATION**

*I cannot understand how so many distinguished men have been of the opinion that matter was uncreated; thinking that so great a work as the universe could exist without an architect or an overseer.*

that point on, hostility grew between himself and the principal of his Catechetical School.

Caracalla's massacre at Alexandria saw the school close and Origen take refuge back in Caesarea. When he returned to Alexandria, Origen made a connection that would soon gain his work a very wide audience. The man's name was Ambrose, and he was a wealthy Alexandrian who had been a dabbler in various religions and philosophies. He had rejected Christianity as rationally untenable until he encountered Origen, who showed him the intellectual depth of the faith. This changed his life; he embraced Christ, and together with Origen established what can only be described as the world's first international publishing house, dedicating all his wealth to the project.

Origen wrote the books, and Ambrose set up a copying team that duplicated and distributed them. He hired Origen a secretary and seven tachygraphers, effectively stenographers, and they established a production line. This became the vehicle which, over the ensuing decades, spread an avalanche of Origen's works to Christian communities all over the empire. They included not only theological and philosophical treatises, but also exhaustive commentaries on the Jewish Scriptures and on many of the works that would soon become the New Testament. In total, his individual writings numbered into the thousands.[2] A

*The tools used to spread Origen's works to Christian communities throughout the empire: instrumentum scriptorium (Roman writing utensils). This is detail from a wall painting in "the bankers house" at Pompeii, Italy.*

much-sought adviser and lecturer, he would travel to Caesarea in Cappadocia to preach, to Nicomedia to settle a dispute over biblical interpretation, and back to Arabia to confront and restore a bishop whose teachings were deemed to have strayed too far from the faith.

The need for such commentaries as Origen produced was self-evident. Gnosticism had captured and deluded the Christians in Egypt, largely by founding doctrines and theologies on isolated scriptural verses that were usually at odds with much else in the Scriptures. Only by a coherent commentary on all the books could a comprehensive picture of Christianity be drawn and taught. It was

---

2. Epiphanius, writing in the next century, puts at six thousand the number of Origen's writings, doubtless counting separately the different books of a single work, his homilies, letters, and his smallest treatises. Jerome in the same century reduces the figure to less than two thousand titles, but his list is known to be incomplete.

# A tycoon-bishop's affluent son rejects the Jews' God and starts his own faith

## The God of Abraham was not the God of Jesus, says Marcion, as he rewrites the New Testament and his churches multiply over Christian denunciations

Thomas Jefferson was famous—or infamous—for producing a version of the New Testament in which all suggestions of Jesus' divinity were excised. This better suited the famous deist's view of the way Christ ought to be seen by enlightened humans. But it was not the first time Scripture has gone under a tendentious editor's knife. In the second century, a religious leader named Marcion went a great deal further, tossing out most of the New Testament and all of the Old, in order to bring the Truth in line with his way of thinking.

Unlike Jefferson, Marcion's theology attracted a host of followers—in critics' minds, the best followers money could buy. So powerful did his movement become that it was officially condemned by most Christians. Indeed, Marcion was long known as the second century's "arch heretic."

He was born in Pontus, the big Roman province south of the Black Sea, to a father who was both a bishop and a shipping magnate. He enjoyed financial security and, like his father, had deeply held beliefs. The problem was with the nature of those beliefs. So bizarre were they that, sometime around 140, his father was forced to excommunicate his own son.[1]

Undaunted, Marcion moved to a larger stage—Rome—where he bequeathed to the Christians there two hundred thousand sesterces and went on with his preaching. By 144, the church fathers followed Marcion's father's lead, giving him back his donation and ousting him. Still undaunted, the twice-excommunicated Marcion established churches across the empire, as Tertullian later put it, "as wasps make nests."

What were these controversial beliefs? They flowed from Marcion's insistence that the God of the Old Testament and the God of the New could not be one and the same. The Old Testament's God was a fierce and unforgiving warrior-god, he said, who caused the sun to linger in the sky in order to prolong a slaughter. A woman suffered his punishment by having her children eaten by bears. In Isaiah 45:7, this God goes so far as to say, "I make peace and it is I who send evil. I, the Lord, do these things."

Yet did Christ not tell us, Marcion argued, that a good tree could not bring forth evil fruit? And therefore how could the Old Testament's ferocious God be the same God who sent his Son to redeem the world through love? Marcion's conclusion: There must be two Gods. The first was the Creator—called the Demiurgos or Cosmocrator—who has served his purpose and has been superseded by the loving God of the New Testament.

His was a breathtaking doctrine, and it caused no small number of problems for Marcion besides excommunication. For instance, which Scriptures were to be preached? The Old Testament was definitely out, but there remained profound problems with the New as well. The Nativity, for instance. It not only fulfilled an Old Testament prophecy, but placed Christ in a human body, thus attaching him to the old Creator God. Marcion's solution: Christ appeared in Capernaum in A.D. 29 as a grown man. Yet he was not really a man, but more of a supernatural being without human essence.

Before the editing was done, Marcion had whittled the New Testament down to a gutted version of Luke plus ten of Paul's letters. His theology rejected bodily resurrection. It offered baptism only to those who were willing to reject worldly pleasures, including marriage, which it considered debauchery.

His ministry, unsurprisingly, was never without voluble critics. Polycarp pegged him as the "firstborn of Satan." Justin Martyr observed that "with the help of demons," Marcion was guilty of "denying that the Maker of this universe is the Father of Christ, and declaring that the universe was made by another, greater than he."

Historian Eric Osborn in his *Tertullian: First Theologian of the West* explains the basic brief against him: "At the deepest level, Marcion's denial opposed the central affirmation of Christian faith, which was that one God was only credible if he had, in Christ, redeemed the world which he had made."

Yet Marcion was not entirely an anomaly. Says historian Paul Johnson in his *A History of Christianity*: "He represents two important and permanent strains of Christianity: the cool, rationalist approach to the examination of the church's documentary proofs, and a plain, unspectacular philosophy of love." As with other controversial teachers, he had a positive effect on Christians by forcing them to more firmly establish the books that were essential to the New Testament, which was then coming together.

Some Marcionite churches may have survived into the fourth century, though by then the movement was largely swallowed by another innovation, notably Manichaeism, which was similarly obsessed with the problem of evil.

Marcion is believed to have died in or around the year 160. The precise date and circumstances of his death are not known. Tertullian relates that Marcion repented and agreed to bring his followers back into the orthodox fold but died before this took place. ∎

---

1. The explanations for Marcion's excommunication by his father extend beyond the purely doctrinal. In two ancient accounts, he is ousted for seducing a virgin, a charge dismissed by many scholars because no such misconduct is laid to him in Rome. Historian John A. Clabeaux, writing in the *Anchor Bible Dictionary*, disputes the claim that Marcion was the son of a bishop. J. P. Arendzen writing in the *Catholic Encyclopedia* of 1910, holds that Marcion was an assistant bishop to his father. Most agree that all this diversity in the records arose out of the controversy that surrounded the man.

this that Origen sought to furnish. In the ensuing years, while running the school at Alexandria, he composed five books of commentary on John's Gospel, eight on Genesis, a commentary on the first twenty-five psalms and on the Book of Lamentations, as well as books entitled *On the Resurrection* and *First Principles* and ten now assembled under the heading *Miscellanies.*

The task was monumental, and Ambrose was the taskmaster. "The work of editing," says Origen in one letter, "leaves us no time for supper, or after supper no time for exercise and relaxation. Even at these times we're compelled to debate questions on interpretation and to amend manuscripts. Even the night can't be given over to the help of a little sleep, for our discussions extend far into the evening. To say nothing of our labor all morning." Origen's friendly tribute to Ambrose's tough production demands also survives. He writes: "You're not content to fulfill the office of a taskmaster when I'm there, but even when I'm absent, you demand that I should spend most of my time on the latest job. For my part, I'm inclined to shrink from work, and avoid the pitfall threatening those

who write about God. I'd rather read the Bible than write all these books."

How long he remained in Julia Mammaea's household at Antioch is not recorded precisely. She was "a very religious woman," says Eusebius. "He remained some time with her, instructing her in all that could serve to glorify the Lord and confirm his divine teachings."

The effects of his teachings redound more visibly in Alexander, who is said in one none-too-reliable account to have placed images of Christ and Abraham before all others in his oratory, and whose policies and appointments when emperor consistently favored the Christians. At one point, he proposed to build for them a great church in Rome, but was discouraged because it could appear he was making Christianity a state religion. At another, when some Christians were disputing the

ownership of a former tavern with those who wanted to restore it, he decided for the Christians. Better God be honored there, he said; Rome didn't need another tavern. Finally, on the walls of the palace he had these Latin words engraved: *Et prout vultis ut saciant vobis homines et vos facite illis similiter*. They were not attributed, and the day had not yet come when Romans would instantly recognize

*Origen had joined the household of Julia Mammaea in Antioch as an instructor for both herself and her son Alexander. His influence appears to have been greater upon the son, who is said to have placed a head of Christ before all the other figures in his oratory.*

3. The historian Herodian states plainly that Julia Mammaea selected a wife for her son, Alexander, from the senatorial class. Her formal name was Gnaea Seia Herennia Sallustia Orba Barbia Orbiana. Alexander loved her, and Mammaea soon grew fearful that this relationship would erode her authority. She banished her daughter-in-law from the palace amidst abuse so violent that the younger woman's father abandoned his position of honor in the imperial household for the army. There, he extolled the virtues of Alexander, but complained bitterly of Mammaea's temper. This got back to Mammaea, and she ordered that he be executed and Orbiana sent further away, to Libya. Alexander opposed these measures, but could not stand up to his mother, says Herodian.

"And as ye would that men should do to you, do ye also to them likewise" as the words of Jesus Christ (Luke: 6:31).

In one instance, Origen may have clashed with Julia Mammaea.[3] As her son grew older and bolder, he began to resist his mother's direction, especially in her habitual enrichment of herself at public expense, or at the unjust expense of others, and her vicious persecution of the woman she found for Alexander to marry. This resistance was likely due to the teaching of Origen. Christians, Origen would have said, do not exempt their leaders from the rules that apply to everybody else—a concept that Julia would not have easily embraced.

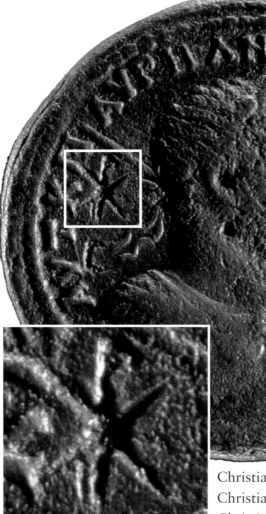

*This bronze coin was minted during the reign of Caracalla (shown carrying a spear). The image of the emperor was sacred, even on a coin, yet behind the head has been scratched a Christian symbol—presumably an act of defiance by a long-forgotten owner. The symbol ☧ made up of the Greek capital letters Chi-"X" and Rho-"P" together forming the first two letters of the Greek name for "Christ," is just visible on the left between the emperor's head and the inscription.*

In any event, the mother-son regime made itself felt rapidly. They first sought to restore the power of the Senate, naming sixteen of its members to a council of advisers, as had Augustus. At the same time, the new regime clamped down on corruption in the courts, prohibited prostitution, closed the disreputable bars, severely punished bureaucratic graft, tried unsuccessfully to establish a national bank for the safe deposit of personal property, inaugurated an economic development plan for the city of Rome, sponsored trade associations, and launched a new imperial building program. While capital punishment was retained for criminal charges, not a single political execution occurred in Alexander's reign, says the historian Herodian.

But the age of persecution was not over, and some Christians knew this. However sympathetic the regime might be to the Christians, and however many held posts in the imperial government, the Christians themselves noted ominous signs. Their fear of the mob mentality still weighed heavily on them. And even Alexander retained as his senior legal counsel Domitius Ulpian, a militant anti-Christian but a man who seemed ready to check the Praetorians, now back in much the same position of power they had held before Severus purged them. Twice the Praetorians tried and failed to assassinate Ulpian, and two Praetorian prefects paid for that failure with their lives. In 228, however, the Praetorians succeeded. Though Ulpian was now gone, the Christians no doubt saw that he had republished all the anti-Christian rescripts of former emperors, thereby providing clear legal grounds for a new crackdown on the Christians if and when the present regime were overthrown.

That possibility was far from remote. Beneficial though their reforms may

*A marble relief showing soldiers of the Praetorian Guard. The once-mighty guard brazenly offered the imperial crown to the highest bidder, but later knew itself no match for the battle-hardened troops of Septimius Severus. Surrendering without a fight, the Praetorians were ordered not to approach within a hundred miles of Rome—on pain of death.*

have been for Rome, Julia and her son had made a fundamental error. They had underestimated the political power of the frontline legions. Indeed, they had come down hard on the army, cutting its pay to pre-Caracalla levels, dismissing entire legions for insubordination, and preventing semi-retired officers from drawing full pay while awaiting appointments that were never intended to be made. Finally, to enable the civil arm to regain control of the military, they turned over to the Senate the power to appoint some of the army's top staff officers. In peace, the military grievances this caused might not matter much. But Alexander, who had never known war, was now about to experience it.

A revolution in Persia had overthrown the Parthian regime, and the new Persian king, Artaxerxes (pronounced as *AR-ta-ZERK-sees*), having raised an enormous army, declared a plan to seize for Persia all the provinces of the Roman Empire east of the Mediterranean and the Aegean.[4] Alexander, now twenty-four, rose to the occasion, drafted new troops from every province in the empire, and set in motion plans to assemble them at Antioch for a major offensive

---

4. The lands adjacent to the east coast of the Mediterranean, including modern Turkey, have been disputed by the powers of East and West almost from the dawn of human history. The ancient peoples from beyond the Tigris and Euphrates—Assyrians, Babylonians, and Persians—held them until the conquests of Alexander the Great brought them into the sphere of the West. They remained under the Romans and Byzantine Empire until the eighth century A.D., when the rise of the Muslim Arabs returned them to the East. The West sought to regain the lands with the Crusades early in the second millennium and ultimately failed. Armed with new technology and a thirst for oil, the West regained a position in them during the nineteenth and twentieth centuries. In the course of this, the West established the state of Israel.

against Persia. Tearfully, he left Rome behind and took up his position as commander of the assembled legions.

A calamity followed for which he was held wholly responsible. He and his commanders laid out a three-pronged attack, one through Armenia in the north, a second through southern Mesopotamia in the marshlands where the Tigris joins the Euphrates, and a third, the largest, under his personal command, through central Mesopotamia.

The first attack clawed its way through the Armenian mountains, defeated the Persian force sent to oppose it, then headed south to join Alexander's main body coming up the middle. But it wasn't there, because the emperor had canceled the main attack. The reason was never explained. The army laid it to sheer cowardice, blaming his mother, who was with him and undoubtedly feared he would be killed. Thousands of Roman soldiers perished in the retreat through Armenia.

Then a second blow fell. The Germans on the Rhine broke through and were moving south towards Roman Illyria on the Adriatic coast. Alexander and his mother rushed north, bringing elements of the Antiochian force with them. Confronted with the German horde, however, Alexander had another idea. He and his mother possessed a great deal of money, he said. He offered a bribe to the Germans if they would withdraw. They accepted, but the Roman troops were aghast. Anxious to regain the pay scale Alexander had taken from them, they were ready to fight. But now the money that had been withheld from the army was being paid to their enemies. The empire, they said, was in the hands of a woman and a mother's boy who had surrounded themselves with Christians.

They also had a new champion: Maximinus, a giant of a man whose reputed

*Gaius Julius Versus Maximinus, identified in some accounts as a former shepherd who rose through the ranks to become one of Alexander's best commanders—and then his assassin and successor. For six years the stern rule of Maximinus prevailed. He trounced the most rebellious of the Rhine barbarians, the Alamanni, so thoroughly it was twenty years before they again attacked. Maximinus also combed the imperial administration, firing all of Alexander's appointees, in particular the Christians, and executing many of them.*

dimensions grew with the years until legend had him standing eight feet tall and wearing his wife's bracelet on his thumb, like a ring. According to tradition, he had once been a Thracian shepherd boy, a barbarian himself, that is, who had risen through the legions to senior rank, first through his skill in training recruits, and then through his competence in command, much of this under Alexander, who saw in the man the military capability he himself lacked.

But by now the Rhine legions, fed up with Julia's covetous ways, Alexander's military ineptitude, and the outrage of the German bribe, seized Maximinus and (whether in farce or in fact) forced him at sword point to accept the purple toga. Acquiescing, he told the troops they must act at once, since both mother and son were now near Mainz on the Rhine. They marched in a body on Alexander's camp. It was March, 235.

Warned of their advance, the young emperor assembled those troops who were with him and appealed for their loyalty. At first it seemed he would get it, but as Maximinus's contingent came into view the mood changed. The arrivees, says Herodian, jeered at the young emperor as "a mean little sissy" and as "a timid little lad tied to his mother's apron strings." Why, they shouted, did they not come to the side of a man who was a soldier, who had lived his life among them, and who fought the empire's enemies with arms, not money—their money?

Herodian describes the end. Alexander ran terrified to his tent and clung to his mother, while blaming her bitterly for causing his ruin. There, Maximinus's centurion-assassins found them both, and swords in hand, put an end to them, to the family of Severus, and to the first genuinely pro-Christian emperor.

For the next six years, the stern rule of Maximinus prevailed. Under his direction the army's pay was raised and the most rebellious of the Rhine barbarians, the Alamanni, were thrashed so thoroughly it was another twenty years before they tried again to break out. Maximinus then combed the imperial administration, firing all of Alexander's appointees, in particular the Christians, and executing most

## The troops jeered at the young Emperor Alexander as a 'mean little sissy,' calling him 'a timid little lad tied to his mother's apron strings' who spent their money foolishly.

of them. No doubt a warrant for Origen's arrest was issued in Alexandria. But he wasn't there. In another twist of fate, his life was saved again, this time because Bishop Demetrius had driven him out of town.

Four years before Alexander's assassination, Origen had been called to Greece to resolve an ecclesiastical conflict there. En route, he passed through Palestine, and once again the bishops asked him to preach. Remembering the rebuke this had caused the last time, they decided to remove the problem by ordaining him to the priesthood. But this set off a much worse explosion. Protesting that Origen could be ordained only by his own bishop in Alexandria, and that in any event his self-emasculation had disqualified him, Demetrius summoned a council of the Eastern bishops to have Origen's priesthood annulled. When the move failed, he called a second council. This time it carried, effectively discrediting Origen as principal of the Catechetical School and forcing him out of his beloved city to Caesarea in Palestine.[5] Forewarned there that he was a

---

5. In his conflict with Origen, Demetrius invariably appears to be acting out of sheer jealousy. However, the fact that two of Origen's former pupils, both in turn successors to Demetrius as bishops of Alexandria, voted for the motion to void Origen's ordination, is evidence that what Demetrius sought was not considered all that unusual and his motive, therefore, not all that vindictive.

# The Great Debate of the third century

**The Platonist philosopher Celsus states the case against the Christians; with Origen's reply sixty years later, some basic issues are set forth**

*Some time in the late second century, a Platonist philosopher named Celsus, apparently well-connected to the imperial government, produced a formal treatise in opposition to Christianity. Entitled* The True Discourse, *it gained wide circulation and may perhaps have been written (says the historian Marta Sordi) at the suggestion of Emperor Marcus Aurelius, to be cited in philosophical circles as the decisive "Case Against the Christians." Some sixty years later, the Christian spokesman Origen, urged by his sponsor and business partner Ambrose, wrote a formal rebuttal entitled, simply,* Contra Celsum, *to which the Christians gave similarly wide circulation. Five of Celsus's principal arguments are given below, along with Origen's replies, paraphrased from the original text, in order to summarize them. Plainly, they prefigure arguments that would continue to be made against the Christians for the next two thousand years.*

## ROUND ONE: Do Christians think they're superior and set themselves apart?

**CELSUS:** Christians (and likewise Jews) set themselves apart, thinking they're better than everybody else, and have some special wisdom. They form into secret and hidden groups, and the people who get involved in them are setting themselves against everybody else. Certainly, the world's religions differ in the names they give the gods and how they make their sacrifices, but they all believe in one supreme God. As the philosophers argue, everyone believes more or less the same things. So Christian threats of eternal punishment for those who don't believe in their Jesus make it evident they are against everybody else.

**ORIGEN:** All people, not just Christians, act on the basis of what they discern as the Truth. There's nothing secret in what Christians believe true. For who is ignorant of the statement that Jesus was born of a virgin, that he was crucified, and that his Resurrection is an article of faith? But unlike Greek philosophy, Christianity is not based on a theory but on an event and on a Person. And anyone versed in Greek philosophy, looking fairly at the gospel history, must see a demonstration of his own philosophy's fulfillment more divine than any theories established by Grecian arguments. He would see in Jesus Christ the reality behind what for philosophers is mere theory. However, by contrast, the idols that ordinary people worship are neither theory nor the Truth. They are either dumb stone or demons. Yet no one is supposed to point this out, and even Celsus's cherished philosophers have constantly been persecuted for doing so. Is it surprising, therefore, that Christians should be persecuted even more when they assert that God offered himself up as a sacrifice to free people from these superstitions and demons?

## ROUND TWO: Was Mary an adulteress, Jesus illegitimate, his miracles faked?

**CELSUS:** Jewish converts to Christianity are particularly foolish for abandoning the laws of their fathers to follow a charlatan punished by the Jews for his crimes. Jesus did not fulfill what the prophets promised in the Messiah. He invented his virgin birth, having been born in a Jewish village of a poor woman turned out of doors by her husband, a carpenter by trade, because she was convicted of adultery—with a Roman soldier. She then disgracefully gave birth to Jesus, an illegitimate child, who later hired himself out as a servant in Egypt because of his poverty and there acquired some miraculous powers—on which the Egyptians greatly pride themselves; he returned to his own country and by means of these powers proclaimed himself a god.

His followers were ten or twelve infamous barkeepers and fishermen—hardly the company of God. His miracles were either lies or magic tricks. What great deeds did Jesus perform as a god? Did he put his enemies to shame or humiliate those who were plotting against him? Nor did Jesus recover the lost glory of Solomon's Jerusalem. He did not even keep the loyalty of his own followers. His prediction of his own death was invented by his followers, and the fable of his Resurrection from death is nothing new—similar tales were told of the philosopher Pythagoras's ghost. If Jesus really rose from the dead, why did he appear only to his disciples and not to his persecutors?

**ORIGEN:** Strange is it indeed that a humble carpenter's son from a nondescript village in a backwater province has been able to shake the whole inhabited world far beyond that which Pythagoras or Plato or any other wise man from anywhere, any prince or any general, has ever succeeded in doing. But it would be even stranger if his disciples hadn't seen Jesus after his Resurrection and weren't really persuaded of his divinity, and yet still they endured the same sufferings as their Master, exposed themselves to danger, and left their homeland to teach Jesus' message—all suffering martyrdom rather than deny his Resurrection. Even Jesus' detractors, spreading stories about his mother's adultery, must admit there was something unusual in his birth. But it is highly improbable that an illegitimate child, living a deceptive life, would then willingly sacrifice himself for his people. Yet the entire gospel history is an account of Jesus' self-sacrifice. Celsus reproaches the Savior because of his sufferings. But we must say that his sufferings were the subject of prophecy, and it was for the benefit of mankind that he should die on mankind's account.

## ROUND FOUR: Could the God of a huge universe care about mere humans?

CELSUS: Christians' supposedly unique revelation is really just warmed-over Greek philosophy. When the Christians tell us that God is a spirit, they're merely repeating the Stoic saying that the God is a spirit penetrating all and encompassing all. And the Christian idea of a future life is borrowed from Greek poets and philosophers; the resurrection of the body is simply a corruption of the old idea of the transmigration of souls. But the Christians maintain that there *has* descended upon the earth a god, or Son of a god, who will make the inhabitants of the earth righteous. This is a most shameless assertion, not needing much refutation—shameless in that it assumes humans are something special in the eyes of the god.

ORIGEN: The god of the philosophers may be Reason itself, but the God of the Christians is both Reason and Love. What the philosophers find shameless is the thought that God could love his creation so much that he would enter into it. We answer, then, that God, not being known by wicked men, would desire to make himself known, not because he thinks that he meets with less than his due, but because the knowledge of him will free the possessor from unhappiness.

## ROUND FIVE: Shouldn't Christians just give up and worship the gods of nature?

CELSUS: Different mythologies simply point to the same natural powers, worshiped in different countries, under different names. Christians are ungrateful for the gifts of nature when they refuse to worship the deities who symbolize nature's powers. And these powers, spirits, or demons mediate between God and man, and are the immediate source of prophecy and wonder-working. So I invite Christians to give up their life apart, abandon their vain hope of establishing their rule over all the earth, and rejoin the majority religion.

ORIGEN: We decline the invitation. This is forbidden to us, for we have been taught not to worship the creature instead of the Creator, but to know that the creation shall be delivered from the bondage of corruption into liberty. So it remains for the readers of this discourse to judge which of the two breathes most of the Spirit of the true God, of piety towards him, and of that truth which leads men by sound doctrines to the noblest life.

## ROUND THREE: Although Jews and Christians endlessly quarrel aren't they really the same?

CELSUS: Both Christians and Jews are given to rebellion. Both believe that the Divine Spirit intended to send a Savior to the human race, disagreeing only about whether the person predicted has actually come or not. They're like frogs and lizards arguing which of them God loves more. But both rest on the same principle: revolution. The Jews revolted against the Egyptians, Christians against the Jews, and now Christians revolt among themselves. They exclude the wise and good and gather only with the ignorant and sinful. In their weakness they call on a Savior, as if God could not by his own power do what Christians say he put Christ on Earth to do. And in their vain self-importance, they believe the world was made for man's use and benefit, rather than appreciating that God has a plan for the whole universe in which humanity plays a small part and individuals none.

ORIGEN: No, Christians are not rebellious. Had they owed their origin to rebellion, they would not have adopted laws so exceedingly mild that when it is their fate to be slain as sheep, they do not resist their persecutors. The real issue is whether the Supreme God could have exerted a providential care for human beings at a particular time and place in history. The answer is found in the history of the Jewish people. How could the Jewish nation have continued to survive had there existed among them no promise of the knowledge of future events? This people alone was taught to view with contempt all those considered gods by the heathens, not as gods but as demons. The whole nation had been taught to despise the deities of other lands. Yet, despite being cast as an enemy among all the world's nations, against all odds the Jews both remained faithful to God and survived in their faith. There have been many prodigious events throughout human history, but in the Jews, providence can be seen to have worked for the good of all, in that their Messiah has come for all.

wanted man, Origen fled to Cappadocia, where he hid out until the Maximinus regime ended.

His publishing partner, Ambrose, wasn't so lucky. He was arrested and jailed in Alexandria, and seemed about to be executed. Origen wrote to him what became a Christian classic of the times. Entitled *Exhortation to Martyrdom*, it urged Ambrose to face up to the ordeal as one who had been liberated from the limitations of bodily existence and was thereby able to behold Christ in all his fullness. But Ambrose was soon released, and the work of the publishing house resumed.

Ambrose's release was evidence of the general chaos into which the imperial administration had dissolved. Maximinus was the first of a long line of soldier-emperors. In his experience, power was retained only by brute force, the force of the frontline army. Keep the troops happy and you can stay in office, he reasoned, and the same view now gained sway in imperial affairs. That overlooked, of course, one critical factor. There was always more than one ambitious general. Consequently, twenty-six men, most of them generals, would succeed one another as emperor over the next sixty years, many of them murdered by their own troops.

Maximinus was the first to suffer this fate. Barbarian by birth and manner, he was seen by the imperial aristocracy as ruining them with the taxes he imposed to keep the army victorious and happy. A rebellion against him broke out in Carthage and spread to Rome under the titular leadership of a father and son, both gaining brief mention in Roman history as Gordian I and II. As Maximinus assembled a huge force to advance on Rome and confront them, a counterrevolution on his behalf broke out in Carthage, where Gordian II was trampled to death in the rout of his followers, and the elder Gordian hanged himself.

The Senate then named from their own number two successor emperors. With such instability of authority, serious riots broke out in the capital, and Maximinus's huge force began advancing upon it. But when he attacked the northern Italian trading city of Aquileia, whose citizenry had very effectively prepared themselves for a protracted siege, Maximinus, to his chagrin, found that he couldn't take the place. Nor could he advance on Rome, because the rivers were all in flood, and he couldn't cross them. Thwarted and furious, he turned bitterly on his own commanders, berating them for incompetence. That was the last straw. The following day, his troops quietly murdered him. Meanwhile, in the continuing riots at Rome, the senatorial emperors met the same fate at the hands of the Praetorians. These now hailed as emperor the thirteen-year-old grandson of Gordian I and proclaimed him Emperor Gordian III.

Young Gordian was to reign more than five years. That was unusual stability for the time, partly because the administrative chaos had exhausted the populace, but chiefly because of new trouble in the East. The Persians again began attacking Roman outposts in Mesopotamia, alarming and in this way uniting the empire. Painfully, the Romans pushed the invaders out of northern Mesopotamia, but neither Gordian III nor his gifted minister, Timesthius, survived the campaign. The latter died of an illness. How Gordian III perished is disputed. Persian records say he was slain in a battle; most Roman accounts say he was murdered by his

*No doubt aware a warrant would likely be issued for his arrest, Origen knew his life would be in danger and left Alexandria. He fled to the rugged mountains of Cappadocia (above), where he hid out until the Maximinus regime ended.*

**ORIGEN ON DEMONS**

*We do not deny that there are many demons upon earth. But they have no power over those who "have put on the whole armor of God" and who are ever engaged in contests with them.*

troops, fomented into rebellion by Marcus Julius Philippus, known to history as Philip the Arab.

Eusebius records the report that Philip was Christian, making him the first Christian emperor, and relates that in the year 244, when Philip donned the purple toga, he was required by Bishop Babylas of Antioch to do public penance before being allowed to attend an Easter service. The penance was imposed for his role in the death of Gordian III. If true, that would have had momentous implications, then and in years to come, for it would mean that a Christian bishop had exercised authority over a Roman emperor.

There was another indication of a link between the Christians and Philip. He came from Bosra in Arabia, where a flourishing church had once sought Origen's help in resolving a theological controversy. The Christian records mention letters that Origen wrote to Philip and to his wife, the empress Otacilia Severa, though none of this is found in Origen's surviving works.

However, most modern authorities doubt Philip's ostensible Christianity, pointing out that Philip's regime was hardly beneficial to the faith. As the historian Michael L. Meckler observes, Philip was indistinguishable from other emperors in his use of pagan titles and symbols, and he made no improvements to the legal status of Christians.

Worst of all, he bought off rather than defeated the enemies on the northern and eastern frontiers, levied heavy taxes to do it, and thereby aroused the hatred of the soldiers. One in particular possessed a deep loathing of both Philip and the

*Origen wistfully recalled the days when Christians went to martyrdom with courage, returning from the cemeteries after burying the slain, and assembling together, united, indivisible.*

Christians. This was Gaius Messius Quintus Decius, Roman commander on the Danube, a devout pagan who saw Christianity not just as a nuisance, distraction, and rival to the gods of his ancestors but as a mortal malignancy afflicting the whole empire that must be stamped out completely in every nook and cranny where it appeared, until all trace of it was gone. Christians feared that a Decian coup would be followed by the most sweeping persecution they had ever known.

By Philip's day, Origen was hard at work in Caesarea. His school there was far more of an evangelical or missionary enterprise than the one at Alexandria, and an intimately nostalgic portrait of it is preserved in the memoirs of one of its students, Gregory Thaumaturgus (the Wonder Worker). En route to law school at Beirut, Gregory heard Origen speak of Jesus Christ and was so enchanted that he abandoned law to become one of Origen's students. The school's goal, writes Gregory, was not simply to capture the mind of the student, but also the soul, and Origen taught not just by word but by example, pausing sometimes when explaining a difficult point to pray for God's guidance, and to ask his pupils to do the same.

Gregory recalls the school as a vision of Heaven itself. "Both day and night,"

*Eusebius records that when Philip became emperor he was required by Bishop Babylas of Antioch to do public penance before being allowed to attend an Easter service. The penance was imposed for his role in the death of Gordian III—says Eusebius.*

he writes, "the holy laws are declared, and hymns and songs and spiritual words are heard; where there is perpetual sunlight; where by day, in waking vision, we have access to the mysteries of God, and where by night, in dreams, we are still occupied with what the soul has seen and handled in the day; and where, in short, the inspiration of divine things prevails continually over all."

Yet Origen's own most vivid memories hearkened back to another school in another era, when faith was tested by deed, and his students one by one paid for their convictions with their lives. "That was when one really was a believer," he wrote as age crept upon him, "when one used to go to martyrdom with courage in the church, when returning from the cemeteries whither we had accompanied

# Wine flows and spectacles dazzle as Rome marks a thousand years

**Wild animals are slain in their thousands, the mobs are gorged with food because the emperor Philip the Arab knew how to throw a great party**

Whatever else he achieved during his five years as emperor of Rome, one thing can be said for certain of Philip the Arab: he threw a great party.

The occasion was the Roman millennium, held in April of A.D. 248—the official celebration of Rome's one thousandth anniversary. Even in Philip's time, no one knew for sure when Rome was founded, but 752 B.C. seemed as good a guess as any, and once the date was declared it stood, just as the year 2000 would later be hailed worldwide, even though that new millennium didn't really begin until 2001.

Philip, recognizing that such a milestone demanded not just ceremony but spectacle, used every promotional device the third century could contrive. Heralds went out to summon the citizenry from far and wide. Coins that would be cherished by collectors centuries later were struck, stamped with images of the elephants, lions, giraffes, and other wild animals that would meet a bloody death during the millennial games. Platforms and stages and other facilities arose everywhere, food was piled high with an appropriate deluge of wine.

Everyone in the city and the surrounding country-

*An elephant is shown being led aboard ship in a detail from a mosaic in the Villa del Casale, Piazza Armerina, Sicily. A fabulous collection of exotic beasts—including thirty-two elephants— was collected for games to celebrate the thousandth anniversary of Rome's founding in A.D. 248. All were loosed in the arenas during the festivities, and most were slaughtered for the crowd's entertainment.*

the bodies of the martyrs, we came back to our meetings, and the whole church would be assembled there, united, unbreakable. Then the catechumens were catechized in the midst of the martyrdoms. . . . It was then that we saw prodigies. Then faithful were few in numbers but were really faithful, advancing along the straight and narrow path leading to life."

He, too, would finally join them. When Origen was about sixty-four, the dreaded coup occurred. The troops on the Danube rebelled against Philip, defeat-

*The emperor Marcus Julius Philippus—Philip the Arab—was according to some accounts the first Christian emperor, but there is no conclusive proof and many historians doubt his Christianity. In any event, his rule was indistinguishable from previous pagan emperors and he did nothing to improve the legal hazards faced by Christians.*

side joined enthusiastically in the affair. There was so much to see and do that many Romans went entirely without sleep for three nights—not that there was any possibility of sleep anyway, the city's inns having filled to the brim and the streets overflowing with visitors and noise.

What specifics history would record of the festivities come secondhand, but the accounts are given credibility by records of earlier, lesser events. The millennial celebration, for instance, was the occasion of *Ludi Saeculares,* the Secular Games, which had been held before, most magnificently in 17 B.C. when, among other things, the Roman poet Horace led a chorus of fifty-four young noblemen and noblewomen in the singing of a hymn that he had composed for the occasion. Upwards of a million spectators had poured into Rome for that session of the games, and when the millennium's time arrived, the crowd was far greater.

Revelers massed upon the city's rolling hills, illumined after dark by the flames of thousands of handheld torches. The *Quindecemuiri,* the sacred college of fifteen men who guarded the holy Sibylline Books, lent appropriate gravity to the opening ceremonies, and Philip himself presided, as along the river Tiber amid the smoke and heat and blaze of the torches, priests sacrificed a bellowing stream of steers, heifers, lambs and sows to the gods.

Carefully selected white bulls were slaughtered to honor Jupiter, the patron god of Rome; and the goddess Ilithyia, credited with aiding childbirth, was worshiped with overflowing offerings of cakes and incense. All over the city, athletes tossed and raced and wrestled, theatrical troupes staged specially commissioned plays, competition-ready chariots rumbled, musicians played, wine flowed freely, and great quantities of wheat, barley, and beans were distributed ceremonially to all.

Spectators thronged, of course, to the Colosseum, where each day brought new spectacles of pageantry and death. In between the energetic jugglers and dancers and clowns, prisoners whose executions had been postponed for the festival were brought out in hordes to die, some in cages with poisonous snakes, some set afire, some gored or trampled. Gladiators stabbed and killed each other in battle as the ecstatic audience feasted and placed bets.

Gordian III, Philip's predecessor, had been collecting exotic animals for the event from the far reaches of the empire, dispatching teams of adventurers into Africa and India to bring back fabulous beasts in cages and chains. The *Historiae Augustae* records that he had accumulated thirty-two elephants, ten elk, ten tigers, seventy lions, thirty leopards, ten hyenas, six hippopotamuses, one rhinoceros, ten giraffes, twenty wild asses, and vast herds of other animals. All were loosed in the arenas at one time or another during the festival, and most were slaughtered for the crowd's entertainment.

The Australian history writer Tony Perrottet offers a colorful summary of Philip's three-day spectacular: "To imagine a modern equivalent, we would have to combine Australia's 1988 Bicentennial festivities with the Olympic Games, High Mass at the Vatican, the Gay and Lesbian Mardi Gras, and a Nuremberg rally."

If Philip had hoped to distract an unsettled populace with bread and circuses, he succeeded—but only briefly. Barely a year later, rebellion erupted, Philip died either in battle or at the hands of his own men, and the Roman general Decius took the throne. Perhaps because the cost was so great and the political outcome was so poor, the Secular Games were never held again. ■

WOOD

*Realizing that a recantation from Origen would have a devastating effect on Christian morale, the emperor Decius subjected him to prolonged and agonizing torture—locked in a dark cell, his feet stretched to a crippling degree. But Origen did not yield. Released when Decius was killed on the German front, Origen later died of his injuries.*

ing his army near Verona and setting off the greatest persecution that Christians had ever endured. Origen was among the first arrested, but he was not put to death. Instead, his captors realized what a prize he would make if he could be induced to recant his belief in the Nazarene Jew, and declare his obedience to the gods of the empire.

In an early-on attempt at what a later generation would call brainwashing, Decius locked Origen in a dark cell, often with an iron collar around his neck, tortured, threatened with fire, and repeatedly tempted with freedom if he would merely give the word. Eusebius describes the torments: "The evil demon, bent on his destruction, brought all the weapons in his armory to bear, and fought him with every device and expedient, attacking him with more determination than anyone he was fighting at the time—the dreadful cruelties he endured for the word Christ, chains and bodily torments, agony in irons, and the darkness of his cell, how for days on end his legs were pulled four paces apart in the torturer's stocks."

But Origen remained steadfast, and Decius was never awarded his prized apostate. Bruised, battered, and greatly weakened, Origen was released in 251, Decius having perished in fighting on the Danube frontier. Origen died about three years later, at Tyre. For centuries his tomb lay in the wall behind the high altar of Tyre's Church of the Holy Sepulchre, destroyed by the Muslims during the Crusades, a calamity from which Tyre never recovered. Today, poor fishermen, who occupy the huts and hovels that stand on the site of what were once Tyre's great palaces, speak of a vault under which lie the remains of a man they call "Great Oriunus."

Origen towers over all others in the postbiblical period as the first great Christian theologian. He was preeminently a student of the Scriptures, and his teachings created discussions and arguments among Christians for the next three hundred years. Then in 553, what had become known as "Origenism" was condemned by the Second Council of Constantinople, because its concept of the soul and of the nature of man's resurrected body were deemed to be deeply flawed, minimizing Christian salvation, conflicting with the resurrection of the body, and creating an unnatural separation between body and soul. It was deemed to be founded on much too speculative a use of the Christian Scriptures.

How Origen might himself have responded to this rejection of his teaching is suggested by his writings, says the Christian historian Michael Green. He would simply have accepted the rebuff. "Is it all that amazing," Origen once wrote, "that if the Lord was willing to be made a curse for slaves, that the slave should be willing to be made a curse for his brethren?" In other words, "If helping your brother costs you your reputation, what does it matter? Christ didn't care. Why should we?" It was this attitude, says Green, that has made many Christians revere Origen ever since.

# CHAPTER 9

# Out of some 50 gospels which ones matter?

## A chaos of books and stories on Jesus' life pose a growing problem, though four retain credibility

By the late second century, a mind-boggling welter of writings about the life and teachings of Jesus had proliferated wildly among Christians. Imagine, for example, a congregation listening to accounts of the child Jesus in the so-called infancy Gospels.

From the *Gospel of Thomas,* they would hear this story about him as a five-year-old: "When Jesus was going through the midst of the city, a boy threw a stone . . . and struck him on the shoulder. And Jesus said to him, 'Thou shalt not go on thy way.' And directly falling down the boy died." Neighbors demanded that the family move Jesus out of town "for he is killing our children."

Then there was the time the young Messiah profaned a Sabbath by making twelve clay sparrows. When Joseph reprimanded him, Jesus refused to answer. Instead he "looked upon the sparrows and said, 'Fly and live and remember me.'" Instantly the clay creatures turned into real birds and flapped away.

Worshipers learned that at age eight Jesus ventured into a den of lions, and the beasts simply fell down and worshiped him. They also heard how he used his bare hands to stretch a board that his carpenter father had cut too short, and how the child laughed after he had so thoroughly outshone his adult teacher that the poor man lamented, "There is nothing for me but despondency and death on account of this boy."

How were Christians to reconcile the spiteful, self-centered show-off of these fables with messages of love and charity they heard in the older, less fantastic accounts of Jesus' life? Such a conundrum was typical of scores of interpretive puzzles created by a growing diversity of texts.

After more than two centuries, Christians faced "a terrifying jungle of scholarly contradictions," observes historian Paul Johnson in his *History of Christianity*. The further in time and distance that the movement spread from its point of origin, the more teachings diverged and discrepancies arose. By the end of the second century, he estimates, there were in circulation some forty-seven hundred relevant manuscripts and one hundred thousand written quotations or allusions to Jesus or early church fathers.

Many factors accounted for confusions and inconsistencies in Scripture: lack of written accounts during Jesus' lifetime; the rich oral tradition ("miasma," Johnson calls it) from which written texts emanated; tensions between Gentile and Judaic interests; rivalries between two evolving loci of church power in the Eastern Mediterranean and Rome; competition of Christianity with mystery cults and Gnosticism; melding of the faith with local traditions and cultures, and attempts at compromise; pressures of politics on spiritual affairs in the Greco-Roman world; mistranslation between languages; simple errors in reading and copying handwriting; and the sheer physical disintegration of papyrus on which most writing was preserved.

The desire of enthusiasts to attract followers often led to overemphasis on the supernatural and embellishments of dramatic detail.

Bitter controversies over doctrine and liturgy also drove selection and editing of texts. There were arguments about everything from relationships between the material and spiritual worlds to apocalypse, judgment, and the imminent return of Christ; about ritual, the nature of Jesus as both man and God, and the concept of a Holy Trinity; about the meaning of parables Jesus told and the stories about him; about the role of women in the church and the function of clergy. But beyond all this, one overarching fact counted most of all: there was simply no controlling ecclesiastical authority to determine what Scripture should be used.

Around almost all great historical figures, the twentieth-century Christian apologist C. S. Lewis observes, there grows up a body of legend. First come the historical, more contemporary accounts of what they said and did, often with great gaps in the chronology, particularly in their earlier years, when their lives go unrecorded. Then, usually a century or more after they died, there gradually accumulates a body of far more colorful, spectacular tales, the basis of a mythology that admirers create and cherish.

Precisely this, he said, occurred around the figure of Jesus. The earlier texts circulating among the first congregations included what Christians now accept as the New Testament. And among these, the four Gospels, from very early times called Matthew, Mark, Luke, and John, had gained general recognition as a group. All contained a critical common core, centering in the story of Christ's Passion. The narrative of Jesus' suffering, death, and Resurrection was at the heart of Christian experience and was the climax of each Gospel.

These accounts were always longest and most consistent in shared detail and clearly the oldest and most important of the early writings. They plainly demonstrated that Jesus was not merely a good man but something beyond that. Son of God, they said, whatever that meant. Clearly intended to be read aloud, these four Gospels contained short, mostly unconnected anecdotes telling about something Jesus said or did.

But there were huge gaps in them. Between the birth and infancy stories in Matthew and Luke, and apart from a single instance in Luke alone, they recount nothing of Jesus until his ministry began at about the age of thirty. This is typical of almost anyone who lived at that time, except, of course, emperors and kings whose childhood was often noted because a significant future was foreseen for them. Gradually, therefore, a distinction was being drawn between the four accounts, which represented the memory of eyewitnesses, and the later fantastic accounts, like the infancy Gospels, written some 150 years after his death, which were the stuff of mythology.

Meanwhile, Paul's Epistles had been collected and shared widely, although there were arguments over the authenticity of some letters attributed to Paul. The Book of Revelation was broadly distributed as well. But it, too, was a source of contention because many Gentiles considered the treatment too much like pre-Christian Jewish literature. The fourth-century Christian historian Eusebius, for example, personally rejected the very idea of apocalypse as unbiblical.

More than fifty texts like the *Gospel of Thomas* had appeared and some dozen or so of these were in fairly heavy use. They fell into two categories: reiterations of primitive tradition, or romantically amplified recastings of synoptic Gospel narratives.

The *Gospel of Thomas*, for example, circulated in four popular versions, two in Greek and two in Latin, and all were quite different. In extravagantly magnifying the divine aspects of the boy miracle worker, it removed almost all traces of humanity from Jesus (other than some disagreeable traits of character, such as a vindictive streak). Much of the book's appeal was its unique description of Jesus' life between ages five and twelve.

Other popular early gospels were:

• *The Protoevangelion Jacobi*, loosely known as the *Book of James*. An example of the early veneration accorded the Blessed Virgin Mary, it includes the story of her own birth, education, and marriage. She herself was the miraculous offspring of the previously childless Joachim and Anna, and was dedicated to service in the Temple at age three. A priest chose Joseph as her husband after the miraculous sign of a dove emerging from his staff and landing on his head.

# The beloved story of Cecilia tells of a girl, a boy, and a martyrdom

**Ships bear her name, and a famed New York choir honors this patron saint of musicians whose convert-husband respected her life-time virginity**

In church stained glass windows, St. Cecilia is usually seated at the keyboard of a pipe organ. As the patron saint of musicians, she has given her name to schools and churches around the world. The Grace Line steamship, *Santa Cecilia*, sailed proudly in the 1940s, and the noted St. Cecilia Chorus performs each year in Carnegie Hall.

St. Cecilia, however, went down into Christian history, neither for elegance nor for an esthetic beauty, but for sheer heroism and deep commitment to Christ in the face of fierce cruelty. She is, in fact, one of the most venerated of Christian martyrs.

Her story first appears in full form in a fifth-century work, *Acts of the Martyrdom of St. Cecilia*. Though widely translated and circulated, it cannot be verified in the usual historical sense. She is said to have been born a Roman, early in the third century, the daughter of a senator, and a Christian from childhood. As a girl, she took a vow of chastity. When her parents gave her in marriage to a pagan boy named Valerianus, she told him that her body was guarded by an angel and that he must not take her virginity.

In love and curious, Valerianus went to see Urbanus, the bishop of Rome, about this, and was shortly convinced and baptized, as was his brother, Tiburtius. The two young men began carrying out works of charity among the Christians, distributing alms and reverently burying the bodies of those executed for the faith. When the Roman prefect, Turcius Almachius, learned of this, he sent an officer named Maximus to execute them, but they so impressed Maximus that he converted too and was killed along with them.

Cecilia buried her husband and brother-in-law before being taken prisoner herself. She had dedicated her home as a church, and she was condemned to die of suffocation in the bath of the house. After three days of heat and steam, she emerged unscathed. The executioner took his sword to her, striking her in the neck three times, but failed to kill her and fled in fear. She lived for three more days during which, according to tradition, she disbursed her worldly goods to the poor.

She was said to be buried in the catacomb of St. Callistus. However, when her remains were discovered by Pope Paschal I (A.D. 817–24) they were found in another cemetery, then moved to the church that bears her name, over the site of her house in the Trastevere quarter of Rome. When the church was being repaired in 1599, her body was reported to have been found and reburied, entire and uncorrupted.

And the music? According to the stories, on her wedding day, while praying that her oath of chastity would not be violated, Cecilia heard musical instruments—organs, in some translations—playing, and she began "singing in her heart to God." Thus, though bloody and brutal her end, she became the patron saint of Christian musicians. ∎

*A reclining sculpture of Saint Cecilia by Stefano Maderno in the church in Rome that bears her name and is said to be built on the site of her house in the bustling Trastevere district. For four hundred years the sculpture faced the wall, but was turned to face outwards during recent restoration.*

• *The Gospel According to the Hebrews*. Popular in the Upper Nile region, it was apparently the only gospel used for many years among the Palestinian Judeo-Christians. The book closely parallels the Gospel of Matthew, which it replaced in some congregations, but also contains other stories and sayings that critics considered attempts to "Judaize" the Scripture.

• *The Gospel of Peter*, probably dating from the middle of the second century, apparently drew upon the Four Gospels for a narration of the Passion, and dates from the first quarter of the second century. Critics contended that it presented a Docetic view (that Jesus was not truly human but only appeared to be so), and were offended by the language and implications in the book's description of Jesus on the cross: "'My power, my power, why hast thou forsaken me?' Immediately he was taken up."

Other such gospels that appeared in the early centuries include the *Gospel of*

# Second-century Christian worship

## Justin's description of a church service is the first postbiblical record

*The second-century Christian evangelist Justin, in his address to the Emperor Antoninus Pius, entitled First Apology (which it's highly unlikely the emperor ever saw), gives a description of a second-century Christian church service in Rome, the first such depiction in the postbiblical period of Christian worship. Written in Greek, it translates as follows:*

At the end of the prayers, we greet one another with a kiss. Then the president of the brethren is brought bread and a cup of wine mixed with water; and he takes them, and offers up praise and glory to the Father of the universe, through the name of the Son and of the Holy Ghost, and gives thanks at considerable length for our being counted worthy to receive these things at his hands.

When he has concluded the prayers and thanksgivings, all the people present express their joyful assent by saying Amen. . . . Then those whom we call deacons give to each of those present the bread and wine mixed with water, over which the thanksgiving was pronounced, and carry away a portion to those who are absent.

We call this food "Eucharist," which no one is allowed to share unless he or she believes that the things which we teach are true, and has been washed with the washing that is for remission of sins and unto a second birth, and is living as Christ has commanded.

We do not receive them as common bread and common drink; but as Jesus Christ our Savior, having been made flesh by the word of God, had both flesh and blood for our salvation. . . . For the apostles, in the memoirs called Gospels composed by them, have thus delivered unto us what was enjoined upon them; that Jesus took bread, and when he had given thanks, said, *This do in remembrance of me, this is my body;* and that, in a similar way, having taken the cup and given thanks, he said, *This is my blood;* and gave it to them alone. ∎

*This fresco from the third-century Catacomb of Callistus, Rome shows the sharing of the Eucharist. The belief that the Eucharist represented "both flesh and blood for our salvation" was seized upon by opponents as proof that Christians indulged in ritual cannibalism.*

*Pseudo-Matthew*, which includes a narrative of Jesus' flight into Egypt, filled with wonders like dragons and palm trees bowing to him; the *Gospel According to the Egyptians*, a Coptic work that circulated in the Lower Nile area around Alexandria and tended toward pantheistic Gnosticism; and five other books—the *Arabic Gospel of Infancy*, the *Gospel of Gamaliel, Transitus Mariae* or *Evangelum Joannis*, the *Gospel of Bartholomew*, and the *Gospel of the Twelve Apostles.*

In addition to the cornucopia of gospels, there were more than a dozen different texts in the category Acts of the Apostles, along with a similar number of apocalyptic books dealing with the "end-times" and several Epistles. There were also three versions of the Lord's Prayer in circulation.

Among the additional epistles in use were three *Epistles of the Blessed Virgin*, composed in Latin; the *Epistle of the Blessed Virgin to St. Ignatius*, which exhorts faith and courage; and the *Epistle to the Messaniense*.

Then, too, there was the *Epistle of Peter to James the Less*, which beseeches him to keep Peter's preaching, and the *Epistle to the Laodiceans*, an apparent attempt to replace a lost document referred to by Paul, along with the *Correspondence of Paul and Seneca*, eight letters supposedly from the Stoic philosopher and six replies, based apparently on Seneca's leanings toward Christianity.

Several attempts were made in the second century to impose order on this chaos. One was the *Diatessaron* of Tatian (c. 170), which wove the four synoptic Gospels into one narrative (see p. 59), and Marcion's compilation based on his own Pauline sympathies and anti-Jewish views (see p. 237).

Even then there was a deep yearning for what would become known as "biblical Christianity," that is, for a Christian book. For instance, Bishop Papias of Hierapolis complained bitterly about the chaos sometime before 165, says Eusebius, and he tried to establish an orthodox New Testament by getting rid of any works that were not demonstrably connected to the original apostles. Around the year 200, these books were listed in a Roman catalog known as the Muratorian Canon. (Discovered in 1740, its earliest surviving version is from the eighth century).

But determining what texts actually represented the divinely inspired "Word of God" presented a challenge that was both monumental and increasingly urgent for the Christian faith. All agreed that the Holy Spirit must decide. But how and through whom? Without an agreed-upon answer, there could be no Christian Bible and no biblical Christianity.

Over the coming 250 years or so, the decision would evolve, not at any specific point in time, but gradually and with protracted argument over what came to be called "the Canon of Scripture," which meant the official list of books. What is known of how this happened will be described in successive volumes.

DUDASH

Early Christians used only burial, not cremation, but little is known for certain about the rituals which were followed. No doubt they observed the national customs of those peoples amongst whom they lived—as long as they were not directly idolatrous. In Rome, this meant burial in the catacombs, as shown in this painting.

# CHAPTER 10

# *The leaven in the bread: steady, silent, relentless*

**Man to man, woman to woman, parent to child, the faith spreads irresistibly—like a disease, says officialdom, moving massively to wipe it out**

I n the year A.D. 256 or thereabouts, fierce Persian warriors attacked the small Roman garrison town of Dura-Europos, on the Euphrates River. During the bloody siege that followed, the city's doomed defenders piled huge embankments of mud and sand against the inside of the city walls to reinforce them against the onslaught, and in their haste and terror they covered up a number of their own buildings. The Persians had no difficulty overcoming such resistance, however, and Dura-Europos disappeared—sacked by the invaders, and buried in part by its own efforts at self-defense.

More than sixteen centuries later, in the 1920s, British soldiers digging trenches in the region encountered the top of a wall. By 1931, archaeologists had begun excavations at the site, located in what is now Syria, near the border of Iraq. Over the next several years, there emerged from the sand a number of remarkable buildings, much of their contents preserved from the vandals and the weather by the mud that had been heaped upon them as a defensive tactic. Among the uncovered ruins stood temples and shrines to any number of gods— not only to Zeus and Apollo and Artemis, but to a wide variety of deities from such places as Phoenicia and Babylon.

The excavations uncovered two private houses as well, both snug against the city's southern wall, about two blocks apart. Both had obviously been converted to religious use. One had been developed into an elaborate synagogue, with spectacular paintings on its walls. The other, smaller but also splendidly decorated, had become a Christian church. Painted on its walls are depictions of Adam and Eve, David and Goliath, Christ walking on the water, Jesus the Good Shepherd, and Jesus healing the paralyzed man. Painted slogans urged worshipers to "keep Christ" in their hearts. One room seems to have been used as a school. Inside the church—capacity about one hundred people—is a stone basin covered by an arch, used as a baptistery. It is one of the oldest Christian churches known to exist, and visitors can still see much of it. The Persian marauders easily conquered Dura-Europos, but the Christians, barely two hundred years after the brutal death of their founder, were on their way to conquering the world.

By the second century, churches had been erected in Rome, Antioch, Edessa, and Alexandria, and even across the imperial border in Persia, or Parthia as it was then called. Indeed, Christian church buildings were so numerous in the third century that persecuting Roman emperors more than once signed edicts ordering their destruction. At the mid-third century, there were thirty thousand or so Christians in Rome, and the faith had made its appearance in Spain and Britain.

The actual number of Christians in the empire at the beginning of the third century is a matter of great uncertainty. The sociologist Rodney Stark in his *Rise*

## After so short a time, Tertullian wrote, the Christians 'fill your cities, your homes, your squares, your municipalities, the council, the tribunes, the palace, Senate and Forum.'

*of Christianity* puts it at 217,000, meaning the Christians formed a tiny minority, with an average of one person in about two hundred an adherent. However, says Joseph F. Kelly in *The World of the Early Christians*, third-century Christianity was largely a city religion, so that in some centers, the Christian concentration was probably much higher.[1] When Tertullian spoke of Christianity as "filling the world," he meant the Roman world. There were Christian communities in all the major centers of his native North Africa, and Christians were common in the legions stationed there. The Christians had become "a vast invisible empire," writes the historian W. H. C. Frend.

Yet they weren't all that invisible. "We see them [the Christians] in private houses, as wool-carders, cobblers, fullers, the most uneducated, and peasants, who dare not open their mouths in the presence of their elder and wiser masters," wrote the anti-Christian writer Celsus. But they did open their mouths,

---

1. The urban nature of early Christianity had a curious consequence in modern English. The word "pagan" came to mean a person in the ancient world who was neither Jewish nor Christian. But it originated as the Latin word *paganus*, which simply means a country person—in other words, a country person came to be synonymous with non-Christian. The French word *paysan* and the Italian word *paisano* come from the same Latin origin, but both mean "peasant." They retain, that is, the original Latin meaning.

sometimes leading their masters to Christianity, and soon the religion whose early followers had called it "The Way" had strong adherents within the imperial government, helping to shape the law, politics, and culture of the time.

*The Euphrates River is seen here from the ruins of Dura-Europos, Syria, site of the discovery of one of the first Christian churches.*

As early as the late first century, for instance, there had been rumors that the emperor Vespasian's brother was Christian or was certainly influenced by them. People had heard about the stirring confession of Senator Apollonius, the witness of Glabrio and Flavia Domitilla under the emperor Domitian. The emperor Commodus's mistress was Christian, as was the emperor Caracalla's physiotherapist. The fourth-century Christian historian Eusebius says that the emperor Alexander and his mother had surrounded themselves with Christian counselors.

"We appeared only yesterday," wrote Tertullian, addressing the pagan world at large, "but now we fill your cities, your homes, your squares, your municipalities, the councils, the tribunes, the decuries, the palace, the Senate, and the Forum. We have left you nothing save your temples. Should we secede from you, you would be terrified by your own loneliness."

It was a gross exaggeration, of course, but it was too close to the truth for those who despised and distrusted the Christians. "Ill weeds grow apace," says the pagan character Caecillus in Minucius Felix's fictional Christian dialogue, *The Octavius.* "Throughout the wide world, the abominations of this impious conspiracy multiply."

How did this happen? How could Christianity possibly have succeeded? Why did a tiny sect, an odd offshoot of Judaism, survive and spread despite brutal, official persecution aimed at stamping it out? It happened, of course, precisely as that crucified Jew had said it would happen—as yeast spreads through a baking loaf of bread (Matt. 13:33; Luke 13:21), quiet, unseen, but constant, until the whole loaf is leavened. But wasn't this Jesus dead, people asked? Weren't his thoughts and sayings, though faithfully preserved by his followers over the years, made ludicrous by the shameful way he met his end?

The Christians said no. For one thing, they said, Jesus wasn't dead at all. He had come back to life and emerged from the tomb under his own unfathomable power to meet again with his followers and to encourage them to persist. For another, the teachings he imparted, and the doctrines that resulted, were surprisingly powerful in their own right, sweeping the world in a movement unparalleled in all of history.

# When Christians met in houses

### Buried during a Persian attack 17 centuries ago, a home reveals the splendor of a very early Christian church

In the 1930s, in what is now Syria, archaeologists carefully uncovered a remarkable ruin: a private home that had been converted into a Christian church seventeen centuries before, in the early 200s. The building, which had lain buried since Persian warriors attacked the Roman town of Dura-Europos where it sat, is one of the oldest Christian churches known to exist. Its walls are covered with large-scale paintings of themes familiar to today's Christians—Christ walking on the water, Jesus healing a paralyzed man, Jesus as the Good Shepherd—along with Old Testament scenes. The home's central room, used for the church services, could hold about one hundred people, and it features a small stone basin—too small to stand in—that held water for baptism. Among the wall paintings is a depiction of five women who have come to the tomb of Jesus after his Crucifixion. They carry large bowls, presumably for use in washing the body for burial, and they hold torches to illuminate the darkened tomb as they approach a huge sarcophagus, flanked by two large stars representing angels. Archaeologists have uncovered other such homes elsewhere, but because of the wealth of insight it offers into early Christian worship, Dura-Europos remains a spectacular favorite of both tourists and scholars. ∎

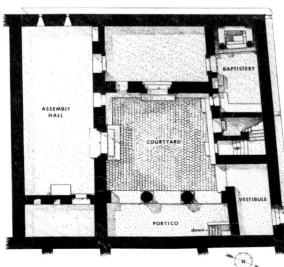

Such was the Christians' explanation for the rapid spread of their faith. Historians offer other explanations. The time, they say, could hardly have been more opportune. Even as the Roman Empire sprawled confidently across the map, seemingly irresistible, it was beginning to show signs of age and decay. Despite its bureaucratic efficiencies, its feats of engineering, and its armies, Rome offered most of its subjects a life of unrelieved and unrewarding toil. "The two centuries preceding the Christian era had been a period of uninterrupted misery," writes the historian Samuel Angus in his book *The Mystery Religions and Christianity*. After the days of Marcus Aurelius, he notes, "happiness departed from the ancient world. . . . Every persecution only strengthened the church. Its competitors were overtaken by mortal weakness when ancient society was tottering to a fall."

The excavated ruins of a third-century house-church at Dura-Europos, in what is now Syria, provide great detail about early Christian life. The building (1) was buried under mud, and therefore preserved, during a Persian attack in about A.D. 256. Inside were a baptistery font (5) and large-scale wall paintings, shown here in a reconstruction in the Dura-Europos collection of the Yale University Art Gallery. An aerial view (3) of the site from the north shows the nearby Euphrates River, and a modern drawing (4) gives the floor plan of the church. Among the paintings are these (2) of the raising of the paralytic (left) and of Jesus and Peter walking on the water (right).

Chief among those competitors was the official paganism advanced by the imperial authorities. But if the people turned in desperation to those far-off gods, they knew these deities held no affection for humans. The gods answered cries for help erratically, if at all, and sometimes quite sadistically. They played vicious tricks on their subjects, finding human suffering and bewilderment amusing. Moreover, they were so numerous as to be bewildering themselves, offering too many options, not enough answers, and absurdities that Christian apologists like Minucius Felix did not shrink from pointing out. He wrote:

> Examine into their attendant rites, how ridiculous, how pitiable they appear! Men running about naked in mid-winter; others marching about in felt caps, or parading old shields; drumming on skins, and dragging their gods to beg from street to street. Some temples may only be entered once a year, some never visited at all. There are rites which a man may not attend, others that may be held only in the absence of women, others where the mere presence of a slave is an outrage needing expiation.—Quoted by W. H. C. Frend from Minucius Felix's *Octavius*.

The officially mandated public adoration of the Roman rulers was no better. Except for keeping the executioner at bay, ceremonial worship enforced at the point of the sword offered little consolation. Even Judaism, the ancient and magnificent faith that recognized one God alone and attributed to him a deep concern for his chosen people, had fallen on hard times. Jerusalem, its spiritual center, was toppled into the dust by Roman soldiers in A.D. 70, its Temple destroyed and its people scattered.

Meanwhile, in place of the noble virtues of the old Roman republic, a general moral squalor had become a tedious way of life for the populace. Adultery, prostitution, idolatry, self-seeking, and uncaring cruelty were the order of the day. Unwanted children were abandoned in the open, left exposed to die.[2] Criminals and political and religious prisoners were thrown to wild animals in arenas for the amusement of bloodthirsty crowds.

Clearly, there was deep hunger for something else, a way out of the pain of despair and oppression, and just as clearly, the Christians offered it. They worshiped a God who, they said, had breached the chasm

*The Maximus Chapel near Salzburg, Austria (below) dates from A.D. 250 and is one of the oldest places of Christian worship in western Europe. Carved out of solid rock, it has been damaged by landslides but is still maintained by local congregations. By the early third century there were thirty thousand or so Christians in Rome. The tomb of one of them, Livia Primitiva (bottom), is engraved with the figure of the Good Shepherd.*

2. Justin expressed Christian opposition to child abandonment in the strongest terms: "We have been taught that it is wicked to expose even newly born children, first because we see that almost all those who are exposed (not only girls, but boys) are raised in prostitution. Anyone who consorts with them, besides being guilty of a godless, impious, and shameful action, may by some chance be guilty of intercourse with his own child, or relative, or brother. . . . Still [another reason against exposing children is] lest some of them would not be taken home, but die, and we would then be murderers. But either we marry, in the first place, in order to raise children, or refusing to marry, we live in continence for the rest of our lives."

chasm separating the human from the divine. Jesus, a real man who lived, taught, and performed miracles—dying and miraculously returning to life on specific days in a specific year, in full public view—was nothing short of God himself, come down to humanity to rescue it from its torment. This God of the Christians was the very Creator who had fashioned the heavens and the Earth and all who inhabited his creation, and rather than an aloof prankster, he was a God who loved mankind and intended to heal its wounds, to save it and build it up, and finally to bring it into joyous union with himself.

"Christianity had a unique advantage over all its competitors including even Judaism," says historian Angus, "in having a historic Person as Founder, whose Person was greater than his teachings. . . . No other religion could placard a real Being in flesh and blood who had lived so near to God and brought men into such intimate soul-satisfying union with the Father."

Frend adds, "They alone of the great religions had the self-confidence and material power to support a long missionary campaign."

Yet the precise nature of that campaign is not easily discerned. Little is known about early Christian missions and how they operated, writes Frend, although the New Testament abounds in references to them and so does the very early Syrian pamphlet called *The Teaching of the Twelve Apostles*, also known as the *Didache* (see p. 53). After the foundational work of Paul and John, there seems to have been a lull in missionary effort until the early second century. The letters of Ignatius, Polycarp, and Clement, and the Book of Revelation lay no particular emphasis on evangelical effort, and, instead, often show a preoccupation with the impending end of the world. As the second century unfolded, however, this appears to change and the missionary zeal of Paul has returned.

"Many of the disciples of that age," writes Eusebius, "whose hearts had been ravished by the divine Word with a burning love for Christ, first fulfilled the command of the Savior and divided their goods among the needy. Then they set out on long journeys, doing the work of evangelists, eagerly striving to preach Christ to those who had never heard the word of faith and to deliver to them the holy Gospels. In foreign lands, they simply laid the foundations of the faith. That done, they appointed others as shepherds, entrusting them with the care of the new growth, while they themselves proceeded with the grace and cooperation of God to other countries and other peoples."

The "shepherds" who were left behind were also evangelists, not only instructing and nurturing the local Christian communities but also visiting and preaching in outlying areas. Irenaeus, appointed bishop in Gaul, writes regretfully that he had spent so much time and effort learning the language of the area's barbarians that his Greek had suffered.

Sometimes Christian apologists like Justin and Irenaeus are portrayed as debating with anti-Christians in the public squares of cities. Open-air preaching was probably another means used to propagate the faith. The author of what are called the pseudo-Clementine *Recognitions*[3] describes a preacher who stood in a public place and declared, "Men of Rome, hearken. The Son of God is come to

  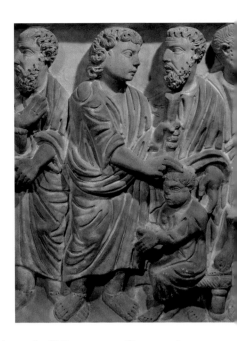

*Reliefs from third-century Christian tombs in Rome, showing the wedding at Cana (left), the multiplication of loaves (center) and Christ healing (right). By this time, the Christian community was spreading rapidly, offering care, justice and the beginnings of social welfare in an age when all were in short supply.*

Judea proclaiming eternal life to all who will, if they shall live according to the will of the Father who has sent him." He then continued to urge his hearers to change their lives and receive the "unspeakable blessings" of eternal life. Otherwise, "after the dissolution of the body, you shall be thrown to eternal fire." No one, says the author, appeared to take him seriously.

One street-corner preacher, the Alexandrian philosopher and Christian convert named Pantaenus, traveled from town to town, addressing informal outdoor crowds. He and others faced the constant risk of being arrested by police or being beaten by infuriated listeners. Heckling might rapidly grow into active hatred. The anti-Christian philosopher Celsus describes such traveling evangelists with contempt: "We see that those who display their trickery in the marketplaces and go about begging would never enter a gathering of intelligent men, nor would they dare to reveal their noble beliefs in their presence; but whenever they see adolescent boys and a crowd of slaves and a company of fools, they push themselves in and show off." Yet, slaves who were thus converted often carried the message into the households of Roman aristocrats.

Far more effective as a missionary tool were the schools, such as those run by Origen and Justin, often attended not only by their students, but by large public audiences who simply came to hear these evangelists speak. But for the most part, says the historian Michael Green in *Evangelism in the Early Church*, people heard of Jesus Christ one-on-one from those who already believed. They heard it from Christians who had heard it from other Christians, and who believed they had the obligation to share it with those still lost in a darkened world, and who invited their neighbors to come and see.

The consequence of this was the phenomenon known as "conversion," a

3. The pseudo-Clementine *Recognitions* are a collection of third-century Christian fables, says the Catholic Encyclopedia, that describe the conversion of Clement of Rome, his travels with Peter, and the rediscovery of his lost family. They are part of a body of Christian legend, all centered around Clement of Rome. The *Recognitions* are historically significant because they preserve a portrait of Syrian-Christian life dating back to apostolic times.

term that would have meant nothing in the ancient world until the Jewish Diaspora had introduced Judaism and the concept of leaving the religion of whatever world you were born into and joining another. This was at some periods forbidden, even in the generally tolerant Roman Empire, because it was considered socially disruptive and, to use a twentieth-century word, "divisive." But Christianity was founded and developed almost entirely by converts, and these became, as they so often would, the most eloquent and outspoken representatives of the faith.

Their conversions had many different causes. "One person would be brought over by means of the Old Testament," writes historian Adolf von Harnack in *The Mission and Expansion of Christianity*, "another by the exorcizing of demons, a third by the purity of Christian life, others by the monotheism of Christianity, above all by the prospect of complete expiation or by the prospect of immortality." Historian Green cites two principal causes for conversion. Some found in Christianity a rational explanation for life. It came upon these people as the truth, revealed either through the path of Greek philosophy or through the Scriptures, or both. Others found in Christianity a sense of freedom—freedom from the fear of death, freedom from some rapture or magic, freedom from ignorance or from some hitherto unconquerable sin.

"The water of regeneration washed away the stains of my past life," writes the Christian Cyprian in the mid-third century. "A light from above entered and

## The convert found a world where people spoke of love and justice, where ethnic distinctions were dismissed and there was no difference between slaves and masters.

permeated my heart, now cleansed from its defilement. The Spirit came from heaven and changed me into a new man by the second birth. Almost at once, in a marvelous way, doubt gave way to assurance; what had been shut tight opened; light shone in dark places; and I found what had previously seemed difficult had become easy, and what I had thought impossible came to be done. You know it all well enough; you understand as I do what it is that brought me to this death to sin and this resurrection to godly living. You know it full well; I am not boasting." This was the "born again" experience, called for by Jesus in his encounter with Nicodemus (John 3:1–9). Down through the ages, from kings to Salvation Army penitents, the testimony of the convert would be the same.

Having found a Christian community, the convert entered another world. It was a world where the inhabitants spoke of love and justice and seemed to practice both, where class and ethnic distinctions were dismissed, where people shared their goods and bore each other's burdens, where it was taught that Jesus Christ recognized no difference between slaves and masters, and a world where people sometimes went to their execution singing hymns and encouraging one another. "Here were societies," writes Green, "in which aristocrats and slaves, Roman citizens and provincials, rich and poor, mixed on equal terms and without distinction, societies which possessed a quality of caring and love which was unique. And herein lay its attraction."

In such communities, the programs for the care of the aged, frail, penniless, and helpless, all duties which Christianity inherited from Judaism, laid the beginnings of social welfare systems that would one day inform the policies of governments all over the Western world. The *Epistle of Barnabas*, written between A.D. 100 and 130 in the name of, if not by, Paul's missionary companion, lays upon Christians their duty to care for widows and orphans. The *Second Epistle of Clement*, a mid-second-century sermon urging self-control and repentance, also stresses the duty of Christians to give alms for needy people. Tertullian emphasizes the duty to provide funerals for the poor, shut-ins, orphans, and those imprisoned for the faith. He urges men to take in widows as "spiritual spouses." From the earliest days, Christians established hospices for the sick and foundling children.

*This is a baptism scene from a third-century Roman sarcophagus. Baptism followed a lengthy period in the catechumenate when the novice was instructed in the ways of the faith.*

The newcomer would also notice a difference between the treatment accorded women in the outside world and their treatment in Christian communities. Paul had taught that "in Christ" women and men are equal (Gal. 3:28). In concluding his letter to the Romans, he mentions twenty-six Christian leaders by name; the first of them, and seven others, are women. In the pre-Roman Hellenistic world, however, women were only marginally better off than slaves in the eyes of the law. Rome had greatly improved their legal status; they could inherit property and run businesses. Still, they rarely played a central part in Jewish or pagan worship or ecclesiastical administration. Though in Christian services Paul required their silence in church (1 Cor. 14:34), he assigned high responsibilities to them.

As Christian communities developed, women assumed the duties of deaconesses, an office that went back to the age of the apostles and was greatly developed during the third century. Deaconesses were responsible for the care of the sick and poor, and for the instruction of women converts. They also attended upon women at their baptism. Since the candidate was often naked, *The Oxford Dictionary of the Christian Church* notes delicately that "for reasons of propriety, many of the ceremonies could not be performed by deacons."

It was within these Christian communities that much personal evangelism was accomplished. Interested inquirers and the merely curious were welcomed to meetings held in Christian homes, where they were made comfortable and offered food and drink, and lodgings if needed. They were encouraged to ask questions, to participate in free-wheeling exchanges of views, and to listen to local leaders or visiting teachers. "Nearly every known Christian congregation started by meeting in someone's house," writes historian Michael A. Smith, in *Eerdman's Handbook to the History of Christianity*.

With his decision to give his life to Christ, the convert joined what was called the catechumenate, the Christian community's beginner contingent, which prepared "the catechumen," as beginners were called, for baptism. The preparation process was no light matter. Candidates might wait as long as three years while the church observed their character and behavior, their personal relations, their occupation, their fidelity in prayer, and whether they rigorously observed the church's fasting rules. During this time they were instructed in Christian doctrine, addressed with a series of questions, and required to memorize a statement of Christian beliefs that became known as the "creed," from the Latin word *credo*, meaning "I believe." Prior to baptism they were exorcized to drive out demons. If they were martyred before baptism, says Hippolytus, they were considered to have undergone "baptism in blood."

For many converts, becoming Christian entailed some distinct changes in living habits. Christians refused to attend the idolatrous theatrical presentations of the time because drama had descended into exhibitions of raw depravity. Nor

*The curious were welcomed to Christian homes, offered food and drink, and encouraged to participate in free-wheeling exchanges of views and to listen to visiting teachers.*

would they willingly go to see the gladiators fight and die. Some wouldn't sign up for military duty or join the civil service, claiming loyalty to Jesus instead of to those who might give them orders that would compromise their beliefs. Some wouldn't teach in non-Christian schools because the curriculum would involve them in the support of pagan gods. Many wouldn't take oaths, and therefore couldn't enter into business contracts. All this could lead to extreme economic and social hardship.

The Christian attitude to wealth was as ambivalent then as it would remain for centuries to come. To Tertullian, the Christian must abstain from all luxury as a preparation for martyrdom. Almost every gainful employment was spiritually dangerous, even tailoring, because to clothe God's sheep in costly raiment was the devil's work. To Clement of Alexandria, however, such severity was absurd. Christians, after all, had to earn a living. Still, many occupations were universally forbidden, such as brothel-keeper, sculptor of idols, actor, gladiator, magician, and astrologer.

Clement, as sternly as Tertullian, vigorously denounced the outright abuse of wealth, particularly the ostentatious luxury of the age—rich gowns, gold-embroidered slippers, and the immoderate gluttony of the wealthy, their fancy meals, and what he called "the empty skill of the pastry cooks." Infatuation with money as an end in itself was particularly condemned. "Those of us who loved money in the olden days now give away all that we possess," writes Justin. To the Christians, says historian Henri Daniel-Rops, "the rich man was to be regarded as a kind of administrator, using his property for the superior interest

Since most Christians were converts, baptism was a great unifying force in the early church. The newly baptized received the bread and wine of the Eucharist, and milk and honey as a foretaste of Heaven.

DUDASH

of the community. Moreover, it should never be forgotten that the riches of the earth were perishable, and that the only true wealth was that of paradise, which was eternal."

A similar ambivalence characterized the Christian attitude towards war and military service. While Christianity for its first three centuries was distinctly pacifist and took literally such injunctions of Jesus as "Love your enemies" (Matt. 5:44), and "Put up your sword" (Matt. 26:52), and while Christians were certainly repelled by the idolatry that seemed such a part of military life, it remained true that Christians were numerous in the army. Moreover, Clement, bishop of Rome, urged Christians to emulate the discipline of the legions, and Christians in the army no doubt observed that almost every occurrence of a centurion in the New Testament left the man in a positive light (Matt. 8:5–10; Mark 15:39; Acts 10:1ff; Acts 27:42–44). Paul, meanwhile, freely used military images to portray the Christian life (Eph. 6:11–17). Finally, whatever their occupation or whereabouts in the empire, observes the historian Joseph F. Kelly in *The World of the Early Christians*, "most Christians would have been grateful for the security that

*This early Christian fresco from the Catacomb of Callistus, Rome (right), showing bread, fish and a glass of wine, symbolizes a Eucharistic meal and the Miracle of the Loaves and Fishes. A headstone from the Catacomb of Priscilla, Rome, (below), shows an anchor and fish; two of the very earliest symbols of Christianity.*

Roman arms provided and would have recognized the need for a strong military to defend the frontiers."[4]

The convert would also encounter sharp distinctions between the Christian and the conventional rules for sexual conduct. While women in the Roman Empire were expected to remain virgins until marriage, men made casual use of prostitutes and their female slaves both before and after marriage. Divorce and remarriage were common for both men and women, the children of divorce usually remaining with the father. Women who cheated on their husbands had a legal claim against their lovers and could demand and get an allowance. This was not regarded as a form of prostitution. Widowers sometimes took a concubine after the death of a wife, though the children of that union would be considered

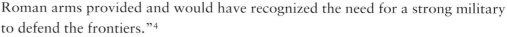

4. Indeed even Jesus' own attitude seems divided, for while he usually opposes armed resistance (Luke 6:29), at another point he instructs each of his disciples to sell his mantle and arm himself (Luke 22:36), though within definite limits (Luke 22: 38).

illegitimate. Paul Veyne, in his work *A History of Private Life*, observes that Roman marriage in the early Christian period assumed a new quality, in that it became more of a life-long companionship than a merely legal relationship. A happy marriage, that is, became a genuinely respected accomplishment.

Among Christians, however, sexual restraint by all parties was expected. Both men and women were enjoined to remain virginal until marriage, and thereafter any sex outside marriage, including sex with slaves, was regarded as adultery. The widely read Christian book known as *The Shepherd of Hermas* lays great stress on family unity and warns that children as well as parents can disrupt it. Clement of Alexandria's powerful defense of legitimate sexuality within marriage was controversial at the time, because celibacy for both men and women was winning intense admiration among Christians. "In striking contrast to the prevailing veneration of celibacy," writes the historian Joseph Wilson Trigg in *Origen: the Bible and Philosophy in the Third Century Church*, "Clement considered marriage the preferred state for the attainment of spiritual perfection." On one point, however, all were agreed. In an age when abortion was a common method of birth control, the Christians spoke out against it. To abort a child before birth was to commit a murder (*Didache* 2:1–2, *Letter of Barnabas* 19, Athenagoras in *A Plea for Christians*).

The Christian concept of marriage differed fundamentally from that of the Romans generally in other respects. The Christians proclaimed marriage to be more than a means of legalizing and socializing the union of a man and woman, so that children could be taken care of and property accounted for. For Christians, marriage meant that a couple would, in Tertullian's words, "sustain one another in the way of the Lord . . . pray together . . . go together to God's table, and . . . face all their ordeals together." The man and woman were to unite in the spirit of love and purity with which Christ is united to his Church. They became, in Christ's words, "one flesh." Among other things, that meant that divorce was permitted only under extreme circumstances and, in the early church especially, remarriage was discouraged or forbidden. (The Athenian Christian apologist Athenagoras called second marriages "adultery made respectable.")

Rapidly the catechumen would become familiar with the Christian home and begin establishing one himself. Christian homes might serve as the location for prayer meetings, worship, organized instruction, Holy Communion services, and baptisms. The house church that was uncovered at Dura-Europos may well have begun as the home of a wealthy family that converted to Christianity.

Archaeologists have uncovered other such homes elsewhere.

Decorations, often subtle and even coded against a raid on house churches by the authorities, provide evidence of their use. Best known of these coded symbols is the "sign of the fish." (Jesus promised his disciples that he would make them "fishers of men," and the Greek word for "fish," *ICHTHYS*, is an anagram for the words "Jesus Christ, Son of God, Savior.") Other symbols included the lamb bearing a T or a cross, the anchor, the sailing-ship, and the cross topped by the dove from Noah's ark.[5]

Though various forms of prayer were written for all seasons and all actions and hours of the day, the Lord's Prayer was certainly in common use. Prayers were likely spontaneous, says the historian Daniel-Rops in *The Church of the Apostles and Martyrs*, but were characterized by the language and expression of the Old Testament. The gift of tongues, now called "*glossolalia*," was widely evident in the first- and second-century church. It was not viewed as odd, but as a sign of the presence of the Holy Spirit.[6]

By the year 150, the Christians had established Sunday as the day for a formal, weekly meeting, when they dined together in a common meal to which members contributed, not unlike the potluck suppers held in churches today.[7]

In the early days, this common meal, known as the *agape* feast from the Greek word for "love," served also as the occasion for the celebration of the Lord's Supper, or the Holy Communion, or the Eucharist, which means "thanksgiving."

However, by the third century, the agape meal and the ceremonial communion service, involving the bread and wine alone, had been separated. The Lord's Supper service often began on Saturday night with a nightlong "vigil," concluding at dawn Sunday morning (a work day for most, before it became a public holiday in the fourth century). A fellowship meeting with a heavier meal was held on Sunday evening, when the day's work was done.

The meetings also included readings, likely with portions of the Old Testament, as apparently occurred in synagogues, though information about such practices in the first century is scanty. It's certain that Paul's letters were read—his letter to the Thessalonians carries instructions that it is to be read "to all the brethren" (1 Thess. 5:27), and his letter to the Colossians says it is to be read in Laodicea. There were probably homilies—sermons—as well, though few survive.

---

5. The early Christians had a square of letters, found at Pompeii in Italy and Cirencester in England. On the surface it appears meaningless, but a slight rearrangement of the letters yields, "I am Alpha and Omega, the beginning and the ending, saith the Lord." If an A and an O are removed twice, it leaves two anagrams of *Pater Noster* (Our Father) in the shape of a cross.

6. The term *glossolalia* is drawn from two Greek words meaning "tongue" and "talking." This "speaking with tongues" makes its appearance in Christian history at Pentecost, when the apostles were "filled with the Holy Spirit and began speaking with other tongues as the Spirit gave them utterance" (Acts 2:4). Paul found the custom in wide use at Corinth, and he spoke in tongues himself, though he regarded it with suspicion at Corinth, and less valuable than "prophecy" (1 Cor. 14:1ff). The same phenomenon often occurs at modern revival meetings. *The Oxford Dictionary of the Christian Church* comments that "its healthiness or otherwise is best judged by its effect on the character and moral resolution of the individual." Oxford also notes that while the phenomenon goes back to the first century, the word *glossolalia* itself has no ancient origin and did not come into use until the nineteenth century.

In *The First Urban Christians*, Wayne A. Meeks observes that "the rich allusions to and arguments from Scripture that Paul sometimes includes in his letters . . . presuppose some means for learning both text and traditions of interpretation. Regular meetings and homilies in the assemblies are the most plausible."

The Lord's Supper was one of the two great observances of the first church communities. The other was baptism. Much of what is known of its earliest form is drawn from the *Didache*. The candidate was "sealed" in the faith by being anointed with oil from the head to the soles of the feet to purge any remaining demons. After formally renouncing sin and pagan ways, he or she went down as "dead" into the water—usually a river, because "running water" was the most

*In the early days, a common Saturday evening meal, known as the agape feast from the Greek word for "love," served also as the occasion for the celebration of the Lord's Supper, Holy Communion, or "Eucharist," a word that means "thanksgiving."*

---

7. How the first day of the week came to be the chosen day of Christian worship is not easily documented. Christ rose on Sunday, the day after the Jewish Sabbath, and the Holy Spirit came on the Christians at Pentecost, also Sunday. Acts relates that on the first day of the week, the Christians assembled to break bread (20:7), and Paul writes to his charges (1 Cor. 16:1, 2) to have their money ready on Sunday, so that he doesn't have to spend time taking up a collection. In his *Letter to the Magnesians*, Ignatius of Antioch, writing at the end of the first century, refers to Christians as "no longer observing the [Jewish] Sabbath, but living in the observance of the Lord's Day." However, no record exists of a specific instruction or decision to establish Sunday as the Christian day of worship. The practice simply grew. Some Christian denominations, including the Seventh-day Adventists, have never accepted the change and continue to observe Saturday as the day of worship.

*"At the end of the prayers, we greet one another with a kiss," writes the second-century evangelist Justin. The "holy kiss" or "kiss of peace" has been preserved for centuries in the eastern churches. It was gradually modified in western churches, from an actual kiss, to a mutual clasp of shoulder and elbow, to a handshake. Reforms of the twentieth century saw its return in some Catholic and Protestant churches.*

honorable of the six Jewish "grades" of water[8]—was immersed three times, and came up "alive," to be anointed with oil again and wrapped in a white garment. Tertullian says that the newly cleansed Christian then received the bread and wine of the Eucharist, and a taste of milk and honey, as a foretaste of Heaven.

If there wasn't enough water available to completely immerse the candidate, the *Didache* prescribes pouring water three times over the head of the person being baptized. From the third century onward, Christian artworks generally show a church official pouring water over the head of the initiate, who stands in water. The baptismal basin found inside the Dura-Europos church is too small to stand in. Meeks, who admits that the early record is sketchy, nevertheless declares that Christian converts were routinely baptized naked. This he derives from the many descriptions in St. Paul's letters that refer to taking off and putting on clothing in the context of baptism. Infant baptism became common in the third century, though Tertullian was opposed to it since the infant could not make a personal commitment to Christ.

Those not baptized were not permitted to be present during the celebration of the Lord's Supper. They departed and the doors were shut behind them.[9]

By the second century, the Christian year was already taking shape, and Easter, not Christmas, was the biggest annual feast or holiday. It was to be celebrated on the anniversary of Jesus' Resurrection, but almost from the beginning there were disputes about the correct date, partly because of problems with the available calendars. As baptisms became a central feature of the Easter celebrations, the period of instruction and preparation for candidates shrank to the period before Easter that is called Lent. Widespread celebration of Christmas did not begin to take hold until the fourth century.

By the third century, the Christians had achieved an astonishing unity across the Roman Empire and even into the great rival empire of Persia. Everywhere he went from Rome to Osrhoene, wrote the Phrygian merchant Aviricius Marcellus, "I found brothers in the faith," and partook of "the mixed cup with bread." Not before and never after, says historian Frend, would Christians achieve the degree of unity that they had accomplished by the year 180. Somehow a form of organization, embracing Christian communities thousands of miles apart, had developed—almost, it seemed, by default.

It had been clear from the start that there had to be some way of managing the church's affairs, administering it, preserving its truths and apportioning out

8. The six Jewish "grades" of water, as preserved in the Eastern Orthodox churches, recognize running water in a river as best for baptism, followed by still water in a lake, still water inside a building in which the candidate is totally immersed, water poured over the candidate, water sprinkled over the candidate, and (least desirable) any other liquid or some other material like sand, used when no form of water is available.

9. The closing of the doors against those not yet baptized survives to this day in the liturgy of the Eastern Orthodox churches. Before the recitation of the Nicene Creed and the celebration of the Eucharist, the order of service calls for the priest or deacon to ask the catechumens to depart, although this is not spoken aloud in most twenty-first-century Orthodox churches. The Prayer of the Faithful follows, after which the deacon chants, "The doors! The doors!" an ancient signal to the doorkeepers that no one should leave or enter. Some Catholic churches reflect this ancient practice by conducting catechism classes for newcomers while the Eucharist is served in the church.

its duties. Jesus established the first such structure himself: twelve disciples, then seventy others. By the time of the book of Acts, Luke wrote of deacons, elders (in Greek, "presbyter"), and bishops.[10] By the year 100, an early administrative schema was well established.

Christians sought for metaphors to describe it. They saw Christ as its head. For the rest, Paul favored the metaphor of the body, with each member doing its part. Clement of Rome employed the model of the army, with its chain of command, common goal, and discipline. Exactly how the details came together has provided grist for scholarship and debate over two millennia.

At the top of the organization were the bishops (from the Greek word *episkopos*, an overseer). Each city had a bishop, and the church was thus divided geographically into bishoprics, generally following the boundary lines of cities, with the bishop selected by the members of the church community over which he held authority. The bishop appears to have had certain main duties. He performed

---

10. The first churches in Palestine appear to have drawn their structure from the Jewish synagogue, which was directed by a board of "elders," the Greek term for which produces the English word "presbyter." In the earliest days, the office of presbyter appears to be the same as the office of bishop, though the two were soon distinguished, the presbyters becoming the assistants to the bishop. The word "priest" is an etymological contraction of the word "presbyter." Therefore elder, presbyter, and priest all originate from the same ancient ecclesiastical office in the Jewish synagogue.

# East vs West: the first big test

## The issue: Could the bishop of Rome excommunicate the whole eastern Church?

The first major controversy to divide Christian communities concerned neither doctrine nor ritual, but the most significant date on the Christian calendar, Easter.[1] The date became a major issue by the middle of the second century.

The churches of the East celebrated Easter on the same day as the Jewish Passover, which began at sunset of the fourteenth day after the first full moon after the spring Equinox, known to the Jews as the "Fourteenth Nisan." The churches of Palestine, Syria, and Asia Minor followed the Jewish precedent they had learned from the apostles.

However, this meant that Easter might fall on any day of the week, and the Western churches had long ago concluded it should always fall on a Sunday, the day of Jesus' Resurrection. The Eastern group came to be called "Quartodecimans" after *quartodecimus*, the Latin word for fourteen.

In A.D. 155, Polycarp, the much respected bishop of Smyrna in Asia Minor, who would face martyrdom at the hands of the imperial government the following year, met with Bishop Anicetus in Rome to try to resolve the controversy. They failed and both sides continued as they had before, though both agreed it was not a sufficiently important issue to cause an open rupture between East and West.

Some forty years later, however, Bishop Victor of Rome took a much tougher line and ordered the Eastern churches to conform and adopt the Sunday celebration, or he would excommunicate the whole Eastern church. Writing on behalf of the Eastern bishops, Polycrates of Ephesus replied that the East would continue as it had. "I am not afraid of threats," he said.

Meanwhile, Bishop Irenaeus of Lyons took Bishop Victor to task for high-handedness. While he agreed with the Sunday observance, he said, excommunicating every Christian in the East was something of an overreaction. Victor should simply have continued the gentlemen's agreement reached by Polycarp and Anicetus, said Irenaeus. In the end, the issue was simply shelved until the Council of Nicaea in 325, when the Sunday observance became universal. ∎

---

1. The term "Easter" was believed by the early British historian Bede to have derived from the Anglo-Saxon goddess of spring, *Eostre*, whose festival was superseded by the Christian one. In the East, the feast is called Pascha from the Aramaic word for the Jewish Passover, and the dispute over the date of the feast is known as the "Paschal Controversy."

baptisms. He supervised religious instruction. He managed the community's worldly goods, which by the third century began to include property, usually bequeathed on the death of members and often seized by persecuting emperors. He presided at gatherings, was expected to lead prayers, and to preach homilies or sermons. Finally, the bishop was responsible for the moral and spiritual supervision of all the other believers, whatever their level within the structure.

*This early third-century fresco from the Catacomb of Priscilla, Rome, depicts the Adoration of the Magi. Christians had a very early tradition of devotion regarding the Nativity, which would later give rise to the celebration of Christmas.*

Beneath the bishop were presbyters or priests, helping and advising the bishop and carrying out the duties that they still carry out today. Below these were deacons and deaconesses, aiding the presbyter with his ceremonial duties, and also carrying out such practical functions as collecting the offerings, administering funds and services for the needy, and generally keeping things in order.

All of that organization, all the prayers, all the faithful observances of religious duty, all the charity, all the instruction, all the discipline and courage they could muster would now become immediately necessary. For at A.D. 250, the Christians were about to face the most severe persecution they had ever confronted, mounted by the powerful new emperor Decius, who intended not only to eradicate every one of them, but to wipe Christianity itself from the face of the earth forever. The question was: Could they stand up to this? They had but one bedrock reason to think they could. For this was the Church, against which, said Jesus Christ, the gates of Hell could not prevail.

# CONTRIBUTORS TO THIS VOLUME

## THE WRITERS
These writers joined the project for Volume II:

DR. IAN HUNTER, who wrote Chapter 6 on the irascible lawyer Tertullian, holds degrees in law and political science from the University of Toronto. He has taught at several Canadian universities and has been a visiting scholar at Cambridge University. His previous books include biographies of Malcolm Muggeridge and Hesketh Pearson; his most recent book is entitled *Brief Lives: Heroes, Mountebanks and Lawyers*. He is a columnist for *Report Newsmagazine* and a frequent contributor to the *Globe and Mail* and the *National Post*.

JOHN DAVID POWELL of Houston, Texas, a former print and broadcast journalist and former public radio network commentator, is an executive speechwriter and an award-winning Internet columnist. He wrote Chapter 5, with its account of the mass slaughter of the Christians at Lyon.

DAVE SHIFLETT of Midlothian, Virginia, who wrote the sidebars on the Montanists and the Marcionites, has also written for the *The Wall Street Journal*, *Reader's Digest*, the *Los Angeles Times*, *The Manchester Guardian*, and other publications. The author of *The America We Deserve* (with Donald Trump) and co-author of *Christianity on Trial*, he has worked as a columnist and editor at the *Rocky Mountain News* in Denver and on the editorial page of *The Washington Times*.

STEVE WEATHERBE of Victoria, British Columbia, is a former teacher, a former staffer of *The Report* newsmagazine, and a current columnist for Sterling News Service who works for the B.C. government. Weatherbe produced Chapter 3, the story of the eloquent second-century Christian apologist and eventual martyr, Justin.

JOE WOODARD, religion editor for the *Calgary Herald*, has taught politics and philosophy at universities in Canada and the U.S., and researched social policy for both the Canadian and American governments. He wrote Chapter 4, recounting the life, times, and despairing death of the brilliant and conflicted Emperor Marcus Aurelius; and the sidebars on the Gnostics and on the Celsus-Origen debate.

Biographical notes on these returning writers appear in Volume I: Charlotte Allen, who wrote Chapter 2 in this volume; and Mark Galli, Frederica Mathewes-Green and Gary Thomas, who collaborated on Chapters 7 and 8. Ted Byfield wrote Chapter 1 and Calvin Demmon wrote Chapter 10; both wrote several sidebars. Director of research Moira Calder, illustrations editor Jack Keaschuk and series planner Barrett Pashak contributed to the text throughout the volume.

## THE ACADEMIC CONSULTANTS

All text appearing in each volume is submitted to a two-member committee of academic consultants, one representing the Evangelical and one the Catholic or Orthodox traditions. These in turn call upon specialist historians where specific subjects require it. The consultant committee for Volume II consists of DR. KIMBERLY GEORGEDES (left), associate professor of History, Franciscan University, Steubenville, Ohio; and DR. DOUGLAS SWEENEY (right), assistant professor of Church History and the History of Christian Thought, Trinity Evangelical Divinity School, Deerfield, Illinois.

Assistance on specific chapters was provided by Dr. William McDonald (Chapters 2-5), Professor Eugene TeSelle (Chapters 6-10, pronunciation guide), and Dr. Samuel H. Moffett (sidebar on Edessa).

## THE ILLUSTRATORS
Joining the team for Volume II:

As a fine artist, CARLO COSENTINO, a native of Montreal, paints mostly with oil on canvas, though he is comfortable with other arts media as well. As an illustrator, Cosentino produces artwork for clients including IBM, Seagram's, Pepsi-Cola, Toshiba, Canon, Celanese, Imperial Tobacco Ltd. and Toyota. His poster art has been used to promote the annual jazz festivals in the cities of Montreal, Toronto, Vancouver, Edmonton and Winnipeg.

JOHN MANTHA of Toronto works with oils and oil-wash. He has designed two gold coins for the Royal Canadian Mint and he serves as a courtroom artist for the Canadian Broadcasting Corporation. Other clients include the Ford Motor Company, Fox Television, Bantam Doubleday Dell, Penguin Books, and Better Homes and Gardens magazine. He has illustrated seven books, including the award-winning *The Kids' Book of Canada's Railway*.

TOM MCNEELEY, who lives and works in Toronto, has won awards from the Society of Illustrators, the Art Directors Clubs of New York and Toronto, and Communication Arts Magazine. The Canadian Association of Photographers and Illustrators in Communications honored him with its Lifetime Achievement Award. His clients have included publishers, theater and opera companies, major corporations and the Canadian postal service.

Biographical notes on returning illustrators appear in the previous volume.

## DESIGN & PRODUCTION

As the illustrations editor, JACK KEASCHUK commissioned the original art and selected the photos for the volume. He has additionally been appointed the art director for the series making him responsible for the layout and general appearance of each volume. Further biographical notes appear in the initial volume of the series.

The pages are laid out by a newcomer to the project, DEAN PICKUP of Edmonton, a graduate of the visual communications program at Edmonton's Grant MacEwan College with a major in design and digital media. Pickup, who assisted Jack Keaschuk, has previously worked in retail promotions and video marketing.

The production editor for the series is REV. DAVID EDWARDS, an Orthodox monk of the Community of St. Silouan the Athonite. An arts graduate of the University of Manitoba, he received his theological training at Durham University in England and took his teacher training at Leeds University. After eighteen years in the Winnipeg, Manitoba, public school system, he came to Edmonton as a pastor at St. Herman's Orthodox Church.

# BIBLIOGRAPHY

## GENERAL

Angus, Samuel. *The Mystery Religions and Christianity: A Study in the Religious Background of Early Christianity*. New York: Scribner, 1925.

Cook, S. A., , F. E. Adcock, and M. P. Charlesworth. *The Cambridge Ancient History*, rev. Vol. 11, *The Imperial Peace A.D. 70–192*. Cambridge: Cambridge University Press, 1954.

Cook, S. A., F. E. Adcock, M. P. Charlesworth, and N. H. Baynes. *The Cambridge Ancient History*, rev. Volume 12, *The Imperial Crisis and Recovery*. Cambridge: Cambridge University Press, 1956.

Cross, F. L. *The Oxford Dictionary of the Christian Church*, 2nd ed. London: Oxford University Press, 1974.

Dowley, Tim, ed. *Eerdman's Handbook to the History of Christianity*. Grand Rapids, MI: Eerdmans, 1977.

Foster, Richard J. *Streams of Living Water*. [San Francisco]: HarperSanFrancisco, 1989.

Freedman, David Noel, ed.-in-chief. *Anchor Bible Dictionary*. New York: Doubleday, 1972.

Garraty, John A., and Peter Gay, eds. *The Columbia History of the World*. San Francisco: Harper & Row, 1972.

Herbermann, Charles G. *Catholic Encyclopedia: An International Work of Reference on the Constitution, Doctrine, Discipline, and History of the Catholic Church*. New York: Appleton, 1907–1910.

Hornblower, Simon, and Antony Spawforth. *The Oxford Classical Dictionary*, 3rd ed. New York: Oxford University Press, 1996.

Runes, Dagobert D. (1959). *Pictorial History of Philosophy*. New York: Philosophical Library, 1959.

Sordi, Marta. *The Christians and the Roman Empire*. Norman: University of Oklahoma Press, 1976.

## BIBLE COMMENTARY

Blomberg, Craig L. *The Historical Reliability of the Gospels*. Downers Grove, IL: Inter-Varsity Press, 1987.

Bruce, F. F. *The New Testament Documents: Are They Reliable?* London: Intervarsity Fellowship, 1960.

—-. *Paul: Apostle of the Free Spirit*. Exeter: Paternoster Press, 1977.

—-. *Peter, Stephen, James and John: Studies in Early Non-Pauline Christianity*. Grand Rapids, MI: Eerdmans, 1979.

—-. *The Pauline Circle*. Grand Rapids, MI: Paternoster Press, 1984.

Griffith-Jones, Robin. *The Four Witnesses*. San Francisco: HarperSanFrancisco, 2000.

Renan, Ernst. *Oeuvres Complètes*, ed. Henriette Psichari. Vol. 5, *Les Evangiles*. Paris: Calmann-Levy, 1961.

Sanders, E. P., and Margaret Davies. *Studying the Synoptic Gospels*. Philadelphia: Trinity Press International, 1989.

Streeter, Burnett Hillman. *The Four Gospels: A Study of Origins*. London: MacMillan, 1964.

## CHRISTIAN BIOGRAPHY

Barnes, Timothy David. *Tertullian: A Historical and Literary Study*, rev. ed. New York: Oxford University Press, 1985.

Eisenman, Robert. *James the Brother of Jesus*. New York: Penguin, 1997.

Foakes-Jackson, F. J. *Peter: Prince of Apostles*. London: Hodder & Stoughton, 1927.

Murphy-O'Connor, Jerome. *Paul: A Critical Life*. Oxford: Clarendon, 1996.

Osborn, Eric Francis. *Justin Martyr*. Tübingen: J. C. B. Mohr, 1973.

—-. *Tertullian, First Theologian of the West*. New York: Cambridge University Press, 1997.

Perkins, Pheme. *Peter: Apostle for the Whole Church*. Minneapolis, MN: Fortress Press, 1994.

Salisbury, Joyce E. *Perpetua's Passion: The Death and Memory of a Young Roman Woman*. New York: Routledge, 1997.

Thurston, Herbert, and Donald Attwater, eds. *Butler's Lives of the Saints*, ed., rev., and suppl. Aberdeen: Burns & Oates, 1956.

## EARLY CHRISTIANITY

Brown, Peter. *The Cult of the Saints*. Chicago: University of Chicago Press, 1983.

Chadwick, Henry. The Early Christian Community. In McManners, John (Ed.), *The Oxford Illustrated History of Christianity* (pp. 21–60). New York: Oxford University Press, 1990.

Daniel-Rops, Henri. *The Church of Apostles and Martyrs*, 2 vols. New York: Image Books, 1962.

Danielou, Jean, and Henri Marrou. *The Christian Centuries*. Vol. 1, *The First Six Hundred Years*. New York: McGraw-Hill, 1966.

Davidson, Marshall B., ed. *The Horizon History of Christianity*. New York: American Heritage, 1964.

Edersheim, Alfred. *The Life and Times of Jesus The Messiah*. Grand Rapids, MI: Eerdmans, 1980.

Eusebius of Caesarea. *A History of the Church from Christ to Constantine*, trans. G. A. Williamson. New York: Dorset, 1966.

Eusebius of Caesarea. *Church History*. Vol. 1 of *The Post-Nicene Fathers*, ed. Philip Schaff and Henry Wace. Grand Rapids, MI: Eerdmans, 1895, repr. 1986.

Frend, W. H. C. *The Early Church*. Philadelphia: Fortress, 1965.

—-. *The Rise of Christianity*. Philadelphia: Fortress Press, 1984.

Gascoigne, Bamber. *The Christians*. London: Jonathan Cape, 1977.

Gonzalez, Justo L. *The Early Church to the Dawn of the Reformation*. Volume 1 of *The Story of Christianity*. San Francisco: Harper & Row, 1984.

Grant, Robert M. *Early Christianity and Society: Seven Studies*. New York: Harper & Row, 1997.

Grant, Robert M. *The Sword and the Cross*. New York: Macmillan, 1955.

Green, Michael. *Evangelism in the Early Church*. Grand Rapids, MI: Eerdmans, 1970.

Johnson, Paul. *A History of Christianity*. Markham, UK: Penguin, 1976.

Kelly, Joseph F. (1997) *The World of the Early Christians*. Collegeville, MN: Liturgical Press, 1997.

Lebreton, Jules, and Jacques Zeiller. *The History of the Primitive Church*. 2 vols. New York: Macmillan, 1949.

MacMullen, Ramsay. *Two Types of Conversion to Early Christianity*. In *Conversion, Catechumenate, and Baptism in the Early Church*, ed. Everett Ferguson. New York: Garland, 1993.

Meeks, Wayne A. *The First Urban Christians*. New Haven, CT: Yale University Press, 1983.

Mohler, James A. *The Heresy of Monasticism*. Staten Island, NY: Alba House, 1971.

Newman, John Henry. *The Miracles of Early Ecclesiastical Christianity*. London: Longmans Green, 1907.

Robertson, Archibald. *The Origins of Christianity*. New York: International Publishers, 1954.

Scholer, David M. *Women in Early Christianity*. Volume 14 of *Studies in Early Christianity*. New York: Garland, 1993.

Stevenson, James. *The Catacombs: Life and Death in Early Christianity*. Nashville, TN: Thomas Nelson, 1978.

## GEOGRAPHICAL REFERENCES/LOCAL CHURCHES

Cadoux, Cecil John. *Ancient Smyrna: A History of the City from the Earliest Times to 324*. Oxford: Blackwell, 1938.

Codrington, Thomas *Roman Roads in Britain*. London: Society for Promoting Christian Knowledge, 1903. Downloaded 24 April 2002 from http://www.ukans.edu/history/index/europe/ancient_rome/E/Gazetteer/Periods/Roman/Topics/Engineering/roads/home.html

Corwin, Virginia. *St. Ignatius and Christianity in Antioch*. New Haven CT: Yale University Press, 1960.

Donaldson, Stuart A. *Church Life and Thought in North Africa, A.D. 200*. Cambridge: Cambridge University Press, 1909.

Downey, Glanville. *A History of Antioch in Syria*. Princeton, NJ: Princeton University Press, 1961.

Drinkwater, J. F. *Roman Gaul, 50 B.C.–A.D.260*. London: Croom Helm, 1983.

Frend, W. H. C. *The Donatist Church: A Movement of Protest in Roman North Africa*. Oxford: Clarendon, 1952.

Giannini, Luca. *Fodor's Holy Rome*. Milan: Touring Editore, 1999.

Griggs, C. Wilfred. *Early Egyptian Christianity: From its Origins to 451 C.E.* New York: E. J. Brill, 1990.

Malaty, Tadros Y. *The School of Alexandria*. Volume 1 of *Before Origen*. Jersey City, NJ: St. Mark's Coptic Orthodox Church, 1994. Downloaded 24 April 2002 from http://www.stathanasius.miss.on.coptorthodox.ca/Extras/Patrology__Sayings_of_the_Fath/The_School_of_Alexandria/the_school_of_alexandria.html

Malaty, Tadros Y. *The School of Alexandria*. Volume 2 of *Origen*. Jersey City, NJ: St. Mark's Coptic Orthodox Church, 1994. Downloaded 24 April 2002 from http://www.stathanasius.miss.on.coptorthodox.ca/Extras/Patrology__Sayings_of_the_Fath/The_School_of_Alexandria_-_Ori/the_school_of_alexandria_-_ori.html

Moffett, Samuel Hugh. *A History of Christianity in Asia*. Volume 1, *Beginnings to 1500*, 2nd ed., rev. and corr. Maryknoll, NY: Orbis, 1992.

Platner, Samuel Ball. *A Topographical Dictionary of Ancient Rome*. London: Oxford University Press, 1929. Downloaded 24 April 2002 from http://www.ukans.edu/history/index/europe/ancient_rome/E/Gazetteer/Periods/Roman/Topics/Engineering/waterworks/home.html

Segal, J. B. *Edessa: "The Blessed City."* Oxford: Clarendon, 1970.

Thomas, Charles. *Christianity in Roman Britain to A.D. 500*. Berkeley: University of California Press, 1981.

Thomas, P. *Christians and Christianity in India and Pakistan*. London: Allen & Unwin, 1954.

## JUDAISM AND JEWISH HISTORY

Chilton, Bruce, and Craig A. Evans, eds. *James the Just and Christian Origins*. Boston, Brill, 1999.

Donfried, Karl P., and Peter Richardson. *Judaism and Christianity in First-Century Rome*. Grand Rapids, MI: Eerdmans, 1998.

Jocz, Jacob. *The Jewish People and Jesus Christ: A Study in the Controversy Between Church and Synagogue*. London: S.P.C.K, 1954.

Lipman, David E. *Bar Kochba: The Bar Kochba Revolt*. Downloaded 1 May 2002 from http://www.jewishgates.org/personalities/bar.stm

Ricciotti, Giuseppe. *The History of Israel*, 2 vols. Milwaukee: Bruce, 1955.

Salstrand, George A. E. *The Time was Right: How God Prepared the World for the Coming of Christ*. Nashville, TN: Broadman Press, 1973.

Yadin, Yigael. *Bar-Kokhba: The Rediscovery of the Legendary Hero of the Last Jewish Revolt Against Imperial Rome*. London: Weidenfeld and Nicolson, 1971.

## NON-CHRISTIAN RELIGION

Chadwick, Nora K. *The Druids*. Cardiff, Wales: University of Cardiff, 1966.

Champlin, Edward. *Fronto and Antonine Rome*. Cambridge, MA: Harvard University Press, 1980.

Kendrick, T. D. *The Druids*, 2nd ed. London: Cass, 1966.

Wynne-Tyson, Esme. *Mithras: The Fellow in the Cap*. Sussex: Centaur Press, 1958, repr. 1958.

## PERSECUTION OF CHRISTIANS

*Acts of the Christian Martyrs*, trans. Herbert Musurillo. Oxford: Clarendon, 1972.

Barnes, Timothy David. Legislation against the Christians. *Journal of Roman Studies* 58 (1968): 32-50.

Frend, W. H. C. *Martyrdom and Persecution in the Early Church: A Study of a Conflict from the Maccabees to Donatus*. New York: New York University Press, 1967.

Hertwig-Jaksch, Michael. *Studies in the Martyrdom of the Christians at Lugdunum*. Unpublished master's thesis. Edmonton: University of Alberta, 1985.

Smith, Lacey Baldwin. *Fools, Martyrs, Traitors: The Story of Martyrdom in the Western World*. Evanston, IL: Northwestern University Press, 1999.

## ROME AND THE EMPIRE
### ANCIENT SOURCES

Cassius Dio Cocceianus. *Dio's Roman History, with an English Translation by Earnest Cary, Based on the Version of Herbert Baldwin Foster* (Loeb Classical Library). Cambridge, MA: Harvard University Press, 1914.

Herodian, Aelius. *Herodian*, trans. C. R. Whittaker (Loeb Classical Library). Cambridge, MA: Harvard University Press, 1969.

*Scriptores Historiae Augustae*, trans. David Magie. Loeb Classical Library. New York: G. B. Putnam's Sons, 1922–1934.

## THE EMPERORS

Birley, Anthony R. *The African Emperor; Septimius Severus*. London: Batsford, 1972.

—-. *Marcus Aurelius: A Biography*. London: Batsford, 1987.

Brauer, George C., Jr. *The Young Emperors, Rome, A.D. 193–244*. New York: Crowell, 1967.

—-. *The Age of the Soldier Emperors: Imperial Rome, A.D. 244–284*. Park Ridge, NJ: Noyes Press, 1975.

Grant, Michael. *The Antonines: The Roman Empire in Transition*. New York: Routledge, 1994.

—-. *The Severans: The Changed Roman Empire*. New York: Routledge, 1996.

Hay, J. Stuart. *The Amazing Emperor Heliogabalus*. London: Macmillan, 1911.

Henderson, Bernard W. *The Life and Principate of the Emperor Hadrian*. London: Methuen, 1923.

Gibbon, Edward. *The Decline and Fall of the Roman Empire*, 4 vols. London: F. Warne, 1887.

Hopkins, R.V. Nind. *The Life of Alexander Severus*. Cambridge: Cambridge University Press, 1907.

Marcus Aurelius. *Meditations*, trans. and ed. A. S. L. Farquharson. New York: Knopf, 1992.

Marcus Aurelius. *Meditations*, trans. George Long (Internet Classics Archive). Downloaded on 23 April 2002 from http://classics.mit.edu/Antoninus/meditations.11.eleven.html

Millar, Fergus. *The Emperor in the Roman World (31 B.C.–A.D. 337)*. London: Duckworth, 1977.

Perowne, Stewart. *Hadrian*. London: Hodder & Stoughton, 1960.

Petit, Paul. *Pax Romana*. London: B. T. Batsford, 1967.

Tingay, G. I. F., and J. Badcock. *These were the Romans*. Chester Springs, PA: Dufour Editions, 1989.

Webster, Graham (1979). *The Roman Army of the First and Second Centuries A.D.*, 2nd ed. London: A. & C. Black, 1979.

## LIFE IN THE EMPIRE

Aries, Philip, and George Duby, eds. *A History of Private Life*. Vol. 1, *From Pagan Rome to Byzantium*. Cambridge, MA: Cambridge University Press, 1987.

Balsdon, J. P. V. D. *Romans and Aliens*. London: Duckworth, 1979.

Carcopino, Jerome. *Daily Life in Ancient Rome: The People and the City at the Height of the Empire*, trans. E. O. Lorimer, ed. Henry T. Rowell. Harmondsworth: Penguin, 1941.

Casson, Lionel. *Everyday life in Ancient Rome*. Baltimore: Johns Hopkins University Press, 1998.

Dilke, O. A. W. *The Ancient Romans: How They Lived and Worked*. Newton Abbot, UK: David and Charles, 1975.

Grant, Michael. *Gladiators*. New York: Delacourt Press, 1968.

## ROMAN CIVILIZATION

Frontinus, Sextus Julius. *The Stratagems, and the Aqueducts of Rome, with an English translation by Charles E. Bennett* (Loeb Classical Library, No. 174). Downloaded on 30 April 2002 from http://www.ukans.edu/history/index/europe/ancient_rome/E/Gazetteer/Periods/Roman/Topics/Engineering/waterworks/home.html

Houston, George W. Roman Technology Handbook. Downloaded 24 April 2002 from http://www.unc.edu/courses/rometech/public/frames/art_set.html

Marcus Vitruvius Pollio. *De Architectura*. Loeb Classic Library. Downloaded 1 May from http://www.ukans.edu/history/index/europe/ancient_rome/E/Gazetteer/Periods/Roman/Topics/Engineering/waterworks/home.html

Smith, Philip. *Aquaeductus*. In *A Dictionary of Roman and Greek Antiquities*, ed. William Smith. London: John Murray, 1895. Downloaded 24 April 2002 from http://www.ukans.edu/history/index/europe/ancient_rome/E/Gazetteer/Periods/Roman/Topics/Engineering/waterworks/home.html

Taylor, Jill. *Lighthouses of Ancient Rome and North Carolina*. Downloaded 24 April 2002 from http://www.unc.edu/courses/rometech/public/content/transport/Jill_Taylor/Lighthouses.htm

Wiedemann, Thomas. *Emperors and Gladiators*. London: Routledge, 1992.

## WRITERS AND WRITINGS OF THE EARLY CHURCH
There are many translations of the writings of the Church Fathers that are widely available. In addition to those cited below, the 1885 "Edinburgh" series, *The Writings of the Fathers down to A.D. 325*, edited by Alexander Roberts and James Donaldson, has been reprinted by Eerdmans (Grand Rapids, MI, 1986) and is available online at http://www.ccel.org/

Arnold, Eberhard. *The Early Christians: Selected and Edited from All the Sources of the First Centuries*. Grand Rapids, MI: Baker Book House, 1979.

Bray, Gerald Lewis. *Holiness and the Will of God: Perspectives on the Theology of Tertullian*. London: Marshall, Morgan, & Scott, 1979.

Chadwick, Henry. *Early Christian Thought and the Classical Tradition: Studies in Justin, Clement, and Origen*. Oxford: Clarendon, 1966.

Crouzel, Henri. *Origen*, trans. by A. S. Worrall. San Francisco: Harper & Row, 1989.

Danielou, Jean. *Origene: Translated from the French*. New York: Sheed & Ward, 1955.

De Genouillac, Henri. *L'église chrétienne au temps de Saint Ignace d'Antioche*. Paris: Gabriel Beauchesne, 1907.

Dechow, Jon F. *Dogma and Mysticism in Early Christianity: Epiphanius of Cyprus and the Legacy of Origen*. Macon, GA: Mercer University Press, 1988.

Eusebius of Caesarea. *A History of the Church from Christ to Constantine*, trans. G. A. Williamson. New York: Dorset, 1966.

Eusebius of Caesarea. *Church History*. In Vol. 1 of *The Post-Nicene Fathers*, ed. Philip Schaff and Henry Wace. Grand Rapids, MI: Eerdmans, 1895, repr. 1986.

Grant, Robert M., Ed. *The Apostolic Fathers: A New Translation and Commentary*, vol. 1. New York: Thomas Nelson, 1964.

—-. *Greek Apologists of the Second Century*. Philadelphia: Westminster Press, 1988.

—-. *Irenaeus of Lyons*. Volume 1 of *The Early Church Fathers*. New York: Routledge, 1997.

Trigg, Joseph Wilson. *Origen : The Bible and Philosophy in the Third-Century Church*. Atlanta, GA: John Knox, 1949.

# PHOTOGRAPHIC & MAP CREDITS

# INDEX